TWO SIDES OF THE RIVER

TWO SIDES OF THE RIVER

A TIME TO CHOOSE

HENRY EUGENE IVEY

iUniverse, Inc.
Bloomington

Two Sides of the River
A Time to Choose

iUniverse books may be ordered through booksellers or by contacting:

iUniverse
1663 Liberty Drive
Bloomington, IN 47403
www.iuniverse.com
1-800-Authors (1-800-288-4677)

Because of the dynamic nature of the Internet, any Web addresses or links contained in this book may have changed since publication and may no longer be valid. The views expressed in this work are solely those of the author and do not necessarily reflect the views of the publisher, and the publisher hereby disclaims any responsibility for them.

Any people depicted in stock imagery provided by Thinkstock are models, and such images are being used for illustrative purposes only.

Certain stock imagery © Thinkstock.

ISBN: 978-1-4502-7861-4 (e)
ISBN: 978-1-4502-7862-1 (hc)
ISBN: 978-1-4502-7863-8 (sc)-

Library of Congress Control Number: 2010918349

Printed in the United States of America

iUniverse rev. date: 3/1/2011

CONTENTS

PREFACE

Time to Choose I invite you to take a journey with me to explore both sides of a metaphoric river, separating very diverse ideologies and ethics. Making the decision on which side of the river to reside is, or should be, a personal decision, made by each individual, without regard to decisions made by others.

For the past fifty years, many Americans have compromised their principles and values in favor of selfish reasons by giving support to politicians they hope will benefit them personally. As a result, we have given free rein to politicians, allowing them to do what they please without reprisal from an apathetic society. We have ignored the threat to our freedoms and now the government is eager to take them from us. As citizens of a free country, we are free to choose our own beliefs and ideology, but consequently, it could divide us like no other time in our history; this threatens our ability to survive as a united people. If we continue on the path we are on, the United States of America will lose its heritage, and there will be no going back. We must have the courage to stand by our principles because without sound principles to guide our lives, there is no other foundation on which to build! The threat to our way of life transcends politics; it is a matter of changes in social attitudes and the erosion of the long-held values of previous generations, who recognized and protected the greatness of our country.

We can no longer ignore the reality of the state of our country. *We the people*, always have either contributed to the solutions or contributed to the problems of our country. If we uphold our responsibility as citizens of this great country, we can contribute to the solutions. However, if we do nothing, we will most definitely add to our problems. America has many problems for us to solve, and there are no easy solutions. Our problems cannot be solved through politics alone; we the people must accept that over the past thirty years the apathy of the American people is responsible for the troubles facing us today. If the American people do not awaken from their slumber and make contact with the reality of the state of our country, America will be lost.

It is not possible to live on both sides of a river concurrently. The time has come to choose one side or the other. Although not everyone will exercise their freedoms, each of us is free to make our own decisions concerning the kind of America we wish to live in. However, no society can survive as fragmented as America is today. We must first defragment ourselves by making personal choices rather than adopting someone else's choices.

To support the opinions in this book, included are many historical quotes, and verses taken from the King James Version of the Holy Bible. It is my hope that reading this book will assist you in deciding on which side of the river you wish to live.

CHAPTER I

THE POLITICAL SIDE OF THE RIVER

My America

On a cold February night in 1940, in the small cotton-mill town of Bladenboro, North Carolina, I was fortunate to take my first breath in the world's greatest country. Good fortune again smiled on me by allowing me to be reared in the company of America's Greatest Generation.

Bladenboro was one of many cotton mill towns that dotted the landscape of the rural South in those days. My first venture away from the place where I was born occurred at the age of twelve, my cousin invited me to join him on a train trip to Florida to visit relatives. It was the beginning of a lifelong quest to explore not only the country but also life itself.

During my formative years, there were never sufficient hours in a day to satisfy my cat-like curiosity and the adventuresome nature of a Huckleberry Finn. I am still pursuing that quest today, and I suppose writing this book is a manifestation of my love and respect for the heritage of this great country and what has happened to it.

Reality is what it is, and we must confront it. Many Americans are living in a fantasyland that, in large part, accounts for our troubles and will lead to our eventual downfall. To be born in the United States of America is a blessing that only a very few of the world's six billion inhabitants are privileged to enjoy. Sadly, many Americans fail to appreciate their good fortune and are about to forfeit what they have taken for granted far too long.

In those days, politics and materialistic pursuits were not an obsession as they are today. Financial gain was necessary for survival, but it was low on the list of priorities for most people. My parents taught me that there are far more important things in life than the pursuit of wealth and chasing rainbows. Strong faith in God, good moral principles, integrity, responsibility, respect for others, and honesty were universally understood to be the proper motivation for dwelling among other human beings. Many people my age long for the America we once knew, when selfishness and self-serving attitudes were not a way of life as they are today. America has gone through many hardships and struggles to maintain the legacy willed to us by our founders and ancestors, and old gravestones display the names of those who sacrificed their lives to protect and defend this great country. Our schoolchildren are denied the true history of America and are indoctrinated with American-bashing falsehoods that shelter them from the reality of what is about to be taken from them.

My earliest clear recognition occurred in May 1945, and it is still fresh in my memory. I was standing on the porch of our small, company-owned house with my mom and dad and being frightened by the commotion and noise taking place in our otherwise quiet neighborhood. People were scurrying about the streets, car horns were honking, police-car sirens were wailing, and whistles at the nearby cotton mill were blowing. I can easily recall the commotion sixty-five years later. After a time, when things quieted down, I asked my dad what was happening; being a man of very few words he simply patted me on head and said, "The war is over." I was not fully aware of what war was, but even at such a young age, I knew it was a very important development.

As time passed, and veterans began to return home and share their experiences, I knew that the military would be part of my future. Those experiences instilled in me a never-diminished respect for the sacrifices of those men and women who would never see their loved ones again. Even as a young child, I recognized how blessed I was to be born in America. Brave, selfless men, and women, continue to die every day to defend our freedoms, but the youth of today give little respect to their sacrifices. The best that America can produce make up our military, and the twenty-two years that I was part of the world's greatest organization are the proudest of my life.

It is impossible not to be sad by the knowledge that children and grandchildren are facing a country far removed from the America preserved by parents and grandparents of people my age. However, things being what they are today, those days are lost forever. America has sacrificed a great deal of wealth and lives to defend against those who wish to do us harm. The threat to our country, however, is not from foreign armies. Like most of the great societies of the past, we are self-destructing from within.

Lessons from History

Edward Gibbon's great historical book, *The Decline and Fall of the Roman Empire*, is a sort of blueprint for the destiny of all great societies, and the reason for America's downfall can be seen in that blueprint. The similarities are striking, beginning with Rome's failure to control the influx of foreigners that breached its borders and took advantage of what it had to offer. Rather than assimilate into the existing society, newcomers worked to change it, and change it they did. Rome's form of government and strong military made it the leader for hundreds of years, but the breakdown of morals; alcoholism, sexual deviancy, idolatry, and the erosion of a stable leadership and discipline in the military, contributed to the failure to defend itself against foreign influences that led to its downfall. As a pagan society, Romans had so many gods to worship, it was impossible to identify them all. To be sure, not to offend one, they would add another god and worship them all. Rome did not disappear; it just disintegrated. I am afraid that a similar fate awaits the United States of America. As Rome, America will not disappear, it will become a mere remnant of its once glory.

There have been many great empires in the past, including those of the Romans, Egyptians, Persians, and Babylonians, among others. Where are these countries now when at the height of their power they were considered too powerful to fail? The common thread that brought about their downfall was the concentration of power among the elite and the apathy of an affluent society that ignored the walls crumbling down around it.

The United States of America is not a young nation; 200 to 250 years seems to be all the time required to cycle a country through its birth, growth, and decline. History has shown that apathy, abundance, and ignorance by the populace—mixed with greed and corruption of the leadership—ensure the failure of a society to sustain itself with any measure of stability, and nations continue to repeat the same mistake, and have for thousands of years.

The Threat of Communism

The same internal threats that existed in this nation at its founding are still with us, but today we have a far different leadership. Rather than build upon the foundation our founders created, current leaders are determined to destroy it. Bigotry, distain, and yes, even racism directed toward the founders and builders of this great nation, has led to pure hatred of all things American by many of those in power today. The underlying theme of their agenda seems to be revenge against a society into which they are unwilling to assimilate. When the government fears the people, there is liberty. When the people fear the government, there is tyranny. Thomas Jefferson is given credit for speaking those words as a warning to both the government and the people—not only his generation but also all who would follow.

Freedom is the God-given right of every human being, and the government cannot suppress it from people forever. When democracy is introduced into a Communist country, it is like a dim light that grows brighter and brighter until it eventually overcomes the darkness of oppression. We can see that occurring in China today, although the light is growing slowly. When oppressed people experience freedom, it is difficult to take it away from them—unless of course, the people allow it to be taken away. People who live in a free country like the United States of America and take their freedom for granted and do nothing to preserve it, face the inevitability of losing it.

People do not leave America and go to a Communist country, because they realize Communism is a failed system; it always has been and always will be. Socialists, on the other hand, view Communism as a panacea, and for those in power in a Communist country, that is exactly what it is. We cannot exclude Communism from this discussion because it is possible, it could come to America. Socialism is the road that leads to Communism, and necessity is the material that paves the road. This current administration is going full steam to create the necessity by gaining control over every aspect of our lives. Most Americans do not yet realize the number of new laws the administration has clandestinely passed, but shock and awe are just ahead.

When one reads the words of some of our previous great leaders, especially our founders, Democrats and Republicans, it is a mystery where all the leaders have gone. It is almost embarrassing to watch some wimpy politicians sashaying around like a bunch of overgrown teenagers frightened by political jocks, afraid they will not be successful if they are not popular with the in-crowd. The majority of politicians from both parties are devoid of courage or conviction to do the right thing for our country. They just go along to get along to protect their own selfish interests to remain in power while our country is imploding. The powerful Socialist juggernaut that is in control of our country today ignores the few who are trying to do the right thing for our country.

Political Correctness

There is nothing in the American lexicon that has affected our country more than political correctness, especially in politics. Long before President Obama came on the scene, America had already gone through a fundamental change by the validation of political correctness by the American people. It takes courage, integrity, self-respect, and character to stand against the implications of political correctness. While I am not a political groupie, I cannot think of more than one or two politicians who display those qualities.

Political correctness is a political tool Liberals use for intimidation. You may not know exactly what the term means, but you certainly understand its implications. Like the word "racism," political correctness often is a solid roadblock against freedom of expression. I suppose it is a harebrained idea instigated by the government to make us all equal; the question is, equal to what. There are no winners or losers; there are no criminals—only those who have been victimized by society. There is no evil—only a different way of expression. There is no self-imposed poverty—only people who have been trampled on by the rich. I could go on, but the point is that political correctness has destroyed self-motivation and goal setting, especially among the young.

The Failure of Our Leadership

One of my favorite Aesop fables is, "The Sick Man and the Doctor." and we can learn a lesson from it.

> A Sick Man received a visit from his Doctor, who asked him how he was. "Fairly well, Doctor," said he, "but I find I sweat a great deal." "Ah," said the Doctor, "that's a good sign." On his next visit he asked the same question, and the patient replied, "I'm much as usual, but I've taken to having shivering fits, which leave me cold all over." "Ah", said the Doctor, "that's a good sign too." When he came the third time and inquired as before about the patient's health, the Sick Man said that he felt very feverish. "A very good sign," said the Doctor; "you are doing very nicely indeed." Afterwards a friend came to see the invalid, and on asking him how he did, received this reply: "My dear friend, I'm dying of good signs."

This fable has a message that is pertinent to us today. My dear friends, America is dying of good signs. Just as the doctor in this fable, our government is hiding the truth from us and deceiving us with false optimism. Death is the fate of any society that ignores reality in favor of more palpable lies and deceptions.

The actions of our present leadership show a slanderous disrespect toward our great leaders of the past like George Washington, Thomas Jefferson, Abraham Lincoln, John F. Kennedy, Ronald Reagan, and many others. Their love and sacrifices for this great republic made these men great leaders. Were their efforts all in vain, are we to discard and forget them like some old black-and-white movie?

I have great respect and admiration for the *few* in both parties who wish to do the right thing but are unable to make their way through the herd led around by the nose by the Speaker of the House. If you are among those who believe our leaders are trying to introduce Socialism to America, you need to get a clue; we are already deep into Socialism. Common sense dictates that the only motivation for attempting such a foolish thing is the accumulation of power over the people. I realize that politicians make every effort to avoid the term Communism or Socialism, but Communism is a reality, and it could come to America. It has been creeping its way into our society since before most of us were born.

The president has said he has a gift without explaining exactly what his gift is. Well, we all have gifts, but to what end do we use those gifts? A thief has the gift for breaking into our house and taking everything we own if we fail to protect what is rightly ours. President Obama appears to have a vision of being the president of the entire world, but his self-aggrandizing view of himself far exceeds his abilities to be even an effective leader of the United States of America.

The Failure of the American People

For many Americans, history is what happened two weeks ago, and the future is the next government handout; our focus has become so narrow that we are constantly groping around in the dark, looking for answers in all the wrong places. Politicians rarely plan anything beyond the next election, and most peoples' knowledge comes from the constant sound bites from people in the media, who are mostly America-hating radicals from the same generation as the leadership now driving us toward oblivion. Politicians do not operate in the sunlight but rather prefer to wheel and deal in the back rooms, shielded from the public, while orchestrating our demise. One by one, the elements of their agenda are being implemented in a slow process unnoticed by the majority of this apathetic generation. Of course, this type of political shenanigan is nothing new in American politics, but whether the media expose it or not, depends on what party is in power.

In the history of man, there never has been more hideous device to distract people from real life than television and the Internet. The world has become addicted to these devices and it is no surprise that it is puts a burden on our youth to survive in a world of fantasy and make-believe, leaving them poorly prepared to cope with the real world. Of course, it plays into the hands of government officials to create a society so uninformed and disconnected that it is unable to survive without their involvement, and that, my friends, is a building block in the creation of Communism.

In 2007, the National Institute of Mental Health, reported on their website—http://www.nimh.nih.gov/health/publications/suicide-in-the-us-statistics-and-prevention/index.shtml—that suicide is the third-leading cause of death among young Americans ages fifteen to twenty-four. Drug and alcohol use is destroying many young people before they have a chance to experience a productive life. It is true that I am cynical about our government; there are millions, maybe a majority of Americans, who share my concern about the decline of our nation. However, recognition or support from the liberal press or elected representatives is not forthcoming.

Conservatives will not tolerate being represented by radicals of any persuasion. Conservative protesters will continue to be peaceful and intelligent, and if it fails, which it probable will, it will be partly due to lack of participation and in-fighting. However, it is also likely clandestine Socialist operatives will infiltrate them and make trouble and disparage the peaceful protesters, while the despicable press will be there to put cameras in their faces. Even so, when others falter, those of us with the American spirit in our hearts will survive. Communism has a limited lifespan, and if it comes, it will eventually go, but most, if not all, of us will be long gone before it runs its course.

There are many, young and old, who are capable of rescuing our way of life from those determined to change it, but the power of the people has been lost by this generation. A foundation of sound moral principles is another of those American benchmarks that Socialists consider outdated nonsense, but they do not oppose America-hating radicals ruling them. In America today, political power rules whether it represents the majority or the minority. As usual, common sense will eventually overcome, but it will not return to America until this generation, or even the next generation, has passed on. When future generations, if there are any, look back at what this generation has done to America, they will certainly never let it happen again. No rational, intelligent person would ever accept Communism or Socialism as a desired way of life.

The Fundamental Changing of America

In any society, change is usually a gradual process, but only those paying attention will recognize its development. Since the early 1900s, there have been those eager to bring radical social change to America, including presidents like Woodrow Wilson, Franklin D. Roosevelt, and, to some extent, President Theodore Roosevelt. More recently, Bill Clinton stuck his foot in the door that leads to Socialism and now the door is wide open. The dark clouds of social change began to form in earnest during the 1920s within the entertainment industry, particularly the fledgling movie industry, which took advantage of the opportunity to bring social change to America by diminishing the strength of our ethics and morality. At that, they have been very successful. The weakness that has brought destruction to every great society since the beginning of time has been, and will continue to be, immorality and the failure of the people to resist it.

Communists have existed in America in one form or another for a hundred years, but they maintained a low presence because the American people certainly would not have accepted them. Today, however, our government treats them as saviors of our nation. It has taken many decades, but now our government accepts them mainly because the current ignorant generation does not have a clue what Communism is or how destructive it is. It is like an ignored cancer; when the pain forces someone to see a doctor and he discovers there is no cure, only then will he realize the seriousness of his affliction.

Since the 1950s, when the darling of CBS News, Edward R. Murrow, derailed the efforts of Senator Joseph McCarthy to warn the country about the threat of Communism, politicians have avoided using the word like the plague. Words like Progressivism or Socialism are new names for the same horse. Mr. Murrow died of lung cancer in 1965, and I wonder whether, had he not smoked himself to death, he would have lived long enough to recognize the threat of Communism to America. On the other hand, like most liberal journalists, would he view Communism as acceptable? The real problem is that too many Americans have no understanding of what either of these terms—Progressivism and Socialism—represents. The best way to get people to tune you out is to talk about Communism. It is like talking about hell; people cannot face either subject without vacating the comfort of their fantasy world.

In the 1930s, President Franklin D. Roosevelt took advantage of the Great Depression and introduced the same tactics of deception and fear that President Obama is attempting today. Many believed that Roosevelt's New Deal would end America's economic woes; he scared people into believing that unless he had the freedom to act immediately the country would be lost. The current administration is repeating the same scare tactics today so that people will pay little attention to the repercussions of all the bailouts and the enormous debt that began under President Bush and has skyrocketed under President Obama. Many of the programs that Roosevelt introduced, such as Social Security, still adversely affect us, and like footprints in concrete, they are difficult to remove. If you are among those who have been taught that Franklin Roosevelt was a god-like figure who saved America during the Great Depression, may I suggest you read: *New Deal or Raw Deal: How FDR's Economic Legacy Has Damaged America* (2008) by Burton Folsom Jr. Mr. Folsom describes the damage that Roosevelt did to our country and how liberal Socialists distort history to cover up their real feelings about America. Following is a quote from 1939, which reflects the result of the progressive movement of FDR, which is just as relevant today.

> We have tried spending money. We are spending more than we have ever spent before and it does not work. And I have just one interest, and if I am wrong … somebody else can have my job. I want to see this country prosperous. I want to see people get a job. I want to see people get enough to eat. We have never made good on our promises … I say after eight years of this administration we have just as much unemployment as when we started … And an enormous debt to boot!"

—Henry Morgenthau, President Franklin Roosevelt's Treasury Secretary, May 1939.

Roosevelt was a racist, but he was the first president to recognize how to use minorities to build his support base by convincing them to believe his deceptions. It turned out to be a very successful tactic, one that has been equally successful for every liberal president who followed. Even though Roosevelt refused to support an anti-lynching law that made it illegal to put a rope around a black man's neck and hoist him up in a tree until he choked to death, he was nevertheless supported by most minorities and to this day is considered by many of all races as the savior of America.

Social engineering was masterfully expanded with President Lyndon Johnson. His so-called Great Society created the massive welfare state that has plagued this country ever since and, with very few exceptions, the only people who have benefited from this program are politicians and those given the responsibility to manage it. Politicians are always ready to cherry-pick examples of a few who have benefited from this program, but for the majority, it is more empty promises. Like all government programs, the welfare program has been plagued with mismanagement and fraud. We need only observe the dismal conditions of many major cities today to witness the failure of the so-called Great Society. The promised cities of hope have evolved into cities of hopelessness. Even so, the enslaved masses continue to give their support to the slave masters, and one of the great mysteries of modern times is why!

Like President Roosevelt, President Obama has mesmerized the nation with his charisma, but unlike Roosevelt, as a community organizer, President Obama had years to hone his skills and develop his agenda, surrounding himself with a cadre of likeminded radicals hiding in the shadows with a clandestine plan to conquer the United States of America. Once again, they roped in the disenfranchised by offering the proverbial T-bone. After waiting more than a year for the taste of victory, the phantom T-bone remains a neck bone. Yet, Obama still enjoys support of the vast majority of minorities.

Prosperity

Prosperity is A) a state of good fortune and especially of financial success. *Synonyms:* abundance, ease, easy street, prosperousness, thriving, well-being. B) *Contrasted words:* misery, suffering; distress, embarrassment, indigence, poverty, straits. (Merriam Webster Collegiate Thesaurus.) It leads me to ask this question: If the government is capable of providing A, is it not also capable of providing B? A free, independent, and self-reliant person can choose for himself: A or B.

Even though most Americans disagree with the path our government is taking us on, politicians choose to ignore their objections. Living in the fantasy world in Washington, they assume the likeminded crowd with whom they associate is representative of the American people and they ignore the masses who disagree with what they are doing. Socialists consider regular folk to be a bunch of numbskulls that have no right to question anything they do. Both political parties give attention and devotion to special-interest groups, particularly their deep pockets, but it is difficult to criticize them when we sit with our hands folded in our laps and let them get away with it.

It was the free-enterprise machine and hard work of the American people, necessitated by World War II, that shoveled this country out of the quagmire into which Roosevelt had dragged us. However, recognition for those efforts was overshadowed by politicians who were eager to get to the front of the line to take credit for the recovery, when in reality they had little to do with the recovery. The task of rescuing the country from the mess politicians continue to make of it has once again fallen to the American people, a burden that seems to have no end. Selfishness, greed, and corruption in our government continue to beat down our citizens, and we do not deserve that from our own government. It is very doubtful our economy will ever recover except in the fantasy world of politics where magic is relied on to make two plus two equal a thousand.

It is not the rich and certainly not the poor who sustain our economy; the middle class and small businesses are the life of our economy and always have been. In addition, most countries that do not have a middle class are dying on the vine. When the president succeeds in destroying our middle class, which is a high priority in his agenda, capitalism will wither and die, and Socialism will sprout.

According to an article printed in the fall 2001 issue of Compensation and Working Conditions, from the Department of Labor's Bureau of Labor Statistics, at the beginning of the Great Depression, around 1933, unemployment reached a devastating level of more than 24.9 percent. If you live in the real world, you will realize that we could face that level of unemployment by non-union workers again. In fact, in spite of what this government wants you to believe, the real figure is probably much higher. (As usual, they embellish figures such as unemployment to their advantage, assuming they consider a 9.7 percent unemployment rate to be an advantage.) Drastically increasing government jobs to lower the unemployment rate is no advantage at all, considering that taxpayers pay government salaries. Government jobs take from our economy; they do not contribute to it. If you are among those riding high after being recently hired into a government job, heed this warning: do not get too used to your job because eventually the government will be forced to stop printing counterfeit money to pay your salary.

We live in a different reality today than those who survived the Great Depression. Most people in those days were self-reliant and determined to survive without giving up their freedom to the government. The only way the government can affect economic recovery is to provide the opportunity and not burden entrepreneurs and small business people with high taxes, crippling regulations, and get out of the way and allow the American people to do what they are capable of doing. President Reagan understood this and applied it; otherwise, it would have taken decades to recover from the economic devastation caused by the policies of President Carter.

Many Americans are dependent on the government and are incapable of surviving without government support. Many people who depend on the government for support have earned that support. However, it becomes irrelevant if the government continues to take money from those that deserve it and give it to those that do not. That, my friend, is the death knell that is going to destroy our way of life. However, the real culprit that is bringing about our ruin is the apathy and indifference of the current generation.

The Disconnect between the President and the People

You may hear Socialists embellish the truth about how well the economic recovery is going, but that will not prevent its eventual collapse. I am no economist, but simple arithmetic is all that is required to know that our economy is built on a house of cards that will continue to grow until it eventually collapses under its own weight. We are straddling a teeter-totter; on one end is the most inept leadership this great country has ever had, and on the other end is the coming poverty, created by super-inflation and devastatingly high taxes.

The quest for power is akin to mental illness; the only cure for people who have power is to seek more power, unaware of the bees of reality swarming around their heads. The voice of the average concerned citizen is but a whisper among the boisterous demands from special-interest groups that surround politicians like hungry vultures.

At the time of this writing, there are pods of protest around the country because many people are confused and worried about what is transpiring. Peaceful protest is as American as apple pie, but apple pie is not as popular as it once was. Politicians pay little heed to protest when they have the power to squelch it; and if it threatens their agenda, they will squelch it. In the first place, they are dumbfounded that anyone would oppose their plans for America, and they do not understand why a majority of Americans disagree with them. Not too many years ago, such peaceful protests were effective, but with the bunch we are dealing with today, it is an overwhelming challenge to mount any effective protest.

With the liberal press as its mouthpiece, this administration's voice is all the American people will hear. Protesters are demonized and vilified to the point that, in frustration, those attempting to exercise their constitutional rights will realize the hopelessness of their efforts. At best, a protest may sidetrack the current efforts of the administration, but Socialists are not about to give up, and they will develop some other tactic to defeat any opposition. The door to

Socialism has been opened to them by very misguided voters, and they are not about to allow the door to be closed. I hope these words scare you and cause you to think the unthinkable because an unimaginable nightmare is about to unfold in America.

The president is growing a tree, but rather than start with a sapling, he has planted an entire tree. If he has to trim a limb here and there to silence the protesters, he will do so, but the tree will continue to grow and produce new limbs, replacing the ones he has cut off to fool the people. The political blight that has infected our country will not allow any opposition against its plans to succeed, even if it has to use force.

Narcissism

In Greek mythology, there was a handsome young fellow named Narcissus. After rejecting the advances of a nymph, he was sentenced by the goddess of retribution to fall in love with the next person he saw. He looked into a pool of water and fell in love with his own reflection and he spent his life staring at himself. His only legacy is a flower that bloomed by the pool and bears his name to this day.

I am not a psychologist, but I suspect that sometime during his youth, President Obama was set on a path that developed in him a distain for the status quo in America. If that is true, he compensated for being dissatisfied with himself by seeing his reflection in a mirror as a victim. He is determined that every person on the planet has the opportunity to see not the real person but the same reflection that he sees. He is indeed a handsome man, but not everyone is as infatuated with his reflection as he seems to be. As the sun goes down, the reflection fades, and he must worry throughout the night until it reappears at the rising of the sun, and the cameras are rolling. Many years from now, he will no longer be infatuated with what he sees in the mirror—neither will anyone else—and eventually he will have to confront the real Obama. His legacy is still in development, but if it involves a flower, I wonder what we will name it? As much as I disagree with what he is doing to our country, I cannot help but have compassion for him or anyone who is unable to live in a world of reality and spreads misery to other people to compensate for his own misery. Now he is in a position to bring misery to millions. I can only surmise there has to be a certain amount of evil in a person who can gain pleasure from doing such a thing to other human beings.

The Good Old Days?

Those of us old enough to remember America when it was under the leadership of America's Greatest Generation can clearly see the devastation that is befalling our country. The government was not involved in every aspect of our lives; we relied on each other and ourselves. Neighbor helping neighbor and those unable to help themselves could depend on neighbors or their church for assistance. There were many poor people of all races in this country then, but we were all Americans who relied on each other. We had no desire to rely on the government and that gave us the freedom to make our own choices about how we wished to live.

Politics was never a topic in my family and the only thing I know about my parents' political views is that my dad once voted for Dwight Eisenhower. Beyond that, I have no idea about their political views, but there is no doubt that they were both patriotic Americans. Like most people at that time, my parents depended on God and themselves, not the government. If they ever talked about depending on the government for anything, I was never aware of it.

Harkening back to the so-called good old days may frustrate some of you, but be assured they were not that good economically. My mom began working in the cotton mill in Bladenboro at the age of fourteen and continued in that job for fifty years. My dad worked for fifty-one years in that same mill and did not retire until he was almost seventy years old. There was no retirement plan, no vacation, and no health plan. Both my parents had to work to support us, but they worked different shifts so one of them would always be home to look after my siblings and me. There were no such thing as air conditioners, but we were not afraid to go to bed at night with the doors and windows left open. In fact, the doors and windows in our house did not have locks. When we were away from home, even for extended periods, our house was safe, not because of an alarm system, but because neighbors kept watch. Even petty crime was so rare most people were never affected by it.

My dad was forty-seven years old before he bought his first car, and he paid cash for it because he would not buy anything if he could not pay cash. It took my parents another twenty years to save enough money to buy their first and only home and, again, they paid cash for it. My dad died at the age of eighty-six and, right to the end, he was the most contented person I have ever known. He lived that way because of his faith in God, because he never had to look back on anything in his life with regret, and there was never a derogatory word spoken against him.

The majority of people in our town were hard working and economically poor, but so very rich in many other ways; One of the most valuable lessons I learned growing up in that environment is that living a happy and contented life is a choice. Bitterness, envy, hatred, arrogance, prejudice, and self-pity are insurmountable road blocks to living a happy and counted life. However, the *most* valuable lesson I learned from my life experience is we will never have true happiness, peace and contentment in our life without God. A person on his death bed facing the end of his life will not be thinking about the size of his house, the number of cars in his garage, his bank account, the winner of American idol, how much he may have contributed to his profession, or how he has lived in poverty all of his life. None of those things will matter. He will die in contentment, or die in misery and regret; it is a choice.

My parents are gone now, but my love and respect for the sacrifices they made in providing for our family remains. Looking back, I realize that it had to be difficult for them in very trying times, but I was unaware of it and I was always happy, and every day presented a new adventure to explore. I was thirteen years old when I saw a television for the first time, but I had no interest in it, because it interfered with my adventures outdoors in the real world.

My parents' life was not unique but representative of hundreds of families in the same circumstances in our small village. For years, union thugs attempted to unionize the mill that would surely have improved the financial situation for the people, but they resisted being beholden to any outside organization. They valued their independence above any financial gain and were equally resistant to any government involvement in their lives. Self-respect was a motivating force, the norm rather than the exception, as it is today. My life experience has taught me that government involvement in our lives is contrary to what our founders intended for this country and is rarely beneficial to anyone except politicians. There are consequences to being ignorant, and when the bill comes due, creditors will demand payment. It is the ignorance and apathy of this generation that has brought us to the brink of destroying America; the sad thing is there are many people who rejoice over the prospect.

Politics is not high on my list of priorities, but the most valued right we have as Americans is the right to vote. Even that right is not free from corruption and behind-the-scenes wheeling and dealing, and it is difficult to distinguish enough differences between a Democrat and Republican to favor one over the other. Conservatives are looking for any politician who shares their views on moral issues, character, and above all, honesty, regardless of what party they represent, but the pickings are slim.

Back in the so-called good old days, we had freedom from the involvement of the government in our lives unless it was necessary for national security. People did not depend on the government; the government depended on the people. The people rarely let the government down, but this government seems to enjoy letting the people down as a demonstration of its power.

My parents, along with the majority of Americans, had the wisdom to understand that no matter how hard the struggle, it was better than having their lives dominated by the government. Given the chance, most people from that era would not hesitate to go back to those times because we had a life that is forever lost to this generation. My parents had a hard time providing for our family, but we were always happy and content with our lives and had far more important things to be involved in than politics. Until around 1960, people trusted our government to do the right thing, and for the most part, it did, but the paradigm changed after the assassination of President Kennedy. The American spirit, which he revived during his term in office, died along with him.

Even when, on occasion, things were tough financially—for all races—people did not sit around smothered in self-pity, looking to the government for support. They did what they had to do to survive on their own and to help others in any way they could. I only share this information to impress on some of you that the current situation we have created for ourselves is not the America our founders created.

The America that has existed for over two hundred years is terminally ill, and I shudder to think what will be left of it. Those of you not old enough to have witnessed what the real America was like have no idea what you have lost. We did not have Medicare, but we had medical care, and it was affordable in most cases. If we were unable to go to the doctor's office, the doctor came to the house whether people could pay or not, for those that did pay, paid the doctor, not the government. Doctors were among the wealthiest people in the country in those days, and they did what doctors love to do, they treated the sick and did not have to spend most of their time dealing with government bureaucracy and insurance companies. We had meals at home, not in fast-food fat houses, and we did not have to gulp down a handful of pills just to get through the day, pills that pharmaceutical companies say we cannot live without.

My dad died from prostate cancer at the age of eighty-six; his older brother died at ninety-nine; God willing, his oldest sister will celebrate her 102nd birthday this year; and his youngest sister will be one hundred. My mom died at age eighty-eight, and her brothers and sisters all lived into their eighties and nineties. There is reason for their longevity: faith in God, which diminishes stress; proper diet; physical activity; helping one another and living a disciplined life. As the saying goes, hard work never killed anyone, and living a contented life can increase one's longevity.

Most people I knew in my youth were poor and uneducated, but they sure knew how to live and enjoy the blessings of being American. The small town I grew up in only required one police officer because the people policed themselves. Today, that same town has a smaller population but ten police officers, so what happened? What happened was that government became involved in people's lives by coddling criminals rather than putting them in jail where they belong, further victimizing the victims of crime.

The late 1950s was perhaps the best time in history to be an American teenager. What made it so special was the anticipation of a great future ahead and what seemed like unlimited possibilities; most of my generation took full advantage of the opportunities available to them. Teenagers today must find it difficult to see anything of real value to look forward to without the government's involvement. Most of my generation was composed of fiercely independent people, motivated by determination, perseverance, self-reliance, and self-confidence. It was true then and is true now, if a person has nothing it is because he has done nothing to obtain it.

Entitlements

There is a word quite prominent in today's conversations, although I have no recollection of ever hearing it during my youth: "entitlement." My natural curiosity led me to Merriam-Webster's 11th Collegiate Dictionary, where I found the following definition: "belief that one is deserving of or entitled to certain privileges." Since the definition represents a belief, it required further exploration, so I went back to the dictionary. There are two words in the above definition that seemed to have some relevance: "deserving" and "entitled." The latter seemed a good place to start, so once again, I went back to the dictionary, which defines "entitled" as follows: "to furnish with proper grounds for seeking or claiming something." The phrase "proper grounds" is intriguing, but things were about to get out of hand, so once again, more research was required. In Merriam Webster Collegiate Thesaurus, "deserving" is defined as admirable, commendable, estimable, laudable, meritable, meritorious, praisable, praiseworthy, and thankworthy. Despite all my research, I could find no explanation of how any of these words could apply to anyone simply because they had been born. There were too many unanswered questions to halt my exploration, so I went back for the last time to the dictionary to search for some way to explain it all. By now, some of you are thinking this is all a bunch of nonsense, and it is, and that is the explanation, Nonsense is language, conduct, or an idea that is absurd or contrary to good sense; an instance of absurd action. I have injected a bit of humor here, but there is a serious side, and there is no humor in it. If carefully analyzed, practically everything in which government officials involve themselves, Democrats and Republicans, *is* nonsense. You are certainly free to disagree, but you will have a hard time justifying your disagreement based on our current situation.

The People versus the Government

A free country like the United States of America provides opportunities for everyone, and except for medical conditions or old age, nothing prevents anyone from achieving a goal he has set for himself if he is willing to do what it takes. Life is not always easy, but making the effort to accomplish something meaningful in one's life is far more rewarding than wasting one's life feeling sorry for one self. The only adult victims are those who make choices to become victims. Everyone makes mistakes, and there are consequences for making mistakes, but if we make mistakes it is our responsibility to deal with them. It is fashionable these days for those who think they are living in poverty to blame society for their problems, but unless we walk on four legs and howl at the moon, we are all members of the society and have no one to blame but ourselves if we make a mess of our lives. People who live beyond their means are seldom forced to do so; it is a choice.

I will make my point and not bore you any further with this rambling. Those of my generation recognize a coming possibility that perhaps many of you do not: the loss of freedom. There is no greater gift than God's gift of freedom; it does not come from man, and no man has the right to take it from us, however, we can willingly forfeit it, as many Americans have done.

It would be foolish to leave the impression that everything the government does is bad, but if government officials confined themselves to the things they are suppose to do—like protecting us from the many enemies who are motivated to destroy us—they would be better appreciated and respected by the people. If they learn how to be leaders rather than wheeling and dealing politicians, maintain the country's infrastructure, help those who cannot help themselves, protect our borders, and keep their noses out of every little aspect of our life, it would be a great benefit to us all. Finally, yet importantly, they should properly educate a generation that is ignorant about the greatness of this country and its history. The few who have any knowledge of the history of this country will know that Socialists will never tolerate any success by an individual or business that does not involve the government.

It has taken many years of living and observing the human experience in many parts of the world to recognize a profound truth: people are the same

21

everywhere. Most people seek only to provide a comfortable life for themselves and their families, and people everywhere appear to be in a constant struggle against their governments' efforts to make it difficult for them to achieve an independent life.

Socialists

Socialists hate everything America stands for because they lack sound principles or the character to fit in with the mainstream of society. This is apparent not only in America but exists everywhere. The problem with Socialists is they have no comfort zone and, as misery loves company, they do not want anyone else to be comfortable and contented. There is no such thing as an independent Socialist; Socialists will latch onto almost anything to identify with because they have nothing worthwhile on which to base their own self-identity. They feign more compassion for a one-inch fish in a pool of water out in the middle of nowhere than they do for their human neighbors. Of course, their perceived compassion is as phony as they are because in reality they would not know, or care, if the fish actually existed or not. If a Socialist were on a deserted island, it would not take more than a day or two before he realized the stupidity of Socialism because he would not have a clue of how to survive on his own. Of course, some conservatives would have the same problem, but they would be less likely to blame someone else for their predicament.

The current generation has little knowledge of the history and function of this great country. If the American people would unite again and work for the betterment of themselves and the country, we could make great progress. If we swap hatred for compassion for each other and acknowledge the power that has watched over this country from its beginning, those who we elect into office would have much less effect on our lives. The government would be subservient to the people rather than the other way around.

Unenforced Law

According to Forbes list of the world's richest people for 2010, released March 10, 2010: Mexico is the home of the world's richest person: Carlo Slim Helu (worth 53.5 billion dollars). To get a glimpse of the possible future of America, take a trip to Mexico away from the popular tourist areas; it will be educational, as long as you are not kidnapped or murdered. The contrast between those in abject poverty and the elite is mindboggling. There are pockets of the elite ruling class here and there surrounded by multitudes of impoverished people who have no hope of improving their circumstances. Given the opportunity, who among us would not flee such a crime-riddled country? It is difficult for me to blame Mexicans for seeking a better life for their families by entering our country illegally. Unenforced laws are no laws at all, and it is difficult to reconcile that Mexicans are breaking the law by coming to America when our government ignores the law in order to gain support from those they allow to come here. Some are eager to blame the Mexicans for breaking our laws but seem unconcerned that our political leaders are ignoring not only the Constitution but also their own legislated laws. The fact that the motives of this administration have become obvious under close scrutiny means that the people have no excuse for allowing their way of life to be destroyed. It is a question of who is more stupid—the administration or the people—and that is a difficult call.

Freedom and Personal Responsibility

Poor people of all races seem to be in a stupor, resigned to the hopelessness of their situation, waiting for the government to provide them with free stuff that other people have worked for to provide for themselves. There are those who are unable to provide for themselves due to old age or disability, and we should be willing to spend tax dollars to help those in that situation, but no responsible person should have to help those who refuse to help themselves.

As a person who loves all people because they are God's creation, it saddens me that many people fail to realize what freedom means. No one has the right to rob freedom from another man. People in prison do not have their freedom taken from them; they voluntarily surrender their freedom by committing a crime. Freedom allows man to make his own decisions, and there are consequences for making the wrong one. God, who gave us freedom, will not take it away from us, but man has devised an unlimited number of ways to make a mess of his life because he has the freedom to do so. Unfortunately, any man who makes a mess of his own life does not do so in a vacuum; it also affects many other people. As humans, we all deserve equal respect, if we deserve it; respect is not a right, it must be earned, and if we do not offer respect, we should not expect to receive it. Life is rarely fair to anyone, but life is what *we* make of it, and if we are under the illusion that people will respect us without some effort on our part, then we are undeserving of that respect.

Personal freedom is balanced against government power, and as one side increases, the other side decreases. The new health-care plan is all about power; it gives the government a tremendous boost to its power, and people do not yet know how much freedom they have surrendered to the government under this new law. Ponder this: Three years from now when you are forced to accept that all those wonderful things the government promised are not forthcoming—and believe me they will not be—what are you going to do about it? The aftermath of this debacle will unravel the fabric of this country and linger into the next generation and beyond.

As a passionate person, I have sympathy for those driven by emotion rather than any rational thought and supported the election of this out-of-control government because when faced with the reality of what is ahead for America, they will probably spend the rest of their lives in regret. It is not difficult for any thinking person to realize the impossibility for the health-care plan to come close to what is projected. The new health-care plan is just the beginning; the president and others in Congress knew from the beginning that it would be a disaster and sold their souls to get it passed. However, they do not care because it gave them what they were after from the beginning: more power to inflict the rest of their agenda onto the American people. The health-care plan was debated for over a year and kept the whole country, well, almost the whole country, distracted from all the other devious and clandestine plans taking place in the dark shadows—financial reform and new environmental legislation (a distracting deception for more bailouts) and comprehensive immigration reform (which is another distracting deception for amnesty for illegals). When those plans are revealed, if they ever are, health-care will fade from the scene, overshadowed by the even more disastrous programs.

The Effect on Our Young

Sixty years ago, there were real towns like Mayberry, and real families like the Cleavers and the Nelsons, and *Happy Days* reflected reality. Honesty, integrity, respect, and moral principles were the norm rather than the exception, as they are today. Looking back to those times is like losing a loved one; we mourn the loss but realize that it will never return. Children of today do not have a clue about what it is like to live in the real world, given their addiction to the fantasy world of video games, television, and computers. They are confined to the house or yard, tethered by their parents' reasonable fears that something bad may happen to them.

Children are victims of Socialist indoctrination by our education system and apathetic parents who do not have a clue about what their children are learning. Because of the social indoctrination in our public schools, by the time they leave middle school they will believe that individual responsibility and self-reliance are kooky ideas that our founders dreamed up, that people in those days were too stupid to know any better, and that it is the government's responsibility to take care of them from cradle to grave. They will grow up believing that and be unprepared to take control of their own lives. It leaves me and many others perplexed that some people think that is a good idea.

Children have no idea what it is like to have the freedom to come and go as they wish without fear and to be able to grow and learn, not based on fantasy but on experience driven by imagination and exploration. If you have young children, I am sure you want them to be happy and protected; but they will not be children forever and, unless *you* prepare them for the future, they will have no future. We may live in a free country, but we have lost the ability to live as free people. We have become slaves to the dictates of a government determined to abolish the freedoms we fail to appreciate. When future generations look back, they will not wish for the past to return; they will curse it, and this generation deserves their condemnation.

There are enough young, bright Americans today with the potential to carry on, preserve our heritage, and return our country to its greatness. We have squandered away, however, their ability to take advantage of the America our parents and grandparents sacrificed to build and will to us. Sadly, for each bright, engaged young person, at least a dozen do not have a clue.

This current generation will be the first in our history to be worse off than the previous one—not only financially but much more importantly, also in terms of freedom. Even if our economy rebounds to a 1990s' level, America's once-free people will lose much of their hard-earned money to support a dysfunctional government. The majority of young people today will spend most, if not all, of their lives struggling with the trillions of dollars of debt this administration will burden them with, and their hopes for a comfortable life in the future will be an unattainable dream. As bad as that may be, there is a possibility that they may have to survive under Socialism or even Communism, which would be far worse than any economic problems they will face.

The Forgotten Greatest Generation

Socialists have no real compassion for the suffering of the masses but are never at a loss for devising methods of pretence to disguise their real motives. They have absolutely no interest in perpetuating and supporting the legacy of this great country; instead, their philosophy is infused with hatred and distain for all independent and successful people who are not one of theirs.

If the destruction of the country continues at the current rate, the president will not need a second term; he will accomplish America's demise in his first term. He seems unable to understand that his responsibility is not to represent only a few targeted groups—unions and special interest groups—but the many millions of citizens who are mostly caring, hardworking, and devoted to this country and its heritage. America has become a forest of cocoons where our fragmented population hides isolated from one another, unaware that the forest is on fire.

During the fifteen years following World War II, the country prospered, thanks to the blessings of God and under the care of America's Greatest Generation. The unique American spirit was at its peak and even for those hindered by racism a brighter future laid ahead. It all began to change in the late 1950s; America began to turn to idolatry (television), and Socialism began to wiggle its tentacles into the education system, resulting in the emergence in the 1960s of a radical antiestablishment generation that began the transformation to the dysfunctional, fragmented society we experience today. The American spirit was skewed and fragmented into selfishness and rebellion, except for the brief period of John F. Kennedy's presidency, when there was a resurgence of the American spirit and recognition of America's greatness.

> Let every nation know, whether it wishes us well or ill, that we shall pay any price, bear any burden, meet any hardship, support any friend, oppose any foe, in order to assure the survival and the success of liberty.
> —John F. Kennedy, January 20, 1961

Can you imagine President Obama making such a statement today and meaning it?

The moral foundation that has sustained America through many trials and troubles began to erode in the 1960s with open drug use, free-flowing alcohol, and deviant sex exploitation. In the 1970s, the young people seemed to turn inward and tune out on the society that began the dummying down of America, which continues to proliferate today.

Idolatry

The early 1980s saw the popularity of a new idol: the personal computer and in the late 1980s, with the worldwide availability of the Internet, the computer became a must-have item for most Americans. Today, America has become a full-fledged idolatrous nation, bowing to television, computers, Internet, iPods, Blackberries, sports, and entertainment. We have now created a tuned-out generation that does not have a clue of what is going on in the real world and is led astray by anything that relieves them of any personal responsibility. A Socialist government is orchestrating our demise, but we are so awash with, and so distracted by, technology and information, that only the few who are still in contact with reality are aware that our beloved country is being destroyed.

> Let us, by all wise and constitutional measures, promote intelligence among the people as the best means of preserving our liberties.
> —President James Monroe, first inaugural address, March 4, 1817

Can we read those profound words of James Monroe and in any way conclude that our country can survive when almost half of the students in many public schools fail to graduate high school and the ones that do probably have never heard of President James Monroe? In most universities, education is nothing more than social indoctrination, so who is going to protect America's liberty? People cannot ward off reality forever; we must accept reality and deal with it. Those who do not wish to give up on America, and cling to love and hope for this country, must face the reality of what is in America's future. Denying the truth will not change the truth; The America of the past is dying and waiting, seemingly in vane, for resuscitation.

Separation of Church and State

Do you believe we will ever stop abortion, or that our children will ever again have the opportunity to express their faith in the classroom? Can you convince yourself that the Ten Commandments will ever again appear in public places? Will same-sex marriage suddenly disappear? What is the hope for our future when Socialists finally succeed in removing any evidence of God from this country? Will we ever be able to convince people that the so-called separation of church and state is misrepresented? It is a misrepresentation of a phrase used by Thomas Jefferson, in a written letter he received from the Danbury (Connecticut) Baptist Association. Following is an excerpt from that letter:

> I contemplate with sovereign reverence that act of the whole American people which declared that their legislature should make no law respecting an establishment of religion, or prohibiting the free exercise thereof, thus building a wall of separation between church and state.

That is it! Based on this statement, the Supreme Court ruled that there could be no display of any religious nature on public property. There are two sides to a wall; on one side is the free exercise of religion and on the other side, the prohibition of a national religion. Is it not strange how the Supreme Court explored only one side of the wall? The following statement is an excerpt from Thomas Jefferson's second inaugural speech (1805):

> In matters of religion I have considered that its free exercise
> is placed by the Constitution independent of the powers of
> the General Government. I have therefore undertaken on
> no occasion to prescribe the religious exercises suited to it,
> but have left them, as the Constitution found them, under
> the direction and discipline of the church or state authorities
> acknowledged by the several religious societies ....

It is beyond my understanding how anyone can use Jefferson's words to justify the separation of church and state as it is applied today. The government is prohibited from creating a state religion and prohibited from interfering with the free exercise of religion, whether it is on top of Mount Rainier or in the chambers of our government. It is difficult to think of a more blatant disregard for our constitutional right to free speech and expression, wherever we choose to exercise it. It is a clear indication of the Socialist distain for religion, especially Christianity. Anyone familiar with the writings of Thomas Jefferson clearly knows that he would never agree with the way his words have been misrepresented today concerning the separation of church and state.

In 1854, the House of Representatives made the following declaration: "The great, vital, and conservative element in our system is the belief of our people in the pure doctrines and the divine truths of the Gospel of Jesus Christ." The representatives in the 1854 were obviously more intelligent than those we have in Congress today. So why did they not come up with the notion that our Constitution prohibits the expression of religion in public places?

How Did It Happen?

Another president with the desire to introduce Socialism to America was Bill Clinton, but no president has ignored our Constitution and all legal barriers in the way of his goals more than Franklin Roosevelt and President Obama. Roosevelt failed in his efforts, but there is no indication that President Obama will fail. With a liberal Senate, a liberal majority on the Supreme Court, and an anti-American press, nothing can stop Socialism in America, except the people. Sadly, I do not have confidence that enough people in this generation care enough to get involved, and even if they did, this government has become so determined to succeed with its agenda, it will use whatever means it has to stop the opposition.

If you were blessed to be born and reared in the company of America's Greatest Generation, you probably learned to love and respect this country and honor the sacrifices of all those who came before, a time when heroes were not entertainers or sports figures. We have become a nation of shallow, unprincipled people without a solid foundation in which to build a meaningful productive life. Selfishness, self-interest, bigotry among all races, and self-imposed ignorance is overtaking the attitude of self-reliance, charity, respect for each other, and knowledge of the heritage of this great country.

Who Is to Blame?

People complain about how we got into this mess without realizing that all of us must share the responsibility for allowing it to happen. Many hope that we can change things in the upcoming elections by voting the troublemakers out of office, but the chances of that are slim to none. If the Tea Party protesters would unite, unify their message, and stand shoulder to shoulder as a united power, they could prevent Socialists from taking control of America. The problem is the Tea Party protesters are as divided as any other group. Even if by some magic the Republicans recapture the House and Senate, it will not prevent President Obama from fulfilling his agenda. More and more, the House and Senate are becoming irrelevant, and all the president has to do is sign his name to an executive order or veto to bypass any interference from the Congress. Thus, he has the power to do whatever he wishes; after all, who is going to stop him? That is the sad reality of what we have allowed to befall our country, so get used to it.

We have this destructive government because not only did we put those officials in office; we continue to keep them in office. The current "it's not my fault" generation of politicians is a scab over the cancer that is eating away at our innards. No one is willing to take responsibility for anything; cheating and lying have become so common, they have become a normal way of life. Too many Americans expect to be deceived by our leaders and accept it as the normal way a government operates. Power is the demon here, and it is not only the desire of our leaders, but the populace as well. Give me what I want, and give it to me now; make it free and do not talk to me about consequences and responsibility—that seems to be the attitude of too many Americans.

A Confused Generation

For many years, Socialist educational institutions have released into our country the most misguided, misinformed, unprepared generation in our history. If you are a Socialist, you are a puppet, to be manipulated by a government that promises everything and gives nothing of real value to prepare for a self-reliant existence. The government cannot improve our lives better than we can do so ourselves. America is a land of opportunity, available to all its citizens, but unless opportunities are taken advantage of, they are of no advantage to anyone. If we have nothing, it is because we do nothing. If we live in poverty, in most cases, it is because we choose to do so.

One does not need to be highly educated or have superior intelligence to make the right decisions; common sense usually will suffice. If we consider ourselves victims of society, then we shall live as victims, and that will get us nowhere. Life is not always easy, but the journey we choose to take is our responsibility. If we are materialistic, we must prepare for an unsatisfied life. Most people believe if they win the lottery, they can live the rest of their lives in bliss and happiness, but that is not reality. A happy poor man who wins the lottery will be a happy rich man; conversely, an unhappy poor man who wins the lottery will be an unhappy rich man. He soon will realize that happiness cannot come from a wallet stuffed with money.

There have always been, and will always be, the rich and the poor, but the middle class is what makes America a great country. They may not get rich, but as long as there is a middle class, there will be opportunity for the average person to better his life. Unfortunately, under Socialism, there is an absence of a middle class, only the rich and powerful—and everyone else.

If you are old enough to remember the real America willed to us by the founders and our ancestors, but now witness this once great country ravished by stupidity, it is depressing. However, it is what it is and, no matter the outcome, we can never go back. America is terminally ill, and the consequences are ours to endure if we continue to ignore our affliction.

> In the midst of these pleasing ideas we should be unfaithful
> to ourselves if we should ever lose sight of the danger to our
> liberties if anything partial or extraneous should infect the
> purity of our free, fair, virtuous, and independent elections.
> If an election is to be determined by a majority of a single
> vote and that can be procured by a party through artifice or
> corruption, the Government may be the choice of a party for
> its own ends, not of the nation for the national good.
> —John Adams, inaugural address, March 4, 1797

Mr. Adams's words are in stark contrast to the babbling nonsense from our selfish, self-serving leadership that we hear today. We cannot learn from the history of our country if we are ignorant of that history, and therein is one of our most fundamental problems. Up until the election of President Obama, most Americans were so comfortable in their apathy; they failed to recognize the threat to our way of life. Many people who went to the polls to vote looked for an "R" or "D" without knowing anything about the person whose name was next to the letter. "What are they going to do for me?" overshadowed any concern about consequences to the country as a whole.

America as a Moral Nation?

Anyone familiar with this country's history will clearly recognize the hand of God in the development of our unique form of government.

> I dwell on this prospect with every satisfaction which an
> ardent love for my country can inspire, since there is no
> truth more thoroughly established than that there exists
> in the economy and course of nature an indissoluble union
> between virtue and happiness; between duty and advantage;
> between the genuine maxims of an honest and magnanimous
> policy and the solid rewards of public prosperity and felicity;
> since we ought to be no less persuaded that the propitious
> smiles of Heaven can never be expected on a nation that
> disregards the eternal rules of order and right which Heaven
> itself has ordained; and since the preservation of the sacred
> fire of liberty and the destiny of the republican model of

government are justly considered, perhaps, as *deeply*, as *finally*, staked on the experiment entrusted to the hands of the American people.

—George Washington, first inaugural address, April 30, 1789

Take note of these profound words: "since we ought to be no less persuaded that the propitious smiles of Heaven can never be expected on a nation that disregards the eternal rules of order and right which Heaven itself has ordained."

> Relying on the aid to be derived from the other departments of the Government, I enter on the trust to which I have been called by the suffrages of my fellow-citizens with my fervent prayers to the Almighty that He will be graciously pleased to continue to us that protection which He has already so conspicuously displayed in our favor.
>
> —James Monroe, inaugural address, March 4, 1817

> I shall look for whatever success may attend my public service; and knowing that "except the Lord keep the city the watchman waketh but in vain," with fervent supplications for His favor, to His overruling providence I commit with humble but fearless confidence my own fate and the future destinies of my country.
>
> —John Quincy Adams, inaugural address, March 4, 1825

> The American people stand firm in the faith which has inspired this Nation from the beginning. We believe that all men have a right to equal justice under law and equal opportunity to share in the common good. We believe that all men have the right to freedom of thought and expression. We believe that all men are created equal because they are created in the image of God.
>
> —Harry S. Truman, inaugural address, January 20, 1949

My friends, before I begin the expression of those thoughts that I deem appropriate to this moment, would you permit me the privilege of uttering a little private prayer of my own. And I ask that you bow your heads: Almighty God, as we stand here at this moment my future associates in the executive branch of government join me in beseeching that Thou will make full and complete our dedication to the service of the people in this throng, and their fellow citizens everywhere. Give us, we pray, the power to discern clearly right from wrong, and allow all our words and actions to be governed thereby, and by the laws of this land. Especially we pray that our concern shall be for all the people regardless of station, race, or calling. May cooperation be permitted and be the mutual aim of those who, under the concepts of our Constitution, hold to differing political faiths; so that all may work for the good of our beloved country and Thy glory. Amen.

—Dwight Eisenhower, first inaugural address, January 20, 1953

The world is very different now. For man holds in his mortal hands the power to abolish all forms of human poverty and all forms of human life. And yet the same revolutionary beliefs for which our forebears fought are still at issue around the globe—the belief that the rights of man come not from the generosity of the state, but from the hand of God.

—John F. Kennedy, inaugural address, January 20, 1961

We remain a young nation, but in the words of Scripture, the time has come to set aside childish things. The time has come to reaffirm our enduring spirit; to choose our better history; to carry forward that precious gift, that noble idea, passed on from generation to generation: the God-given promise that all are equal, all are free, and all deserve a chance to pursue their full measure of happiness.

—Barack Obama, inaugural address, January 20, 2009

Freedom and equality for every human is not a mere promise from God—it is his statute. Below is the Scripture alluded to in the above quote:

> When I was a child, I spake as a child, I understood as a child, I thought as a child: but when I became a man, I put away childish things. For now we see through a glass, darkly; but then face to face: now I know in part; but then shall I know even as also I am known.
> —1 Cor. 13:11-12

It would take several pages to include all such speeches from our formal leaders, and I can say with confidence that many of you have never read many of these words. Certainly, most children attending public schools today are not familiar with them. I include another revealing quote from President Obama's inaugural address:

> And those of us who manage the public's dollars will be held to account—to spend wisely, reform bad habits, and do our business in the light of day—because only then can we restore the vital trust between a people and their government.

Speeches are one thing, viewed through "glass darkly" (a reflection). Conversely—action is viewed face to face. "But then shall I know even as also I am known."

Apathy and Ignorance

What little history our children are taught in our Socialist school system is so distorted by political correctness, it is unworthy of being called history. People should be cognizant of their history because to be ignorant of it is to be incapable of protecting and participating in the future. America has not had a perfect past, and to be aware of the less-than-desirable events is a great guide for shaping the future. We cannot relive the past; nor should we. However, the biggest problem with most Americans is their lack of appreciation for the greatness of this country, and that is a result of their ignorance about our history. There is no appreciation for the sacrifices of the founders and our ancestors, who created and willed to us the greatest form of government the world has ever known. There is little appreciation from Socialist radicals for our military and those who voluntarily risk their lives to preserve and defend our freedoms.

Hardworking, successful people are vilified for enjoying the fruits of their labor, whether they are the CEOs of large corporations or regular citizens who drag themselves from bed every morning and spend ten or twelve hours a day trying to support their families. On the other side of this line are the shiftless and lazy that do not create anything but a burden on those who work to support them. Thousands, maybe millions, of people in America—of all races and backgrounds—have never done an honest day's work in their lives to provide for themselves. If one is familiar with the history of this country and the great men and women who created what no other country has, one will know it will not survive if occupied by apathetic, lazy, and ignorant people, and our founders were well aware of that danger.

If we get satisfaction from feeling sorry for ourselves, that is our choice, but no one else is obligated to feel sorry for us. Life on this planet is not always easy, no matter on which rung of the economical ladder you stand. Self-pride and self-respect are what motivates people to do what they have to do to make a living for themselves. We are all born free by the will of God, and if we are in poverty, it is because of the choices we make, particularly if we are physically able to do something about it. If a person has a houseful of malnourished and mistreated children, it is his responsibility to take care of them. If he does not, he should go to jail for child endangerment, and his children should be taken from him. If we are irresponsible, we have no right to expect responsible people to share our burdens, neither by the will of man nor the will of God.

Many, if not most, mothers work outside the home rather than stay home and raise their children—not out of necessity but for that bigger house, big-screen television, a second or third car, or a closet full of junk for the kids to play with (which they tire of the first day you bring it home). If we try to keep up with the Joneses, then the Joneses enslave us. What will we do when we can no longer make payments on all the stuff we accumulate? When they can no longer have all the gadgets and toys they are used to having, what will we tell our children? The only way many grandparents can have a relationship with their grandchildren is through material gifts.

The current generation has seen the greatest explosion of information and technology the world has ever seen. Unfortunately, man's wisdom is in decline at a comparable rate resulting in misuse of all that knowledge and technology. In other words, the contemporary man, guided by his own arrogance, is convinced that he has reached the pinnacle of intelligence and knowledge and is much more advanced than any previous generation; in reality the opposite is the truth. An intelligent person cannot easily be fooled—obviously, a person does not need a collage education to be intelligent—unfortunately, America is not infected with an epidemic of intelligence.

The current generation is the most detached and ill informed that America has ever produced. That is a harsh indictment, but America is in desperate need of a reality check. We have greatly accelerated the time it takes to destroy a nation and, compared to previous great nations, we are dying before our time. This is a bleak commentary, but it needs our attention to prepare for the consequences of our folly, which no amount of false optimism will alter.

Tough times are coming to not only America but to the entire world. You may ignore this if you choose, but it is now clear to see what results from ignoring reality. An apathetic population, trade unions, trial lawyers, the "me first, America last" Congress, special interest groups, and those pulling the strings of those who are supposed to represent the people have in a very short time destroyed the future of our children and grandchildren. I cannot tell you how to prepare for the coming storm, but I can tell you this: doing nothing will not prepare you.

To control any country, a government needs to control the money, education, industry, and the press as well as eliminate personal firearms, thereby making the populace powerless. Four of the five criteria are close to fruition. Any government motivated by maximizing its power over its people will fight to maintain that power by persuasion, deception, and, if need be, by force; once that power is secure it will not be relinquished. If Socialists are successful in dragging this country into Communism, those of you who bravely proclaim that the government will never take your personal firearms away will find out that you are fooling yourself. When a squad of government goons knocks on your door demanding that you turn over your firearms and threatening you with twenty years in prison for lying about owning a firearm, you *will* turn them over.

Some of the world's most caring, hardworking people, devoted to the great heritage of America, are privileged to reside here; that is why America has always rebounded from economical disasters. However, to hope that we shall always be able to do so is not realistic. We soon may surpass the worst employment and economical crises of the Great Depression; the irrevocable damage to our future has never been so precarious. Administrations in the past have attempted to introduce Socialism to America, but never has an administration created the circumstances for Socialist success as has the one now governing our country.

Economics is far from our only problem; moral collapse is what got us in this mess, and no measure of economical recovery will solve that problem. If we accept that never in our history have we been in a comparable situation to what we are facing today, we will have to deal with it eventually. We only have to look at the situation in California, New York, and many other states to preview the fate of our nation; there will be no one to bail us out except the Chinese, and that will not be a bailout, it will be a takeover.

Thousands of individuals and businesses have divested in the hyper-taxation of California and New York and moved to other states to protect their wealth. This has left these states with fewer wealthy taxpayers to support their welfare system. Only a naive and ignorant person would fail to see that a similar situation is in our nation's future. When push comes to shove, and businesses and wealthy people must choose to either turn over a crippling portion of their wealth to the government, or find opportunities outside this country to invest their hard-earned money, it does not take a genius to know what will be their choice. We may finally get a border fence erected, not to keep people out, but to keep them in. However, the current situation will produce nothing to enhance our life; it will ultimately turn us into a third world or

Communist country; neither choice is something to look forward to, unless, of course, you are a politician.

Our founders and forefathers planted the seeds to grow America, but the American people nurtured it and made it grow into the world's greatest experiment. Politicians did not create America, it was men with vision and ordinary hardworking people, and by the blessings of God. It is our inheritance, created by the blood, sweat, and tears of our predecessors.

This current government has already accomplished things that only a few would have foreseen a few years ago, but that could not have happened without the support of many misguided people. If you are one of those who believed the American people would not stand for such things as this government is doing to our country, let me remind you that the American people put this government in power. I must admit that when I hear the phrase "the American people," I no longer know to whom it refers.

The physical, political, and economic elements of America may someday be destroyed, but the American spirit held by many Americans will not be destroyed. Even if America sinks into the deepest pit of Communism, many of you who share my love for America will keep that spirit alive in our hearts. However, we are becoming a minority, and one day we will fade away, replaced by those who do not share the same respect for the heritage of America. Respect is due for people, like Tea Party members, who get involved in efforts to rescue this country from pending disaster, but unfortunately, it may be too little, too late. Those in touch with reality have no illusions about the determination of this administration to forge ahead to their ultimate goal.

If you are among those sitting around waiting for something to happen, you can wake up because it has already happened. The absolute minimum we could hope for is to recapture the situation that existed before the election of President Obama, and the reelection of George W. Bush, but even if we could, we would still be in a dire situation. An opportunity not taken is an opportunity lost. The house is on fire and the heads of the fire department are in the back room, wheeling and dealing, figuring out ways to benefit from allowing the house to burn to the ground.

This administration has gained sufficient power to implement its agenda without fear of failure. Who is going to stop it? It will not be a liberal Supreme Court, or the Republican Party that is just as inept and power hungry as Democrats are. Moreover, we the people relinquished power to the Government a long time ago, so, who is left? A minority of Americans, 30 to 35 percent, favor more government power, and a socialized country. The same percentage, 30 to 35 percent, is on the other side of the teeter-totter, favoring less government and more freedom from government involvement. The 30 to 35 percent in the middle, who are indifferent and tuned out, will vote for whoever benefits them personally. Those in the middle will decide the future of America, and it has been part of American history for over sixty years, the blind leading the blind!

Reality Check

When faced with reality, it can be a devastating experience when one realizes that real life is not a computer game with an undo button. However, there is that thing we call the American spirit, and as long as there is a country called the United States of America, there will be true Americans who keep that spirit alive. It is not possible to know the number of Americans, like me, who live their lives motivated by good moral principles and values and a patriotic love for the heritage of this country. In my heart, I believe we are in the majority.

Conservative Americans may not have a strong voice in our government, but they will survive because they are independent thinkers and do not need a politician to lead them around by the nose. Intelligent people will resist manipulation by the government, no matter the situation; they will resist any attempt to destroy this country, even if it becomes fruitless to do so.

There is no way of knowing what the situation will be by the time you read this book, but whatever is to come will come in time. The economy may be booming, but it will not last. Your 401K might be growing, but it will not continue. You may hear that the country is recovering from its economic crises, but America has not yet arrived at real economic crisis; that will not occur until after 2012. No matter how bad the economy becomes, there will always be those who know how to manipulate the system and become even richer as the majority become poorer.

There is one thing I give the president credit for; he made no bones about his plan to change America and pronounced it loud and clear, so we cannot blame him for the ignorance of those who voted for him. I realize that President Obama is a politician and, like all politicians, he is doing what politicians do, even though, again like most politicians, he has no real leadership skills. That is not much of a disadvantage when you are dealing with people who have no skills for living.

Our very intelligent and devoted founders gave to us a form of government that gave ultimate power to the people. Along with that gift was the warning that unless we take the responsibility to monitor our leadership, they will destroy the fabric of our society. If you really want to know who is responsible for what has befallen our country and you participated in putting this government in power by voting for them or failing to vote for the opposition, look in your mirror.

Socialism

The dilemmas we are facing began to materialize during the first presidency of Bill Clinton. He made it obvious that an ominous change was coming to America, and when he was reelected for a second term, it was clear to anyone paying attention that we were being set up for Socialism. Soon after he came into office, it was obvious to most people that character does not matter to a Liberal, and there was nothing sacred about the office of the president. President Reagan would not set foot in the Oval Office without wearing a coat and tie, and, well, you know what Clinton did in that same office. He turned the White House where Abraham Lincoln agonized over the Civil War into a hangout for all his cronies and celebrities, and he did much more to degrade the sanctum of our sacred emblems of power. Clinton's actions were indicative of Socialist distain and disrespect for our great heritage; when that is destroyed, what is left of our foundation? President Clinton is out of office, but he is still out there promoting the Socialist agenda of this administration.

No one in their right mind would opt for Socialism, and that is why the perpetrators have to use deception and lies in a slow, methodical way to conquer the unaware masses. People now are witnessing the culmination of what was the desire of Bill Clinton: a Socialist government is in control of America. Maybe you do not see it yet, but reality will soon prove it to you. The attitude of some to wait and see what happens is that attitude that allowed Socialism to take over this country. While many were waiting to see what happens, it was already happening, but they failed to see it. This is a perfect representation of the devious and cunning mind of the Socialists, and it is their standard modus operandi in conquering weak-minded people. In order to succeed, Socialists have to prey on the disenfranchised and minorities, offering them a life of ease while in reality enslaving them and turning them against the productive people in our society.

It is amazing that many people seem to be ignorant of the source of all the money our government delights in wasting. The government does not produce one penny; it only knows how to spend it. If industrious entrepreneurs and business people cannot make a profit and hire workers because of over controlling government regulations, and crippling taxes, what will be the source of all the money that the government will waste? It is obvious where it comes from: The government turns to the printing presses to print more soon-to-be worthless dollars, which will result in paying five dollars for something that now costs a dollar.

The blueprint for the presidencies of progressives like Wilson and FDR is the same blueprint on President Obama's desk. American people during the era of Presidents Wilson and FDR were far better equipped to survive on their own than they are today. People of all races were independent and hardworking and relied on themselves to survive. Even under the scourge of racism, black Americans realized that promises did not put food on the table and did the same as poor whites: what they had to do to survive. Blacks and whites knew the source of all blessings and filled their churches every Sunday to worship their provider. It was faith in God that kept them going, not faith in the government. Being poor will not prevent one from living a happy and contented life any more than being rich guarantees it.

With each little step made by previous progressive presidents, President Obama came along at the right time with the most favorable opportunity to succeed. Socialism always has been doomed to fail in America, until now. There is a simple reason why America has avoided Socialism. Americans are not like Europeans or any other society; we inherited the greatest form of government in the world and that made us unique. Millions from all over the world come here to share the American dream, but if that dream turns into a nightmare, where will people go to find a better life?

Racism

It takes a racist to promote racism. The overwhelming majority of people in America, of all races, are not racist and do not know anyone that is. Of course, racism exists among all races, and if you look for it, you can find it, but you will have to look way out on the far fringes of our society. In the sewer of American politics, any politician will cower in trembling fear if anyone points the finger of racism toward him, lacking the courage to defend his honor if he is falsely accused. After I injected the word honor, it occurred to me that, evidently, most politicians do not care much about honor. If there is one thing that has withered and died among American politicians, it is courage and self-respect—and honor.

Segregation was a reality in the small, rural North Carolina town where I grew up. I witnessed firsthand the plight of black Americans and the discrimination they had to endure every day. The jobs that were available to them were nothing more than slave labor, but they survived, and they did so like poor white people; they did what they had to do. Nevertheless, not everyone with a white face looked down their nose at black Americans, but those who did are the ones that get attention.

As terrible as the bigotry and prejudice I witnessed in my youth, it pales in comparison to what is being done today to minorities—blacks and Mexicans— not by white Southerners but by liberal Democrats. The government cannot end racism; only the change in the people's hearts—that is, people of all races—can accomplish that. In my seventy years, I have witnessed tremendous improvements in relations among the races, especially in the South.

Thirty years ago, Martin Luther King, Jr., was held in high esteem by black Americans and rightly so; he did more to help them than any politician ever has, but is it not strange that today his name is rarely mentioned? President Obama is no Martin Luther King, yet he is worshipped by, not all, but the majority of black Americans, who are being unwittingly duped by him. Liberal politicians, for their own political gain, continue to exploit minorities. "Get out the vote"; that is their mantra, and it has been going on for over half of my life. They do not give a hoot where that vote comes from, legal or not, just get the vote. I do not wish to imply the Republicans are any less guilty of this; they are just not as proficient at it. There is one thing to understand about liberal politicians' philosophy: they hate all success except their own. Success equals power, and Liberals regard the quest for power and dominance over the masses as their God-given right. Their comfort comes when they have more power, and the people have less; and they will use and abuse anyone to maintain their power.

The accusation of racism is the nuclear weapon in the arsenal of Liberals for the war against Conservatives. It would bid well if organizations like, the National Association for the Advancement of Colored People (NAACP) and activists like Al Sharpton and Jesse Jackson, rather than continue to stir up racism in America, actually do something to help members of the black community rather than themselves. The so-called race card is nothing more than a "Joker Card", used in the game of "Jokers Wild"; it is time for them to change their mandate to a more productive endeavor before they become irrelevant. The majority of Americans have heard enough of their rhetoric—including many minorities. If these people are truly trying to help minorities, they should encourage them with possibilities rather than perpetuate their self-pity. God does not look at the color of a man's skin, but his character and the contents of his heart. We should look at each other the same way.

Anyone who willingly depends on the government for his welfare becomes a ward of that government and will never have a fulfilled life. We did not choose the color of our skin or the shape of our face, but we all have the same free will given to us by God. It is up to us to exercise that free will in whatever way we choose. Personal responsibility is what determines our development, and with that, we can be or do whatever motivates us. If we are comfortable depending on the government, then our reward will be whatever the government chooses it to be, but if we depend on ourselves, our reward will be whatever *we* choose it to be.

Before we leave this subject, consider this: Wealth and material things never will provide happiness and contentment, but no matter how many times they hear it, most will reject that premise. One does not have to be rich to live a happy and contented life. Happiness is a state of mind that provides contentment, and we can choose to be content regardless of our circumstances. The choice is ours.

Materialism

America is a materialistic society and has been for a long time. All the material things we cherish can, and probably will be, easily taken from us, as many Americans are experiencing today. There is nothing wrong with having material possessions unless they dominate our life. Unfortunately, most modern people live for "things" and "stuff," and they are the only meaningful things in their lives. People's garages and attics are overflowing with old stuff they did not think they could live without when they bought it, and that is why yard sales are so popular in this country. Any satisfaction we may get from material possessions is temporary; the item eventually becomes *old stuff*, tossed aside and replaced with more temporary and unsatisfying possessions. Materialism is the primary cause for Americas' social transformation; compassion has been replaced by snobbery, humbleness by vanity, and understanding by condemnation. I have lived long enough to witness those transformations firsthand. For many people today, poverty means not having a flat-panel TV in every room of the house, no computer and internet, no free vacation, no cell phone for each member of the family, and a car over three years old. I may have exaggerated a little here, but not by much. The poorest person in America today is richer than the majority of the people on this planet.

Capitalism, Socialism, Communism, Fascism, and Anarchy

Capitalism is "an economic system characterized by private or corporate ownership of capital goods, by investments that are determined by private decision, prices, production, and the distribution of goods that are determined mainly by competition in a free market." (Merriam Webster11th Collegiate

Dictionary) Capitalism is the system to which America owes its prosperity. Whether one agrees with it or not, even if we disregard the economical advantages of capitalism, what it provides beyond any other system is freedom of the individual to make his own choice how to live. This freedom provides opportunities for everyone except the lazy.

Socialism is "1: any of various economic and political theories advocating collective or governmental ownership and administration of the means of production and distribution of goods; 2a: a system of society or group living in which there is no private property; b: a system or condition of society in which the means of production are owned and controlled by the state; 3: a stage of society in Marxist theory transitional between capitalism and communism and distinguished by unequal distribution of goods and pay according to work done." (Merriam-Webster 11th Collegiate Dictionary)

Only uninformed people will view Socialism as a good thing; unfortunately, too many Americans are oblivious to what is taking place in our country. Of course, if you happen to be one of the elite in our government, Socialism is joy unspeakable because it gives them absolute power, the life-support system of a politician. The people who suffer the most from Socialism are the same people who wished for it because in reality, it never produces what it promises. It puts a ring on the finger of one hand, and then breaks the fingers of the other hand. Reality speaks for itself; the president has failed to keep almost all the promises he has made because they were rash and unattainable when he made them. Of course, we can say that about most presidents. The magic potion called the new health-care plan is no longer prominent in the news, but it continues to brew in a cauldron of ruin monitored by the president's wizards.

If the captain of a cruise ship forces all the passengers who paid for the expensive upper deck state rooms to vacate those rooms and turn them over to the low-cost, lower-deck passengers, who benefits if the ship is sinking? That is a simple metaphor to expose the stupidity of Socialism.

Communism is "a totalitarian system of government in which a single authoritarian party controls state-owned means of production: a final stage of society in Marxist theory in which the state has withered away and economic goods are distributed equitably." (Merriam-Webster 11th Collegiate Dictionary)

This definition sounds rather benign, but what is not included is the method used to establish such a system. It would work fairly well for a farmer raising sheep, but people, especially freedom-loving people, are not predisposed to have every aspect of their lives dictated by another person. Freedom is never appreciated as much as when it is lost and, once it is lost, it takes more than a lifetime to regain it.

First, there is Socialism to create the mindset necessary for the development of Communism. Socialism is the easiest to understand because we can see it developing today. To define it in simple terms: When the government takes control of commerce, education, banking, state and local governments, and the media, that is Socialism. To simplify it further, the federal government controls everything. If we summed it up in a ten-chapter book, we are currently on chapter seven or eight. The next quest for power is Communism; personal freedom will perish, and Communism will be born.

Under Communism, the only freedom left is to do what the government tells; if you commit a crime, even a minor one, you may spend the rest of your miserable life in prison. Criticize the government, and you will disappear into a black hole. There are no free elections, and the thugs who run the local governments will be appointed by the thugs in the national government, headed by Comrade so and so. It is not necessary to be an expert on Communism, but if you educate yourself sufficiently, you will recognize its coming. We will not wake up one day and discover we are a Communist country; it does not happen that way. It is a slow, methodical process, but it is already well into its development.

Fascism is "1: a political philosophy, movement, or regime (as that of the Fascisti) that exalts nation and often race above the individual and that stands for a centralized autocratic government headed by a dictatorial leader, severe economic and social regimentation, and forcible suppression of opposition.

2: a tendency toward or actual exercise of strong autocratic or dictatorial control." (Merriam-Webster 11th Collegiate Dictionary)

Is it possible for Fascism to come to America? You decide!

Anarchy is a "state of lawlessness or political disorder due to the absence of governmental authority." (Merriam-Webster 11th Collegiate Dictionary)

Anarchy is the worst of the worst; however, it is usually short-lived. There is an example of anarchy just across the border in Mexico. There are also examples of it in our country today: the gangs in many of our cities; they have no respect for the law and are a subculture within themselves. They make their own rules, and mete out their own justice. Some of these gangs are so dangerous; the police are reluctant to confront them. If our economy collapses, which is a very real possibility, criminal elements will run rampant all over this country while politicians hide under their desks, blaming everyone but them for the mayhem. If you think gangs only exist in cities like Los Angeles or New York, here is a news flash for you: If you live in a town or city of any appreciable size, there are gang members in your neighborhood today.

The chaos will be so unmanageable, at least using ordinary means, some people and even some states will fight back. The country will be in chaos without a shred of normalcy. The anarchy eventually will run its course, but only after thousands lose their possessions and even their lives. When it is safe enough, politicians will emerge from hiding, driven by their fanatical desire to regain power, and will, through coercion or force, regain control of the country.

If you think this scenario is a fantasy, you need a reality check. America is only a few steps away from becoming a full-fledged Socialist country and only time will tell where it will lead. The blood is in the water, and hungry sharks are circling. We have relinquished our country to a bunch of mad, greedy, self-serving politicians and sixties' radicals, giving them the power to do as they wish. Unfortunately, nothing we can do will stop it, and little we can do to halt the ship of destruction. Our government is in power because of many very misguided people, and if you are happy with it, enjoy it while you can before it destroys your life. If you are unhappy with it and you voted for a liberal Socialist and looking for someone to blame, look at you. You may say you did not know you were voting for a Socialist, but that is a worthless excuse. You should have known!

Our founders willed to us all the power necessary to remain free in a free country, but many Americans are more interested in having a good time or watching some brain-numbing television program than in the systematic destruction of our country. Unless you are among the elite, misery and hardship is in your future.

The Truth about Communism

Each day, events develop convincing me that Communism could come to America. We may not be there yet, but this government is already using Communist tactics to get what they want by ignoring the voice of the people. Politicians today do not use the word Socialism or Communism; they disguise it by using some other more acceptable phrase, like Progressivism. However, the disguise is unnecessary because most people do not have a clue as to the meaning of either term. It is not that difficult to drag a country into Communism. There are three easy steps: First, you pit the have-nots against the haves. Second, you side with the have-nots in blaming the haves for all the problems to foster a revolt against them. Third, you open the door to a share-the-wealth plan to make everyone the have-nots, except, of course, for the few elites running the government. Can you not see evidence of this scenario in America today?

You will be spied upon from the time you drag your worn-out body from bed to go to work until you drag it back in after a grueling day at a job you probably hate. Welfare will be something you remember from the good old days, but you will no longer have access to it. You will exist in a world where the government controls every aspect of your life. Adequate health care will be available only to the elite, and you will be hungry more often than not. If you doubt the validity of what I express here, talk to one of the many refugees from Communist countries now living in America. I guarantee that you will not be eager to support someone that is determined to bring Communism to

America. Socialism gives much power to a government, but power begets the quest for more power, and the next step from Socialism is Communism.

Liberal and Conservative

<u>Conservative</u> means, "Tending to favor established ideas, conditions, or institutions. *Synonyms*: old-fashioned, orthodox, reactionary, traditional, unprogressive."

Related Words: conventional; faithful, loyal, steadfast, true-blue. (Merriam-Webster Thesaurus)

Conservatives suffer from a trait that makes it difficult to compete with Liberals: they are generally happy, courteous, trusting, and respectful, with malice toward none. God, family, and country are incorporated into most conservative belief systems, as opposed to government, selfishness, and hatred. Conservatism is not a political party nor is it currently supported by a political party. The Republican Party traditionally supported Conservatives until George W. Bush's presidency, when the Republicans abandoned their Conservative base. There are Liberals and Conservatives in both parties, but Conservatives are more independent-minded, do not blindly follow either political party. They usually support Conservative politicians regardless of their political affiliation. It appears that due to the current circumstances, the Republican Party once again is turning to Conservatives. However, Conservatives are looking for politicians who share their values and beliefs, and it is reasonable to assume Liberals are doing the same. However, if many Conservatives had separated themselves from the couch, got off of their backside and voted in the last election, we would not be in this mess. I will not say that all Conservatives are lazy, but it is very difficult to get them motivated. It is sad, and amazing, but many of the Conservatives I know, have never voted in their life.

<u>Liberal</u> means, "not bound by traditional ways or beliefs." *Synonyms*: broad-minded, nonconventional, non-orthodox, nontraditional, open-minded, progressive, radical, unconventional, unorthodox." (Merriam-Webster Thesaurus)

Like Conservatives, Liberals are free to support whomever they wish. Although the two groups have differences in beliefs and philosophy, we are all Americans, and there are always consequences no matter which type of government we choose to govern us. At no time in our history has an administration produced such radical and destructive changes to our country as the current administration. The most destructive aspect of our political system reveals itself when people tag themselves with labels without any understanding of what the labels represent. That is a direct result of the inability of many to think for themselves; instead, they run with the herd, even though they are racing toward a cliff. The most dangerous enemy to any country is the ignorance of its citizens. Throughout history, all great societies eventually self-destruct, and that is the fate that awaits the United States of America. The opportunity to delay the inevitable is wasted by this generation and, as previously stated, an opportunity not taken is an opportunity lost.

The Real Culprit

America did not crown the president as a king; he is honored with the temporary privilege of being the political leader of our country. Unless this country goes completely crazy, as it did in Franklin Roosevelt's time, the president's time in office is limited to two terms. However, the election of a president is not as important as the current dysfunctional and out-of-control Congress, as represented by both parties. At no time has that been more important than today.

Term limits would have spared us from the last forty years of the inmates running the asylum, but it is probably too late to think about that now. The worse the country's economic situation gets, the more politicians seem to prosper. The balance of power shifted from the people to the leadership long ago, but politicians are never satisfied unless they are busy seeking to obtain more power over the people, and that trend will probably never stop.

The erosion of morality and sound governing principles is what is killing America, as it has every other great society. To think that we can reverse that situation is a pipe dream. Unfortunately, it is part of our history to remain complacent about the state of our country until the sky falls in, and 9/11 is a good example. Our complacency is much to blame for our current crisis, and the more it progresses the less chance we the people have in affecting any change. The time has long passed when we can depend on our government to do the right thing for our country. Keeping the government in check is, and always has been, the people's responsibility.

Until the American people live up to their responsibility, they have no right to demand that politicians live up to theirs. Very few things in life are free, and it is certain that freedom can only be achieved and maintained by sacrifices made by those to whom freedom is awarded. For those who ignore the sacrifices made by our military are undeserving of the freedom that our people in uniform voluntarily risk their lives to protect. Many people, especially Socialists, are front and center when it comes to demanding their rights to do or say whatever they wish, but they have never done a single thing in their lives to defend those rights.

This country is awash with problems, and many, if not most, are self-inflicted. If we the people do not start living up to our responsibility, our children and grandchildren will look back on this generation with disgust because we failed to preserve for future generations, the greatest form of government the world has ever known.

> … And so, my fellow Americans: ask not what your country
> can do for you—ask what you can do for your country.
> —John F. Kennedy, January 20, 1961

With those few words, President Kennedy revitalized a spirit in America that had been sorely missing because of the ongoing cold war with Russia. Unfortunately, that spirit died in Dallas, Texas, on November 22, 1963. That spirit can live again in America. If you wish to know who can take part of its rebirth, look at the person looking back at you in your mirror, and remember those words from President Kennedy. What have *you* done for your country? Better yet, what have you done for your neighbor or a friend? There are people in your neighborhood that could use a helping hand; do you know or care who they are? Regardless of how poor or busy we are, there is always something to do to help others.

If you are one of the many Americans flopped down on your couch munching on a bag of Doritos, watching some mind-numbing television program, and waiting for someone else to do something, consider yourself part of the problem. You are that someone else on whom other people are depending. If you are proud to be an American, then start doing something for your country. You can start by educating yourself on what America is all about; however, that television you are addicted to will not provide the answers. If you have access to the Internet, there is a wealth of information at your fingertips, but remember to look for facts not opinions. The following excerpt is from a letter written by Thomas Jefferson on Sept 23, 1800. The letter was in response to a promise he made to his friend Benjamin Rush, concerning his views on Christianity.

> I have sworn upon the altar of God eternal hostility against
> every form of tyranny over the mind of man.

When a government bans free speech concerning religion, is that not tyranny leveled against Christians and other religious groups? Are church leaders and their congregations going to continue to do nothing while the government succeeds in kicking God out of America? Sadly, the answer to both of those questions is yes.

If we elect into office those who continue to strip us of our freedoms, then we deserve to lose those freedoms. The power is, and always has been, with the people, at election time, but if we are not wise enough to know or care about whom we vote for, then we will, as always, get the government we deserve.

Where is the brave, little child to stand up and shout, "The emperor is naked?" Are we so blind that it takes a child to recognize what we refuse to see? If you are not familiar with Hans Christian Andersen's fairytale "The Emperor's New Clothes," you can read it on the Internet. (See "Sources," at the end of the book.) It is a brilliant comparison to the fantasyland created by the President. Even a child, one who is paying attention and has not been *educated* in our Socialist education system, can clearly see how his future is being destroyed and how little effort is made to prevent the destruction.

This generation, and previous generations that called America their home, owe an undying gratitude to our founders. But there is little evidence that many in this generation know or even care about the true history of our Founding Fathers, and their reward will be the loss of the country those remarkable men created for them.

The Inevitable Future of America

The powers controlling America today are on a fast track to drag the country into Communism. It is up to the people whether they succeed or not, but if you see any possibility of the people halting their plans, you are living in a different reality than most. Forget for a moment about what is coming, and concentrate on what is already here. While most American people were slumbering in their apathy, the major agencies of the government were taken over by America-hating radicals with direct contact with the president and unaccountable to anyone but him.

A Lesson from the Past

When Adolph Hitler began to implement his long-awaited plans to change Germany into what he saw in his demented visions, he had a well-planned agenda that he implemented little by little. Most German people were mesmerized by Hitler's oratory skills and fantasy visions of a utopia and world dominance. Still recovering from the disaster of World War I, the people were receptive to Hitler's promise to return Germany to its previous glory and failed to recognize the demonic evil in the man. Some Germans did oppose Hitler, but their voices were silenced by assassination or by his powerful propaganda machine, which squelched any speech that did not support and praise the Nazis. Hitler's supporters, eager for power and prestige as members of his inner circle, seized the opportunity to exercise their long-held radical views, gave him their full support. At the same time, they also created their own little empires.

Hitler knew he would probably need force to control the people once they became more aware of his agenda. To prepare for that occasion, he chose Heinrich Himmler; the only man in Germany more evil than he, to command his personal police force. The group Hitler chose as his personal enforcement police was known as *Schutzstaffe* ("Protective Squadron") or SS. In their apathy, the German people were unconcerned about the SS until its ranks grew, and the SS began to display the same evil as their leader, Himmler. Hitler's vision for himself went far beyond the borders of Germany, he wanted to conquer the world, and the German people were nothing more than pawns in his chess game of world dominance and any serious opposition was quickly disposed of. Himmler's primary mandate was to force Hitler's will onto the German people, who ignored the development of his shadow government, which consisted of the like-minded radicals and madmen who surrounded and supported him. When people awoke from their slumber, they found themselves in the clutches of Fascism, which eventually destroyed their country and caused the death of over fifty million people during World War II.

Hitler failed in his efforts because not only was he a dope-addicted maniac, he was surrounded by mad men who were so mesmerized by him that they willingly assisted him in the destruction of Germany. I do not give President Obama high marks for intelligence, but he is a shrewd and cunning, manipulating community organizer, totally focused and determined to succeed in bringing Socialism to America. He has cleverly placed a shield of supporters around him, consisting of like-minded radicals and at least one self-proclaimed Communist (Van Jones) to provide him with support that makes it unnecessary to abide by the Constitution and the normal channels of our form of government. We can recognize a comparison between the German people during the rise of Hitler and the complacent and apathetic generation in America today.

At the beginning of Hitler's rise, there was no SS, no assassination squads, no propaganda machine, and no gas chambers. However, little by little, over several years, all these things materialized but did not get the attention of the German until they found themselves overpowered by forces they were unable to resist. Could the same thing happen in America? If you had asked the German people in the late 1920s if such a thing could happen to them, their response probably would have been a chuckle—the same response you would get from many Americans today. Apathy and ignorance can cost you your livelihood, or even your life. Chuckle if you wish, I pray that your laughter will not turn to tears. It does not take an Adolph Hitler or a Stalin to oppress people and ignore their humanity, but oppression cannot be perpetrated by rational people either. In our government today, it appears that irrational people far outnumber the rational, and they are capable of bringing total destruction to our way of life.

The Determination of the President

The America that has existed for more than two hundred years is dying. Believe it now, or be forced to believe it when you can no longer ignore it. The blame for our destruction rests with the American people of both political parties for allowing our country to be commandeered by people far removed from the mainstream of our society. As the saying goes, ignorance is bliss. The time will come when we will be ejected from our apathy, thrust into the world of reality, and be forced to realize that our complacency has ruined our way of life. There has not been any evidence of real intelligence in our political landscape for more than twenty years; it appears that among politicians, stupidity has become a virtue.

The president's vision is so monolithic there is nothing to divert his attention from forging ahead toward his goal. He has proven to be untrustworthy and deceiving, a characteristic most Americans will not accept. However, 30 to 35 percent of Americans blindly support him without the slightest knowledge or concern about the consequences awaiting them.

Along with the lack of interest of the majority of American people to take an interest in shaping our government, the Senate, Congress, and the Constitution are becoming irrelevant; what will be left is a dictatorship. Perhaps you are among the millions of Americans who doubt that the United States of America ever will be under the control of a dictator. If I had the opportunity, I would ask you this: What are *you* going to do to prevent it?

The Hideous Nature of Socialism

Anyone who is not guided by the emotions of pessimism or optimism, but relies on his knowledge of facts and reality, can see clearly that this administration will succeed with its agenda. For forty years or more, Socialists have corrupted our education system, brainwashing students into believing America is the scourge of the world, and have all but succeeded in removing any mention of God from our society. I fail to see any grounds for optimism that it will somehow change; the horses are out of the barn and any effort to close the door now is a desperate act of futility.

The Tea Party movement would have been very effective four or five years ago and could have changed our current course. Unfortunately, it may be too little, too late to effect any change. If the many protest rallies around the country maintain their momentum until November 2012, they certainly could have an impact on the elections. However, this administration will do whatever it takes to prevent Republicans from taking the House and Senate; whether or not they succeed, depends on rational people making wise decisions on Election Day. So far, few wise decisions are made by anyone. Even if Republicans take back both houses, do not think for a minute it will end President Obama's quest to socialize America. After the 2012 elections, we will be in the same situation we are now. If the Republicans are in power, who do you suppose liberals will blame during the following two years for the mess we are in. Actually, the upcoming elections could be a win-win situation for Liberals.

America has survived through many tough times before, but we have never faced the situation we are in today. This country has survived for one primary reason: the solid core of Americans with a true love and respect for this country, and faith in God, prevented any radical change to our way of life. The failure to enforce immigration laws has allowed millions to cross our borders illegally, and if the president grants them citizenship, which is part of his agenda, the Liberal support base will increase by millions. These occurrences are no accident; they are part of the Liberal agenda. The core of true Americans cannot be eliminated, but their influence is being diminished by an influx of foreigners who do not share the American spirit. Moreover, the President appears to be on their side. It is a painful thing for many Americans to accept, but it is the reality of the future of America. Conservative Americans need to acknowledge a reality when they hear the term, *the American people*, it is a different demographic than during the era of Ronald Reagan. Our dysfunctional Emigration Department, has left our borders wide open since Bill Clinton's presidency and do not have a clue who is in this country. When you hear the term the, *American people*, do not assume they are all people like you that share your respect for the values of America. *The American people* of thirty years ago are becoming a minority. If you doubt that assessment, when you go into large gatherings anywhere in America today, look around you.

The reason most people are dazed and confused by what is happening in America is due to complacency. They have no idea of the extent of the destruction that has occurred already to the fabric of our country. The reason the president and his supporters do not seem to be concerned about the wishes of the people is that they are not concerned. They have their agenda, and they will do whatever it takes to succeed because they are confident of success. Any obstacle put in their path will be overcome one way or the other. If they do not already have the power, they will create the power, and who can stop them? The president and much of Congress have all but ignored the Constitution or any other law that deters them and no one has stopped them. Aside from the Constitution, there is no other power to stop them. Unfortunately, the American Constitution, written by our founders under the tutelage of God, is considered by this administration and all progressives, past and present, as an outdated relic.

Politicians do what politicians have always done, they are put into power by the people, and if we throw a rotten apple in a barrel, who is responsible if it rots the entire barrel? I know many of you have faith that the Republicans will retake the House of Representatives, but you should realize the Republican Party of Ronald Reagan no longer exists. It now is dominated by the John McCain Republicans, who are as liberal as many Democrats. The Democrats will not defeat the Republicans; the Republicans will probably defeat themselves as they did in the last presidential election—If there is a single opinion expressed in this book, that I pray is wrong, it is this one.

The Danger of Appeasement

The President has traveled the world trying to appease every despot and dictator he can get to talk to him. Even though it is a result of his naiveté and inexperience, the results could be devastating for America. To appease an enemy is to surrender to that enemy, and it only emboldens that enemy to plot our defeat. Following is a timely warning from another one of Aesop's fables, "The Farmer and the Viper":

One winter a Farmer found a Viper, frozen and numb with cold, and out of pity picked it up and placed it in his bosom. The Viper was no sooner revived by the warmth than he turned upon its benefactor and inflicted a fatal bite upon him. As the poor man lay dying, he cried, "I have only got what I deserved, for taking compassion on so villainous a creature. Kindness is thrown away."

There are many around the world to identify as a "villainous creature," but my pick is the little man ruling Iran, Mahmoud Ahmadinejad. If this man does not scare you, it is because you do not know what he is capable of doing. He is in an ongoing dream of wiping Israel from the face of the earth; the major roadblock to his dream coming true is America. There are three possibilities for America to be taken out of Ahmadinejad's way: the president will turn against Israel, leaving it to the mercy of its many enemies; America will suffer a total economic collapse, from which there will be no recovery; or Ahmadinejad will destroy America's power. It is a matter of which scenario occurs first. There is a high probability that any of these scenarios could occur very soon. In either event, America will be the loser.

If you chuckle at the thought of a small country like Iran having the ability to bring America to its knees, it is not as farfetched as you might think. There is a way Ahmadinejad, and many others who have the motive and means to do so, could paralyze America in a flash: with a high-altitude electromagnetic pulse (HEMP) weapon. Do not doubt for a minute that Ahmadinejad would use such a weapon against America if he ever obtains the capability. It does not appear that anyone is seriously trying to stop Iran from acquiring a nuclear weapon except Israel, and it is getting very little serious encouragement or support from the rest of the world. According to a report published by Israel News, on 5 November, 2008, 78 percent of American Jews voted for President Obama, and from that it can be deduced that an overwhelming majority of Jews in America are no more concerned about Israel than President Obama is.

The possibility of a HEMP weapon is nothing new; it has been known about for at least fifty years that I am aware of, but it was not until the proliferation of microprocessors that the full potential of such a weapon was realized. Practically everything in modern times is controlled in one way or the other by computers. Microprocessors operate under very low voltage and are very sensitive to power surges, which makes them vulnerable to an attack by a HEMP weapon. If an atomic bomb is detonated high enough above the earth's atmosphere, it interacts with the earth's magnetic field, releasing a powerful EMP that would destroy every microchip within the area of disbursement.

If a HEMP weapon were detonated high enough above the center of the United States, in a flash, practically everything in the United States, northern Mexico, and southern Canada would cease to operate. Vehicles would stall, power grids would fail, water would stop flowing from taps, sewer treatment plants would shut down, and aircraft electronics would fail, leaving pilots without navigation equipment. Within an hour, America would be transported back two hundred years. Cell phones would not work, emergency services would be immobilized, supermarkets would run out of food in a day or two, and only the very rich would be able to afford the inflated prices for the little food that will be available. Anarchy soon would spread over the country like wildfire. You may be forced to kill, or be killed, while protecting what little food you may have stored in your house. You and your family would be alone, forced to survive on your own. In a very short time, millions would be dead or dying. This is not science fiction; it is a real possibility in this crazy world in which we live. It would take a mad man to use such a weapon against a country, but make no mistake: Ahmadinejad would use such a weapon, given the opportunity, even if it resulted in the destruction of his own country.

No doubt, Iran would have to overcome the many obstacles provided by our military defense systems, that is, if our military continues in its present state. Where there is a will, there is a way. Ahmadinejad has the will, but this administration does not seem to be interested in denying him the way.

Global Government

I leave you with something that requires you to think outside of the box; that is a fancy way of saying, use your own common sense, and think for yourself. The world is being prepared for a global government. What role

President Obama may play in its development is unknown, but he is certainly in a position to be a major player even though our country may not be. The economic collapse of Greece is a prelude to what will spread all over the world, including America, and will facilitate the rise of a global economic controlling authority. The radicals who now are in charge in our government are seeing their long-held dream of introducing Socialism to the world take shape. What this administration fails to realize is that America will not be a major player in the coming globalization. The question is who will be a major player? We will find the answer in the next chapter.

> The two enemies of the people are criminals and government, so let us tie the second down with the chains of the Constitution so the second will not become the legalized version of the first.

Although, it is not verified, Thomas Jefferson is believed to have made the above quote. Whether it was Jefferson or someone else, America is destined to suffer the consequences because it has ignored those words. Optimism and pessimism are feelings and emotions that prevail until they are validated by reality. If you are optimistic that politics alone can solve the problems in America, your optimism will never be validated. Is it hopeless? It depends on which side of the river you reside.

Nothing more can be added about life on this side of the river, and quite honestly it has become tiresome to continue. Our journey will now take us to a different reality, a reality where optimism *is* validated.

CHAPTER 2

THE SPIRITUAL SIDE OF THE RIVER

Some readers will be familiar with life on this side of the river, some will be somewhat familiar, and others will not have any knowledge at all. With that in mind, we will take a simple approach in exploring what life is like here. Politics rules across the river, spawning confusion and uncertainty. However, God rules this side of the river and, through him, there is hope, promise, peace, and contentment.

Who Is God?

If you look into the heavens through a telescope and marvel at the rings of Saturn or the storms of Jupiter, it is comforting to know they are out of reach of man's meddling. The vastness of space is so enormous it is incomprehensible. Even traveling at the incredible speed of 186,000 miles per second, it takes light 100,000 years to transverse the Milky Way Galaxy. On a clear night, Andromeda, the nearest spiral galaxy to our own, is visible to the naked eye, but what we see is what it looked like over two and a half million years ago. It is difficult enough to reconcile such distances, but our galaxy is a mere speck in the vastness of the universe.

The world's space scientists seem to be obsessed with exploring the universe to find any form of life apart from life on Earth. It is a mystery what motivates scientists to pursue such a quest. Apparently, they believe finding even the smallest microbe aside from anything born on Earth somehow will disprove the existence of God. Suppose a space probe exploring some distant planet sent back pictures of a boy in a straw hat sitting by a river with a fishing pole in his hand. Imagine the impact such a discovery would have around the world; nevertheless, would scientists be able to explain where the boy came from? Such a discovery certainly would embolden those who do not believe in God, but it would have little impact on those who do. It is not necessary to explore space to discover the existence of God; the evidence of his existence is all around us, if we care to look for it.

Do we really know God for who he is, or think of him in the abstract as some entity beyond comprehension? No one has ever seen God the Father so how can we know him. "He that hath seen me hath seen the Father." —John 14:9. Jesus is God who is revealed to us almost two thousand years ago. "All things are delivered unto me of my Father: and no man knoweth the Son, but the Father; neither knoweth any man the Father, save the Son, and he to whomsoever the Son will reveal him." —Mathew 11:27. If we accept as true only what we can understand, we only add to our ignorance. The Trinity of God is a good example; who can understand it, who can explain it?

> And God said, Let us make man in our image, after our
> likeness: and let them have dominion over the fish of the sea,
> and over the fowl of the air, and over the cattle, and over all
> the earth, and over every creeping thing that creepeth upon
> the earth.
> —Genesis 1:26

We start with what is in the Bible: "Let *us* make man in *our* image, after *our* likeness."—Geneses 1:26. "Us" refers to the Father, the Son, and the Holy Spirit, three spiritual persons but not three separate persons. Problems arise when we try to identify a power structure for the Trinity; there is the Father of the Godhead, the Son of the Godhead, and the Holy Spirit, yet there is only one God. God the Father is revealed through the Son, Jesus Christ; the Holy

Spirit is the communication link between man and God the Father through our intercessor Jesus Christ.

> But God hath revealed them unto us by his Spirit: for the Spirit searcheth all things, yea, the deep things of God. For what man knoweth the things of a man, save the spirit of man which is in him? even so the things of God knoweth no man, but the Spirit of God.
> —1 Corinthians 2:10–11

The Holy Spirit is not a cleanup man; he is God, and he knows all things about God. We are able to understand the things of humans because we are human. However, we cannot understand the things of a butterfly because we are not butterflies, and butterflies have no means to reveal themselves to us. The things of God are a mystery to the carnal mind of man, but the Holy Spirit can reveal God to anyone with a desire to know him, and it is a unique relationship in the human experience.

The more we explore the Godhead, the more perplexed we become because we are not able to understand it. If we accept anything in the Bible, through faith, as being true, we must accept everything in the Bible as truth, even if we do not fully understand it.

> Jesus saith unto him, I am the way, the truth, and the life: no man cometh unto the Father, but by me. If ye had known me, ye should have known my Father also: and from henceforth ye know him, and have seen him. Philip saith unto him, Lord, shew us the Father, and it sufficeth us. Jesus saith unto him, have I been so long time with you, and yet hast thou not known me, Philip? "He that hath seen me hath seen the Father; and how sayest thou then, Shew us the Father? Believest thou not that I am in the Father, and the Father in me? the words that I speak unto you I speak not of myself: but the Father that dwelleth in me, he doeth the works. Believe me that I *am* in the Father, and the Father in me: or else believe me for the very works' sake."
> —John 14:6–11

To know the Father, we must first know the Son and, through faith, accept him for who he says he is. We cannot separate the Father from the Son, but anyone who accepts Christ belongs to him. He purchased us with his blood and to please him is to please the Father, but to reject the Son is to reject the Father. It can be confusing, but remember this: we can have no part with the Father aside from Jesus Christ. Christ is the Father revealed to us.

God does not provide proof of his existence that will satisfy the carnal man; he reveals himself only to those without closed minds but with open hearts. The Holy Bible is the only reliable source to reveal the things of God. As we explored life across the river, it should be obvious that God does not intend for man to live apart from him. As we explore this side of the river, we will recognize a way of life that is not obtainable on the other side of the river.

Everything in the universe was created by Jesus Christ; it was created by him and for him, and any microbe found floating around in space was put there by the Creator. The universe is so mysterious and beautiful that man cannot accept that it is beyond his ability to understand or to manipulate. This little speck in the universe we call Earth was created as a temporary abode for us by Jesus Christ, and it is not for us to know what else he may have created. Man is much too ignorant to understand the things of God, and he reveals to man only what is in accordance with his plan and purpose for man to know.

You are invited to take a journey into a different world and way of life that can give you peace and provide a ray of light to guide you and your family out of the darkness that is spreading over the whole earth.

The Holy Bible

The Holy Bible is a bridge that provides a passageway from man's world to God's world. The power of the Bible remains hidden from majority of the world because people fail to realize that the answers to all questions and solutions to all problems are contained in this wonderful book. The reason people have difficulty solving problems; they look for answers in all the wrong places. Of all the books in the world, the Holy Bible is unique; men have been blessed or cursed by it for thousands of years, and it is as relevant today as at any time in its long history. The Bible survives because it is more than a book; it is the inherent word of Almighty God kept fresh and alive by the Holy Spirit. The Bible is a complete and comprehensive work, not a mere hodgepodge of writings of ancient history. It is beautifully organized and structured and is the only source to reveal God's supernatural world revealed to us through the Holy Spirit.

One would not thumb through any book, read a page here and there, and expect to get much from it. The Bible is no exception. God is a spirit; he resides in the spirit and deals with man only through the same Holy Spirit as he relied on to deal with the authors of the Bible. During its existence, men have attempted by every means to discredit the Bible's authenticity, and after thousands of years, none has been successful. There are no contradictions in the Bible, only misunderstandings by its readers. The Bible will not prove anything to a doubtful mind; its truth is revealed only to those with the desire and unwavering faith to accept it as the word of God. The Bible is all about Jesus Christ; the Old Testament is about the promise of a coming Messiah, and the New Testament reveals the fulfillment of the promise. Whether Jew or Gentile (a Gentile is anyone that is not a Jew), it is important to study the entire Bible.

There is no advantage to reading the Bible unless we accept, through faith, that it is the true word of God. The Bible provides the knowledge of God to anyone with a sincere desire to learn about him and not to be debated by sinful men. We may boast and declare that we believe in God, but how are we to believe in whom we do not know? God is not who man says he is; he is revealed only through his word and the Holy Spirit. We delude ourselves if we think we can truly know God without reading and studying the Bible. The Bible was not casually compiled, and it certainly cannot be casually studied if its truth is to be revealed.

The Bible is a complete work, not sixty-six separate works. There are no exclusive verses in the Bible, each verse is relevant, when joined together they reveal the truth of God's plan and purpose for mankind, and to be sure of receiving the message, it is necessary to study the entire Bible. Unlike the knowledge in man's head, knowledge received from studying the Bible resides in the heart, and God gave man a heart with unlimited capacity for receiving knowledge about him.

I have stressed the necessity of being familiar with the Bible because there is no other source that can reveal an in-depth understanding of who God is. No matter how many times one reads the Bible, each time is a new experience. The more devoted we are to studying the Bible, the more the Holy Spirit reveals to us; in other words, we get out of it what we put into it. America is in the mess it is in today because of the laziness, apathy, and ignorance of its inhabitants, but ignorance of God leads to dire consequences far more severe than anything created by man.

Before we move on, there is one final thing about the Bible you may not realize: There is a personal message in the Bible just for you. We are all put on this earth for a purpose, and most people acknowledge that belief without ever learning what the purpose is. If you wish to know what your purpose is, read the Bible and you will find it. The Bible is not just for scholars and church leaders but anyone with a sincere desire to know God's plan for his life.

The Bible is pertinent to every generation. There are things in the Bible that are easy for us to understand but were a mystery to our parents or grandparents. There are not many mysteries left in the Bible, which gives me confidence to believe we are very close to the end time. The average person has not always had access to God's written word, but I believe we have advanced to a point in time when we can accept that the Bible was written for the individual. The first time I read the Bible with that as a mindset, I developed a new perspective on God's word and a clearer understanding of how he deals with the human race.

In the Beginning

The best way to begin our journey is to start at the beginning.

> In the beginning was the Word, and the Word was with God, and the Word was God. The same was in the beginning with God. All things were made by him; and without him was not anything made that was made. In him was life; and the

life was the light of men. "And the light shineth in darkness; and the darkness comprehended it not.
—John 1:1–5

And the Word was made flesh, and dwelt among us, (and we beheld his glory, the glory as of the only begotten of the Father,) full of grace and truth.
—John 1:14

Jesus saith unto him, I am the way, the truth, and the life: no man cometh unto the Father, but by me. If ye had known me, ye should have known my Father also: and from henceforth ye know him, and have seen him."
—John 14:6–7

We learn from the above verses that the "Word" refers to Jesus Christ; "And the Word was made flesh, and dwelt among us." The world was not created for man; it was created by, and for, Jesus. We are about to explore the land called Christianity, and Jesus Christ is the foundation upon which the land was created. Permanent residents here are members of the Christian church. To say Jesus Christ created the universe and everything in it, as declared in the above verses, confuses some people. To say Christ created the universe is the same as saying God created it. We cannot separate the two into two separate entities. Man cannot fully understand the structure or the Godhead, so, we must allow the Bible to speak for itself.

The Infallibility of the Bible

For the entire history of the Bible, man has tinkered with it, dissecting every dot and title, looking for flaws. Satan always will provide evidence to support their opinions if it produces doubt in people's minds about the authenticity of the Bible.

Man's ignorance and arrogance keep him separated from God. Only those who accept Jesus Christ as their Lord and Master and receive the gift of the Holy Spirit can have a relationship with God. The Holy Spirit knows what God intended the Bible to be; it was relayed through him to the authors and in spite of man's effort to pollute the Bible with other writings, the Holy Spirit will reveal only what is intended for man to know. The point is, unless we have total, undoubting faith in God, Jesus Christ, and the Holy Spirit, we are just ignorant people.

> For with the heart man believeth unto righteousness; and with the mouth confession is made unto salvation. For the scripture saith, Whosoever believeth on him shall not be ashamed. For there is no difference between the Jew and the Greek: for the same Lord over all is rich unto all that call upon him. For whosoever shall call upon the name of the Lord shall be saved. How then shall they call on him in whom they have not believed? and how shall they believe in him of whom they have not heard? and how shall they hear without a preacher? And how shall they preach, except they be sent? as it is written, How beautiful are the feet of them that preach the gospel of peace, and bring glad tidings of good things! But they have not all obeyed the gospel. For Esaias saith, Lord, who hath believed our report? So then faith cometh by hearing, and hearing by the word of God.
> —Romans 10:10–17

At the time the Apostle Paul wrote these words, the New Testament did not exist, and the Gospel was taught by the word of mouth, as it continues to be today. However, we are blessed to have the Bible teach us God's word. How tragic it is that most people never realize the power available to them through the study of the Bible.

The King James Version that I use for the scriptures in this book is, and always will be, my Bible of choice. More than forty of the brightest Bible scholars in England devoted three years to producing the best and most accurate translation of available manuscripts. After four hundred years, their version has not been improved on, but it is a matter of personal preference. I provide these few facts in hope you will realize how fortunate we are to have access to the wonderful book we call the Holy Bible. Not everyone prefers the old English style of writing used in the King James Version, but there are many modern translations available today, and I believe the Holy Spirit can reveal the truth of God's word through any creditable Bible. However, it is advisable to get guidance from someone familiar with the different versions of the Bible; most Christian bookstores can provide such guidance.

It is suggested, those new to the study of the Bible should start with the Gospel of John, which is a wonderful book and easy to understand. However, almost everyone is interested in the book of Revelation, and many people attempt to launch their study of the Bible with that book. However, unless one is familiar with the Gospels and Old Testament, the book of Revelation will be difficult to understand. Many Christians neglect to read the Old Testament, but in what book other than the Bible would you remove over half the pages and expect to understand what remains? It is a mistake to ignore the Old Testament because you think it does not pertain to Christians. Jesus Christ is revealed throughout the Bible, and seeking him out is a fascinating experience. References to Jesus are throughout the Old Testament as well as the new, and the book of Isaiah is a good example. The important thing is to study the entire Bible. God promised us the wisdom to understand his word if we ask for it. If you are serious about studying the Bible, make it a priority in your life. Once God's word speaks to you, the worldly things you now spend time with no longer will seem important. Do not be discouraged if you have to read several books of the Bible before they begin to make sense. The Bible is not for casual reading.

The Folly of Man

As important as it is to know who God is, we need to understand who we are and why we need God in our lives. King Solomon, reputed by some to be the wisest man that ever lived, summed it up very well.

> The words of the Preacher, the son of David, king in Jerusalem. Vanity of vanities, saith the Preacher, vanity of vanities; all is vanity. What profit hath a man of all his labour which he taketh under the sun? One generation passeth away, and another generation cometh: but the earth abideth forever. The sun also ariseth, and the sun goeth down, and hasteth to his place where he arose. The wind goeth toward

71

the south, and turneth about unto the north; it whirleth about continually, and the wind returneth again according to his circuits. All the rivers run into the sea; yet the sea is not full; unto the place from whence the rivers come, thither they return again. All things are full of labour; man cannot utter it: the eye is not satisfied with seeing, nor the ear filled with hearing. The thing that hath been, it is that which shall be; and that which is done is that which shall be done: and there is no new thing under the sun. Is there anything whereof it may be said, See, this is new? it hath been already of old time, which was before us. There is no remembrance of former things; neither shall there be any remembrance of things that are to come with those that shall come after. I the Preacher was king over Israel in Jerusalem. And I gave my heart to seek and search out by wisdom concerning all things that are done under heaven: this sore travail hath God given to the sons of man to be exercised therewith. I have seen all the works that are done under the sun; and, behold, all is vanity and vexation of spirit. That which is crooked cannot be made straight: and that which is wanting cannot be numbered. I communed with mine own heart, saying, Lo, I am come to great estate, and have gotten more wisdom than all they that have been before me in Jerusalem: yea, my heart had great experience of wisdom and knowledge. And I gave my heart to know wisdom, and to know madness and folly: I perceived that this also is vexation of spirit. For in much wisdom *is* much grief: and he that increaseth knowledge increaseth sorrow.

—Ecclesiastes 1:1–18

There is no ambiguity in God's word. God promised Solomon wisdom that exceeded any that would ever be bestowed on man again. Based on God's word, I accept that Solomon was the wisest man that ever lived, although he certainly did not always use his wisdom wisely. Even so, we can learn from Solomon because learning is the purpose of the Bible. Following are more words of wisdom from Solomon that should convince us that man cannot live a satisfied life apart from God, regardless of the circumstances.

> I said in mine heart, Go to now, I will prove thee with mirth, therefore enjoy pleasure: and, behold, this also is vanity. I said of laughter, It is mad: and of mirth, What doeth it? I sought in mine heart to give myself unto wine, yet acquainting mine heart with wisdom; and to lay hold on folly, till I might see what was that good for the sons of men, which they should do under the heaven all the days of their life. I made me great works; I builded me houses; I planted me vineyards: I made me gardens and orchards, and I planted trees in them of all kind of fruits: I made me pools of water, to water therewith the wood that bringeth forth trees: I got me servants and maidens, and had servants born in my house; also I had great possessions of great and small cattle above all that were in Jerusalem before me: I gathered me also silver and gold, and the peculiar treasure of kings and of the provinces: I gat me men singers and women singers, and the delights of the sons of men, as musical instruments, and that of all sorts. So I was great, and increased more than all that were before me in Jerusalem: also my wisdom remained with me. And whatsoever mine eyes desired I kept not from them, I withheld not my heart from any joy; for my heart rejoiced in all my labour: and this was my portion of all my labour. Then I looked on all the works that my hands had wrought, and on the labour that I had laboured to do: and, behold, all was vanity and vexation of spirit, and there was no profit under the sun.
> —Ecclesiastes 2:1–11

King Solomon lived thousands of years ago, but who can argue with his assessment of the folly of man, which continues from generation to generation. The wildest and most extravagant dreams of fame and fortune cannot exceed what was a reality for Solomon. His wealth and wisdom were gifts from God, but at times he misused them both. When he was "but a young child," he inherited a powerful kingdom (Judah) from his father, King David, and experienced periods of being next to God and periods of being away from God. During a period when he turned away from God, he enslaved thousands and overburdened them with high taxes to satisfy his selfish pursuit of fame and fortune. After his death, his naive and inexperienced son, Rehoboam, ignored the advice of his elders to reduce the devastating taxes against his people and did just the opposite. Rehoboam followed the advice of his young and equally stupid friends and actually raised taxes even more, ignoring the plight of his people. Therefore, God drove a sickle through his kingdom and divided it. Rehoboam remained King of Judah and Jeroboam formed the kingdom of Israel and almost immediately turned toward idolatry. (Jeroboam was the chief superintendent over Solomon's labor force before he became king of Israel.) Both kingdoms were eventually led into captivity: Judah, to Assyria, and Israel, to Babylon. "so Israel rebelled against the house of David unto this day." —1 Kings 12:19—even unto our day! Solomon was correct, there is nothing new under the sun, and today God is standing over America with a sickle in his hand.

Like all of us, King Solomon was flawed. However, he was wise enough to leave us with the phrase "there is nothing new under the sun" as a warning to man of his vain and delusional vision of living apart from God. Generation after generation, part of Solomon's life experience is repeated by one despot after another, and that will continue until no despots remain.

We learn from Solomon that there is no lasting peace and contentment when we live apart from God. No amount of earthly fame or fortune can provide what God freely gives to all who choose to live in his world. I encourage you to read about King Solomon in your Bible—books of Kings, and Ecclesiastes; and learn how the influence of seven hundred wives and three hundred concubines turned him away from God and toward idolatry and the lust of the flesh. Like many before and after, he was destined to learn the hard way; man cannot play games with God, although he never stops trying. Unless man overcomes his arrogance and delusional sense of superiority, accepts the reality of God, and advances his knowledge of God's word, he will remain in the kindergarten of man's world and die in ignorance.

One quote from King Solomon is perplexing until we examine it more closely. "For in much wisdom is much grief: and he that increaseth knowledge increaseth sorrow." Obviously, he is not referring to the wisdom and knowledge of God, so how can wisdom and knowledge produce grief and sorrow? Being older than many, if not most, of you, perhaps I have more insight into his meaning. Today an average ten-year-old is exposed to more knowledge, information, and technology than an eighty-year-old man a mere fifty years ago, but where are the benefits? Is the world not in the throes of grief and sorrow, living under the threat of rogue nations that possess nuclear weapons? Each advancement made by sinful man puts yet another obstacle between man and God and has brought America to the brink of self-destruction. Man's ignorance and arrogance prevent him from learning from history of others because power causes one to believe he is wiser than any predecessor. However, he will end up only in the same graveyard of fools.

Nothing changes; man slogs along on the same treadmill of life without getting anywhere. As we look around the world today, it is obvious; we owe it to the sinful nature we are born with. We are all sinners born into a sinful world unable to escape its curse on our own. Aside from being born with a sinful and wanting nature, there is one thing all humans have in common: We are born with an empty space in our soul, intended to be dwelling places for the spirit of God. Everyone can recognize it, but not everyone knows what it is. People living across the river are in a perpetual quest looking for an alternative to occupy the empty space, but it will elude them. Regardless of our education—we are offered, by God, sufficient wisdom to understand his word if we ask for it.

Man's Wisdom versus God's Wisdom

The carnal man delights in aggrandizing himself by proclaiming that he will accomplish what no one else has done. In reality, his efforts will result in the same failures. We learn from history that after thousands of wars and thousands of peace treaties, man is incapable of bringing peace to the world or to his own life. The carnal man is a god unto himself and brings nothing into his life but trouble and strife.

No one loves technology more than I do, but man is losing the ability to use his common sense to accomplish things on his own. We are awash with mechanical and electronic gadgets that we have do things for us without giving much thought to the process. Personal responsibility and ingenuity is replaced by pushing buttons or relying on the government to relieve us of any bothersome inconvenience. Young children are losing the ability to deal with reality because they spend most of their time in the fantasy world of video games and television. Many teenagers are growing into adulthood with fun as their only motivation and believing drugs and alcohol are essential food items.

Undisciplined parents raising undisciplined children are so occupied with selfish interests they are unable, or unwilling, to manage their own households. They relinquish responsibility for raising their children to a Socialist education system that is brainwashing them into zombies. In addition, many adults have surrendered their lives to political leaders they allow into their lives every day through television rather than accept responsibility for their own lives. That pretty much describes much of life across the river, where the dummying down of America has come full circle in this generation, and grief and sorrow will surely follow. The inevitable result is that God will be pushed into the shadows and ignored.

Man's wisdom did not enable the bridge builders to construct a perfect bridge (the Bible). It was wisdom received from God because the carnal man's wisdom cannot understand things of God. Anyone with a desire to learn about him, is given the wisdom to understand through the Holy Spirit, but God is not deceived by insincerity. He knows what is in our hearts and demands faith, dedication, and commitment if we are to have any part with him.

> "If any of you lack wisdom, let him ask of God, that giveth to all men liberally, and upbraideth not; and it shall be given him. But let him ask in faith, nothing wavering. For he that wavereth is like a wave of the sea driven with the wind and tossed. For let not that man think that he shall receive any thing of the Lord."
> —James 1:5–7

As mentioned above, man's wisdom cannot understand the things of God, but Gods wisdom is available for the asking to "all men." However, there is a prerequisite: We must have absolute faith in God's promise; faith is the bone marrow of a child of God, and we cannot learn and grow without it. If you are among those who try to read the Bible but it does not speak to you, perhaps now you know why. Even so, it does not end there; there is another missing link, and that is the Holy Spirit. The only means we have for communicating with God is through the Holy Spirit, the same Holy Spirit that interpreted God's word to the authors of the Bible. Take note of the phrase "all men"; we are all unique individuals, and God deals with us as individuals.

The Land of Christianity

The land we will journey through—Christianity—is in perpetual sunlight emanating from the glory and majesty of Jesus Christ. This land has existed for almost two thousand years, surviving all attempts to destroy it or usurp the authority of its rightful owner. Residency is available to anyone committed to abide by the rules conveyed through the Bible and Holy Spirit, and there are many of them and they are nonnegotiable. We accept the rules or reject them; it is our choice.

It is a mystery how anyone can cope without God in his life, or why he would want to. Life apart from God is a constant struggle through peaks and valleys, unsettled in all its ways. Anyone whose life is governed by man is at the mercy of man, and the conditions across the river are the inevitable result. History reveals the inability of man to sustain any lasting peace in his life apart from God. In fact, our earthly life is an enigma; and sinful man is ill equipped to deal with it on his own. If you have not yet realized it, you will if you live long enough. However, God does not leave us without hope. We have the opportunity to turn to him and rely on his promises to sustain us through any trials and troubles we may face in this life.

> Behold, I stand at the door, and knock: if any man hear my voice, and open the door, I will come in to him, and will sup with him, and he with me. To him that overcometh will I grant to sit with me in my throne, even as I also overcame, and am set down with my Father in his throne.
> —Revelation 3:20–21

> Come unto me, all ye that labour and are heavy laden, and I
> will give you rest. Take my yoke upon you, and learn of me;
> for I am meek and lowly in heart: and ye shall find rest unto
> your souls. For my yoke *is* easy, and my burden is light.
> —Matthew 11:28–30

The promises of Jesus are comforting thing to contemplate in the times in which we live. How easy it is to abandon the worry and strife of man's chaotic world and experience a peace and contentment that defies man's understanding. It is not necessary to go through some religious ritual or ceremony to establish a relationship with Jesus Christ. We do not have to go searching for him because he is not the one lost. Take him at his word, open your heart to him, and he will draw you to himself.

> Love not the world, neither the things that are in the world.
> If any man loves the world, the love of the Father is not in
> him. For all that is in the world, the lust of the flesh, and
> the lust of the eyes, and the pride of life, is not of the Father,
> but is of the world. And the world passeth away, and the lust
> thereof: but he that doeth the will of God abideth for ever.
> —1 John 2:15–17

We cannot separate from the world in which we live. It is part of us, but we do not have to be part of it. God is in the spiritual world, and like oil and water, they do not mix. Many people try to be part of both worlds, without realizing that it is impossible. We must choose one side or the other. God will not play second fiddle to man, and turning our back on man's world and clinging only to things of God is certainly the most difficult hurdle to overcome, but that is what is required if we are to be part of his family.

We are all God's children, and we all have the same opportunity to turn to him and reap the blessings of a loving father. Like any child, we must obey him and adhere to his Word; otherwise, we are cut off from him. God has many loving and obedient children and will have no part with those who reject him. He did not intend man to live apart from him and did not separate himself from man; man separated himself. God created a perfect world and two perfect people to inherit it, but when Adam and Eve disobeyed him, they introduced sin into the world and that is our inheritance. We are born as sinners into a sinful world and without Jesus Christ we are unable to separate ourselves from its curse. The essence of God is love. It is a mystery, at least to me, how he can love us, and I can think of no greater rebuke than to reject the one who loves us the way he does.

Satan

Clearly, we cannot live on both sides a river at the same time. Anyone who chooses man's world and the things of man can have no part with God. Every person has the freedom to make the choice of how to live. God gave to each of us a free will, and he will not interfere with us exercising it. If we turn to him and do his will, we are recipients of his promise of eternal life with him. However, if we make the choice to turn away from him, the alternative is spending eternity with Satan; there is no middle ground. The reality of Satan is not a topic most people care to address, but Satan exists whether or not we want to think about him. Satan is a powerful supernatural being who roams the earth looking for future tenants, and today he is working overtime.

There are endless enticements across the river, beckoning those living on this side, and some residents are in a constant struggle to resist crossing the river. Some, because of a lack of faith, cross back and forth without choosing either side. A double-minded man cannot have any part in God's world, and if one is not committed to living on this side of the river, his presence will cause strife among the permanent residents here. We are bound to this physical world, but it does not prevent us from living in God's world through a relationship with Jesus Christ, who protects us from the influence of Satan.

If you have any doubt about the existence of Satan, here is something to ponder and you can draw your own conclusion. If Satan did not exist, would man, on his own volition, do the stupid and destructive things he delights in doing? If Satan did not exist, there would be no sin in the world, and we would enjoy a life like Adam and Eve had before Eve bit into the apple. There would be no sickness or death, and we would have heaven on earth. However, Satan caused Adam and Eve to sin and brought sin upon the human race, and we are cursed by it as long as we are on this earth. What other influences other than Satan could cause man to be so destructive to him and others as well? Would people like Hitler, Stalin, and other maniacs have murdered untold millions without a hint of remorse unless they were under Satan's influence? God certainly did not create those men to do the terrible things they did. There are two forces in the world—good and evil—all humans are free to choose one or the other.

> And the devil, taking him up into an high mountain, shewed unto him all the kingdoms of the world in a moment of time. And the devil said unto him, All this power will I give thee, and the glory of them: for that is delivered unto me; and to whomsoever I will I give it. If thou therefore wilt worship me, all shall be thine. And Jesus answered and said unto him, Get thee behind me, Satan: for it is written, Thou shalt worship the Lord thy God, and him only shalt thou serve. And he brought him to Jerusalem, and set him on a pinnacle of the temple, and said unto him, If thou be the Son of God, cast thyself down from hence: For it is written, He shall give his angels charge over there, to keep thee: And in their hands they shall bear thee up, lest at any time thou dash thy foot against a stone. And Jesus answering said unto him, It is said, Thou shalt not tempt the Lord thy God. And when the devil had ended all the temptation, he departed from him for a season."
> —Luke 4:5–13

Satan tempted even Jesus, but Jesus did not use his divine power against Satan; he rebuked him with the written word. Satan has temporary power over the earth, and it is a mighty power that can be defeated only by the power of Christ. Unless we are in Christ, and he is in us, we have no chance to defend ourselves against Satan: "All this power will I give thee, and the glory of them: for that is delivered unto me; and to whomsoever I will I give it. If thou therefore wilt worship me, all shall be thine." Satan has temporary lordship over mankind and promises great things to any who will worship him; he has the power to make good on his promises. There is evidence all around us of the awesome power Satan has over people, but it is not total power. If Satan had his way, he would kill every human on the planet, but the Holy Spirit restrains Satan's total control over mankind. Later, we will explore what happens when that restraint is removed.

For his own purpose, God has allowed Satan a season to dominate mankind with his devious and cunning evil. Satan is very clever at devising ways to entrap people by turning them away from God. Satan is revealed by the word of God, and we would not know about him—or what sin is, without the Bible. Satan is a master at persuading those under his influence not to concern themselves with the things of God.

God's Plan and Purpose

God does not create chaos in the world, Satan's influence has created the conditions we experience today but, even so, it is all according to God's plan. America has turned away from God, and it is foolish to expect that we can escape the consequences. It rains on the just and unjust alike, but Jesus the Good Shepherd always provides shelter for his sheep.

People who live apart from God are living in darkness, ignorant of the power of his spirit to guide their lives. Jesus Christ is the light of the world, and without him, we live in darkness. Nothing in man's world can shield us from fear, anxiety, dread, and worry. A personal relationship with Jesus Christ, however, can provide peace in our lives, no matter what the circumstances. If we live our lives in constant contact with Jesus and put our faith and trust in him, he will always comfort us and lead us to do his will, shielding us from the influence of Satan.

It was previously stated that nothing occurs that is not according to God's plan and purpose. It was God's plan to give us life, and we are all part of his plan. Most people sense that there is some purpose to their lives, but only a few ever discover what that purpose is. We are given life to serve and worship our creator, and we are rewarded for fulfilling our purpose and condemned if we fail to do what God intends for us to do. God did not create junk or useless things, and he certainly did not create man to live a useless life. If one lives apart from God, he is living a useless life. Yet, no matter how far man may sink into the mud, God can pull him out, clean him up, and use him in many ways. There is nothing discovered or invented that will not be used by God to support his purpose at the time of his choosing and that includes everybody and everything in the universe.

Earthquakes do not occur by magic; they occur as the result of movement of tectonic plates in the earth's crust—put in motion at the time the earth was created. According to the book of Revelation, earthquakes will be of major significance during the tribulation period that is coming to the earth very soon. The Bible tells us there will be earthquakes and other natural disasters in various places around the world, and they are increasing in number. Nevertheless, most people fail to realize they are warning signs of things to come.

> And there were voices, and thunders, and lightnings; and there was a great earthquake, such as was not since men were upon the earth, so mighty an earthquake, and so great. And the great city was divided into three parts, and the cities of the nations fell: and great Babylon came in remembrance before God, to give unto her the cup of the wine of the fierceness of his wrath.
> —Revelation 16:18–19

If we observe the fault lines that encircle the earth, it is easy to see how a single, great earthquake could affect the entire world. Aside from fault lines, there are other examples of how easy it is for God to direct world events. The Ogallala Aquifer that lies beneath six states in the center of the United States supplies water for what is colloquially known as America's breadbasket. Imagine the impact on the country if that aquifer dried up. The fact that the water level of the aquifer is declining does not cause any great concern because it will probably be many years before it has any great impact. Nevertheless, here is the point: God could dry it up in a day if he chooses to.

The order in the universe is maintained by gravity, and it keeps us grounded to the earth. However, the mystery of gravity escapes our understanding. Einstein wrestled with the mystery of gravity until his death, without ever furthering his understanding of what it is or where it comes from. We may not know what gravity is, but we can witness the effects of its existence. Electricity is another phenomenon that is incomprehensible to man, but if we poke a finger into a light socket, we can certainly prove it exists. God's spirit is like that; we cannot explain what it is, but once it touches our life there is no doubt of its existence, and its power.

Studying the Bible reveals that, as Solomon said, there is nothing new under the sun. Civilizations come and go; those who turn to God prosper, and those who reject him suffer his wrath. That is consistent throughout the Bible. America is moving away from God, and we are transitioning from his blessings to his wrath. God is not vengeful; he gives warnings in two ways—first through his word, and second through signs. Those who ignore his written warnings by not reading the Bible will ignore his signs because they will not recognize them as warnings. Hurricane Katrina; 9/11; the increase in floods, earthquakes, and tornados; economic problems; problems on the border with Mexico; the increase of the influence of Muslims in America; and the decline of America's influence around the world are all signs from God that are being ignored by this generation. He is telling us loud and clear to turn back to him, but who is listening? America cannot ignore reality forever. Because there is a large population of Christians in America, and for our support of Israel, God is giving us more time than we deserve to wake up. We can expect more frequent and more severe warnings before he gives up on us, but his patience is not without limits.

What is a Christian

We can avoid complicating the simple if we take a systematic approach to why we need God in our lives. From the moment we are born into an earthly body, we advance toward physical death without pause, but that is not where it ends. Because of the sins of Adam and Eve, we are born under a sentence of death, bestowed upon us by Satan. Our physical bodies are perishable, but our souls are eternal. Only Jesus Christ can grant a reprieve from the death sentence of sin, and Christianity provides the opportunity to gain that reprieve.

> Ye worship ye know not what: we know what we worship:
> for salvation is of the Jews. But the hour cometh, and now is,
> when the true worshippers shall worship the Father in spirit

and in truth: for the Father seeketh such to worship him.
God is a Spirit: and they that worship him must worship him
in spirit and in truth.
—John 4:22–24

I lived over half of my life believing I was a Christian, and I was; A Shakespearean Christian—a play actor a religious Christian. I was a Sunday school teacher, sang in a choir, and went to church every time the doors opened, *read* the Bible and thought I was God's right-hand man. It was not until I got into serious Bible study that I realized I was not a true Christian and never was. The essence of true Christianity is neither about feelings or emotions nor a religion. It is all about knowledge of God's word (truth) and a personal relationship with Jesus Christ (spirit). Organized religion has brought more pain, suffering, and death to mankind than the worst despots. During the Crusades and the Inquisition, hundreds of thousands of people were systematically slaughtered in the name of religion, and this very day, people the world over are dying in the name of radical Islam. The opportunity to establish a personal relationship with the creator of the universe is what sets Christianity apart from religion.

How can we expect God's continued blessing on America when religion has become big business and professional sports is a fast-growing religion? Everyone seems to have their own definition for "religion," and I suppose I have also. The word religion appears very rarely in the Bible; it appears in the News Testament of the King James Bible only five times. I will first give my opinion of what religion it is not: Christianity is not a religion; it is a person—Jesus Christ. However, I will concede that if a true, born again Christian has Jesus Christ living in them, I will not object to saying he has a religion. Anyone who has anything living in them, apart from Jesus Christ, such as an addiction to sports or entertainment, most definitely has a religion. The English word Religion comes from the Greek world *Thrace-ki-ah*, which also means, "Worship." I will leave you to deal with this subject yourself. If any man loves the world, the love of the Father is not in him. Dealing with earthly things is a constant struggle for a Christian, and it is why it is essential to have a day-to-day personal relationship with Jesus Christ. Without that relationship, eventually earthly things will crowd him out of our lives.

"Christianity" is more than a label; it is a reference to a personal relationship with Jesus Christ. That is the only definition that says it all and needs no further explanation. The most common proclamation by some is that they are followers of Christ; Christ said we should pick up our crosses and follow him. The problem is Jesus is walking much faster than many Christians are because they are bogged down in the mud of man's world. If we are to walk with Christ, we must keep up, and that means ridding ourselves of worldly baggage. There are times when we will lag behind Christ, but we should never lag so far behind we lose sight of him.

The actions of a Christian should inspire non-believers to seek that which a relationship with Christ offers and not be an obstacle, turning people away from Christ. If one understands what it means to be a Christian, one will realize that it is an awesome responsibility, which requires more giving than receiving. All blessings come from God, and we should never fail to thank and praise him for his blessings. To seek rewards from man is to put man above Christ, and no true Christian would ever do such a thing. Jesus Christ gave his life to cover our sins, and we cannot merely acknowledge it and move on with life in man's world.

A Personal Relationship with Christ

Christianity is not a show-and-tell program or a Shakespearean play performed by actors who call themselves Christians. True Christianity is not about rituals. His church is not a conglomeration of Baptist, Methodist, Pentecostals, the church of this or that and hundreds of other factions; it is a personal relationship between Christ and saved individuals throughout the world.

Christ did not intend for his church to be fragmented and divisive as it is today, but he knew it would come to that from the beginning. Christ does not offer salvation to churches or denominations. He saves individuals, and those saved individuals make up his church. It is a church without doors and windows to be breached by interlopers. However, divisions among the church are nothing new; it has been a problem from the very beginning.

> Now I beseech you, brethren, by the name of our Lord Jesus
> Christ, that ye all speak the same thing, and that there be no

divisions among you; but that ye be perfectly joined together in the same mind and in the same judgment. For it hath been declared unto me of you, my brethren, by them which are of the house of Chloe, that there are contentions among you. Now this I say, that every one of you saith, I am of Paul; and I of Apollos; and I of Cephas; and I of Christ. Is Christ divided? was Paul crucified for you? or were ye baptized in the name of Paul?

—1 Corinthians 1:10–13

Churches in America today are as fragmented as at any time in our history, and the question is why. The early church had the same problem, so what is the solution? Before we can address the solutions, we must recognize the problem. Christ does not deal with church A differently than he deals with church B, because there is no church A or B. The church consists of born-again individuals scattered throughout the world, so how can we all be in one accord? There is only one way, and that is through a personal relationship with Jesus Christ, which will ensure we are all of one mind.

One cannot have a meaningful and personal relationship with someone he does not know. In addition, a Christian must have more than a superficial knowledge of Christ or a casual understanding of Christ's world. Only the Bible provides the knowledge and understanding of God's world, and it takes commitment and dedication to discover it. We cannot rely solely on a pastor or a teacher to teach us about God. Each one of us has a personal responsibility to verify the truth, and the Bible is the only reliable source; any reputable pastor or teacher will agree. Pastors and teachers have an awesome responsibility, and sometimes they are disrespected by apathetic parishioners who are exposed to God's word only once a week without any desire for personal study. God is first in our lives, or he is last; he is the most important thing in our lives, or he is of no importance. We believe, trust, and worship him, or we do not.

Christianity is all about salvation; in our physical world, everything has a beginning and an ending. However, the spiritual world of God has always existed and will never end. It is difficult, if not impossible, for man to comprehend eternity, but although our physical bodies will die, our spiritual souls will go on forever. There are only two destinations for our soul to reside and residence in either place is voluntary. Compared to eternity, a life span on this earth is less than the blink of the eye. Those simple facts are what the Bible is all about; it is not a book of condemnation but a book of hope and promise for those who accept it. However, there are dire consequences for those who reject it.

God is not an old grandfather type, sitting on a throne, nodding off somewhere out in the ether. God is the master of the universe and a dictator who made the rules for man to obey; we ignore those rules at our peril. He sees all and knows all; nothing is hidden from him, and from the time of birth to the time of death, our every word and deed is recorded in his book of remembrance. He has given to us a free will to choose how we wish to live, but he has not given to us a free will to alter his word to conform to our feelings or personal beliefs. We either accept him or reject him, and if we accept him, we must be prepared to abandon our will and accept his.

The same God who talked to Abraham thousands of years ago is the same God who controls world events today. God is all-knowing. He knows the number of ants crawling around in the grass in the backyard, and he certainly knows the thoughts racing around in our heads. Nothing is hidden from him, and nothing exceeds his ability to do whatever is in accordance to his will. He created this universe simply by speaking it into existence, and at his appointed time, he is going to remake it anew.

> And I saw a new heaven and a new earth: for the first heaven
> and the first earth were passed away; and there was no more
> sea.
> —Revelation 21:1

The First Step

The first step in becoming a child of God is to accept, without any doubt, that Jesus Christ is not only the Son of God, he is God revealed to us. He left his heavenly throne to come to the earth in the flesh by way of a Virgin birth to redeem mankind from the curse of sin that man is unable to do for himself. Christ was not forced to leave his throne and come to the earth in the flesh; he did so because of his love for us—the entire human race. He covered our sins by willingly shedding his blood through an agonizing death on a Roman cross. He was resurrected from the grave and returned to his rightful place at the right hand of the Father, where he now resides looking after his redeemed church.

> And as Moses lifted up the serpent in the wilderness, even so must the Son of man be lifted up: That whosoever believeth in him should not perish, but have eternal life. For God so loved the world, that he gave his only begotten Son, that whosoever believeth in him should not perish, but have everlasting life. For God sent not his Son into the world to condemn the world; but that the world through him might be saved. He that believeth on him is not condemned: but he that believeth not is condemned already, because he hath not believed in the name of the only begotten Son of God. And this is the condemnation, that light is come into the world, and men loved darkness rather than light, because their deeds were evil.
> —John 3:14–19

When Moses was leading his people through the wilderness, they were constantly complaining and blaming Moses and God, for making them wander in the desert without food or water even though God had delivered them from bondage in Egypt. Because of the rebellion of the people, God sent poisonous snakes to inflict fatal bites on them, and many of the people were killed. God instructed Moses to fashion a brass serpent and lift it up on a pole, so anyone who was bitten by a serpent could look upon the brass serpent and live.

> And the people spake against God, and against Moses, Wherefore have ye brought us up out of Egypt to die in the wilderness? for there is no bread, neither is there any water; and our soul loatheth this light bread. And the LORD sent fiery serpents among the people, and they bit the people; and

much people of Israel died. Therefore the people came to Moses, and said, We have sinned, for we have spoken against the LORD, and against thee; pray unto the LORD, that he take away the serpents from us. And Moses prayed for the people. And the LORD said unto Moses, Make thee a fiery serpent, and set it upon a pole: and it shall come to pass, that every one that is bitten, when he looketh upon it, shall live. And Moses made a serpent of brass, and put it upon a pole, and it came to pass, that if a serpent had bitten any man, when he beheld the serpent of brass, he lived.
—Numbers 21:5–9

In the same manner, Jesus Christ was lifted up on a wooden cross so that anyone bitten by the curse of sin, which is everyone, could look to him for salvation and live. We have seen what Christ did for us, but what can we do for him? The only things we can do for him is love him, worship him, and do his will.

And they brought young children to him, that he should touch them: and his disciples rebuked those that brought them. But when Jesus saw it, he was much displeased, and said unto them, Suffer the little children to come unto me, and forbid them not: for of such is the kingdom of God. Verily I say unto you, Whosoever shall not receive the kingdom of God as a little child, he shall not enter therein. And he took them up in his arms, put his hands upon them, and blessed them.
—Mark 10:13–16

When we first begin a relationship with God, we do so as little children, innocent and naïve, in need of nurturing and guidance. "Whosoever shall not receive the kingdom of God as a little child, he shall not enter therein." God has little use for proud and vain people; after all, of what do we have to be proud? Children do not have a strong sense of discernment or reasoning; they develop these traits over a period of learning and exposure. We must view ourselves from his perspective; it could take a lifetime to mature in the knowledge of the things of God, and it has to be a lifetime commitment.

A Personal Decision

The true Christian church is not about buildings or denominations; it is about individuals that have separated themselves from man's world and surrendered their lives to Jesus Christ as their Lord and Master. God created people as individuals with distinct abilities and personalities, and he deals with them on that basis. In man's world, not everyone is treated equally, but through God's grace and mercy we are all welcomed into his world as equals—just the way we are—because he is capable of cleaning up the worst of the worst. We were all created for a purpose, and the primary purpose for each of us is to first worship our creator.

Satan is in constant battle with Jesus Christ for the souls of man, and based on the condition of the world, Satan is in his heyday. Only faith in God and his power can provide the strength to resist Satan's influence, but sadly, only a few will accept Christ as their protector to prevent Satan from conquering their souls.

> Now there was a day when the sons of God came to present themselves before the LORD, and Satan came also among them. And the LORD said unto Satan, Whence comest thou? Then Satan answered the LORD, and said, From going to and fro in the earth, and from walking up and down in it. And the LORD said unto Satan, Hast thou considered my servant Job, that there is none like him in the earth, a perfect and an upright man, one that feareth God, and escheweth evil? Then Satan answered the LORD, and said, Doth Job fear God for nought? Hast not thou made an hedge about him, and about his house, and about all that he hath on every side? thou hast blessed the work of his hands, and his substance is increased in the land. But put forth thine hand now, and touch all that he hath, and he will curse thee to thy face. And the LORD said unto Satan, Behold, all that he hath *is* in thy power; only upon himself put not

forth thine hand. So Satan went forth from the presence of
the LORD.
—Job 1:6–12

The book of Job is thought to be the first book to be written in the Bible,
and it would be a challenge to choose it as the first book to read. However,
if you begin with Genesis, by the time you reach the book of Job, you will
find it an excellent source for gaining a better understanding of the power of
faith and the relationship between God, man, and Satan. Once one makes a
decision to have a personal relationship with the master of the universe, life
will never be the same.

> Therefore I say unto you, Take no thought for your life,
> what ye shall eat, or what ye shall drink; nor yet for your
> body, what ye shall put on. Is not the life more than meat,
> and the body than raiment? Behold the fowls of the air: for
> they sow not, neither do they reap, nor gather into barns;
> yet your heavenly Father feedeth them. Are ye not much
> better than they? Which of you by taking thought can add
> one cubit unto his stature? And why take ye thought for
> raiment? Consider the lilies of the field, how they grow;
> they toil not, neither do they spin: And yet I say unto you,
> That even Solomon in all his glory was not arrayed like one
> of these. Wherefore, if God so clothe the grass of the field,
> which to day is, and to morrow is cast into the oven, shall
> he not much more clothe you, O ye of little faith? Therefore
> take no thought, saying, What shall we eat? or, What shall
> we drink? or, Wherewithal shall we be clothed? (For after
> all these things do the Gentiles seek :) for your heavenly
> Father knoweth that ye have need of all these things. But
> seek ye first the kingdom of God, and his righteousness; and
> all these things shall be added unto you. Take therefore no
> thought for the morrow: for the morrow shall take thought
> for the things of itself. Sufficient unto the day *is* the evil
> thereof.
> —Matthew 6:25–34

Do you have faith to believe those words of Jesus? Do you lie awake at night worrying about the things heaped on you by this world? Have you ever solved a problem with worry? The result of worry is stress, and stress will not solve problems, but it can kill you. Do you wish to live a worry-free life? We can have worry-free lives if we claim the promise of Jesus, but there is a qualifier: But seek ye first the kingdom of God, and his righteousness; and all these things shall be added unto you. God's promises are not available to those living in man's world; only those clothed in the righteousness of Jesus Christ are recipients of his promise of peace and salvation.

As we continue to explore God's world, we cannot help but realize that across the river is a deceiving world, but reality exist on this side. There are no lies, deceptions, false promises, or uncertainty, only truth and assurance. God is all-powerful and able to accomplish whatever pleases him; he does not make a promise he will not keep. Even if he could, God has no reason to lie. If you are not yet a member of God's family, the heavenly Father is willing to adopt you and accept you just the way you are with unconditional love. We are all sinners and unable to change our sinful natures, and without the righteousness of Jesus Christ, we are lost.

We are saved from Satan's clutches, not by any effort on our part, but by the grace and mercy of Almighty God. If an earthly father takes care of his children with limited resources, our heavenly Father is not bound by any limits, and as his children, there is no doubt he will take care of us. He does not promise to satisfy our wants, but he will not fail in his promise to satisfy our needs if we trust him to do so. God responds to our faith and love, and the more we display it, the more we will recognize him working in our life.

Apostasy

Apostasy comes from the Greek word *Apostasia*, meaning to fall away or forsake as in turning away from or forsaking the true teachings of the Bible. In the following verses, such people are referred to as false prophets. Apostasy is on the increase, not only in America but also in the entire world. It is from apostate churches that a global religion will develop and be the dominate religion during the tribulation period. The true Christian church will be removed from the world in the rapture prior to the tribulation period, and we will further explore this subject later.

> But there were false prophets also among the people, even as there shall be false teachers among you, who privily shall bring in damnable heresies, even denying the Lord that bought them, and bring upon themselves swift destruction. And many shall follow their pernicious ways; by reason of whom the way of truth shall be evil spoken of.
> —2 Peter 2:1–2

We would not be warned about false teachings if they did not exist, but they do exist and have many titles or labels. It is far beyond my ability, or desire, to identify apostate churches in America today, but suffice it to know they are on the increase. Liberalism has infected this side of the river with the same fever as the other side. The only way to identify apostasy is to know God's word; otherwise how are we to know if we are being taught the truth. If a preacher or teacher teaches that which is contrary to the truth in the Bible, they will face their judgment, but we will not be held guiltless for accepting their false teaching: *"who privily shall bring in damnable heresies, even denying the Lord that bought them, and bring upon themselves swift destruction."* That does not imply we should not listen to a preacher or teacher but that they are human, fallible, and have a very demanding responsibility. It is our responsibility to support our church leaders by educating ourselves with the truth of God's word and presenting ourselves as meaningful participants in church worship, not mere spectators.

We discussed man's eagerness to attach a title or label to identify his allegiance to something, and there is nothing necessarily wrong with that practice. Nevertheless, it would be foolish not to know what such labels represent. The Christian church in America has become so fragmented and divisive that the true brotherhood is difficult to identify, and that is not God's will for his church. More and more, it appears that people never tire of devising ways to make God's word conform to their personal desires rather than accept his word as the only truth, and one that is not to be manipulated.

One beautiful spring morning in Arizona, I was on my patio reading my Bible when the sweet and pleasing aroma from a nearby cocktail tree drifted by. For those not familiar with a cocktail tree, it bears more than one kind of fruit. It was originally a lemon tree but through manipulation and grafting, it bore lemons, oranges, and grapefruits. After a couple of years, there were no more grapefruits, and a couple years after that the oranges were gone. On this particular morning, all there was on the tree were lemon blossoms. As I sat there enjoying the aroma and observing the tree and its beautiful blossoms, it occurred to me that that tree was similar to God's word. A lemon tree was created to produce lemons and, regardless of mans meddling, it eventually will regain its original intent. The true word of God remains the same, no matter how man may manipulate it or try to add something that does not belong. The truth always will overcome any attempt to alter its intended purpose.

The truth of God's word is revealed to man through the Holy Spirit, so why are there so many different interpretations of the Bible? There is only one truth, so who has the correct interpretation? The key lies in God's word; the carnal mind of earthly man cannot understand the things of God. What do you know about God, and where did you learn it? Did you learn about God from man or from the Bible? The sole purpose of the Bible is to reveal God to whoever wishes to know him. I am attempting to tread lightly regarding this subject because I do not wish to give the impression we should ignore the teachings of a preacher. We are discussing, however, the future of your eternal soul and, as formerly stated, nowhere in the Bible is the responsibility for learning the truth given to anyone other than the individual. Before the New Testament was written, God's word was taught by word of mouth by apostles and disciples, ordained by Jesus, but fortunately, today we are blessed by having the written word, and I thank God for that blessing. In biblical times, people ignored the teachings of the prophets, the same way people today ignore the Bible.

How can we be sure that what we assume to know about God is true unless we get it directly from the only reliable source? We are given a brief time on earth to prepare for the life to follow, and if we squander that time away in man's world, we will forfeit any chance of salvation.

For what man knoweth the things of a man, save the spirit of man which is in him? even so the things of God knoweth no man, but the Spirit of God. Now we have received, not the spirit of the world, but the spirit which is of God; that we might know the things that are freely given to us of God. Which things also we speak, not in the words which man's wisdom teacheth, but which the Holy Ghost teacheth; comparing spiritual things with spiritual. But the natural man receiveth not the things of the Spirit of God: for they are foolishness unto him: neither can he know them, because they are spiritually discerned.
—1 Corinthians 2:11–14

Man cannot have any true knowledge of God unless it is revealed by the Holy Spirit. There are apostate churches that make it apparent what they are, yet their pews are filled every Sunday morning. Being clever and deceitful, Satan does not waste time with these churches. His goal is to spread his influence in every true Christian church, and he has a very clever modus operandi. There is not a true Christian church in the world that is not a target for Satan, and his minions are all around looking for any weakness in the faithful.

Every church has its weak link, and Satan is constantly seeking it out. If a church has only two or three members, Satan will attempt to influence the weak one, and he is working overtime, emboldened by his progress. His favorite tactic is to spread his influence over a church one member at a time, so he will go unnoticed until he has succeeded in fragmenting the entire brotherhood. Of course, his prime target is always the church leadership; conquer them, and he conquers the members.

The process of researching for information to obtain a consensus on how many Christians there are in America, resulted in futility. In reality, there is only one reliable source to determine the number of Christians in America. It is—the Lord Jesus Christ. First, we would need a universal agreement on what is a Christian. That also is futile. As there is no reliable source, however, an unreliable deduction from my research is that more than 70 percent of Americans profess to be Christians; unfortunately, for many, this profession is also is unreliable. This is not done deliberately but because of ignorance of what a Christian is. As I stated, Jesus Christ knows what a Christian is, and the answer is in his word. If *you* wish to know the answer, read the Bible. If one studies the Bible, the Old and New Testaments, when you get to the New Testament, you will discover that Jesus did not dwell on theology and dogma. Jesus presented things simple and uncomplicated so people like me could understand. He led his Disciples to do the same.

As undeserving as we may be, God's grace and mercy give to each of us the opportunity to separate ourselves from man's sinful world, enter into his world, and partake of his promises. There is nothing we can do to earn such a blessing; all we can do for God is to accept his son, Jesus Christ, as the Lord and Master of our lives, and surrender ourselves to his care and guidance. That is the truth of the Gospel.

It is important for Christians to fellowship with other believers, but unless we have a personal relationship with Jesus Christ—who reveals the truth to us through the Holy Spirit—how are we to know if we are living according to his will? It is not what we may assume it is, or what other people may say it is. Only God's word and the Holy Spirit can reveal it to us.

Before we were born, God foresaw each moment in our lives, and he knows who will accept him and who will not. He gave us the freedom to make our own decisions. You have the choice: Throw this book in the trash, go back to the other side of the river, and continue to seek the elusive things to fill the empty space in your soul. Alternatively, if you have not already, you can open your heart to Christ and surrender the rest of your life to him. Once he takes control, perhaps for the first time in your life you will experience a peace you never before imagined. If you find this simplistic, it is that simple, but God knows your heart. If you are sincere, he is ready to accept you with all your sinful baggage. There is no new sin; whatever you may have done, someone else has done it already. We are all sinners, unable to abandon our sinful natures. Only through the blood of Jesus Christ, are we able, through his grace and mercy, to be rescued from an eternity with the master of sin.

Once we become children of God, we learn things about ourselves we never recognized before. The most profound revelation is that without God, we are empty shells without depth or substance. Compared to the reality of God's world, man's world is filled with pretense and playacting, supported by self-induced illusions. The primary reason people will accept lies and deception from man but refuse to believe the truth of God's word is because man will tell people what they want to hear, relieving them of any guilt. The gullible will fail to realize that there is no lasting advantage to be gained from lies and deceptions. Know the truth, and the truth will make you free.

Pride

I have mentioned many times how man's ignorance and arrogance keeps him separated from the things of God, but the greatest of all barriers is pride—a thing God hates and with good reason. Pride is man's effort to put himself at the top of the heap, above everyone else, even God. Pride is the antonym of humbleness, and God loves the humble but has no use for the proud. A proud person is constantly on guard to shield himself from embarrassment or criticism because he thinks more highly of himself than he should. A humble person usually is contented and at peace with himself, but a proud person will never know true happiness and contentment because he is under the illusion that every eye is on him, watching his every move. The truth is no one really cares. What we should be conscious of is that God's eyes are always on us, and he does care. Not all pride is bad; it is good to be proud of who we are, but it is pure vanity to be proud of what we are.

Prayer

We cannot have a relationship with Christ without communicating with him, and we do that through prayer. A child of God has a private line directly to the ruler of the universe, and nothing offered by man can trump that privilege. Unless we are in Jesus Christ and he is in us, acting as our mediator, the Father will not hear our prayer. Christ is our arbiter; he must affirm that we are justified through his blood before we are granted access to the Father with our prayers. "Jesus saith unto him, I am the way, the truth, and the life: no man cometh unto the Father, but by me."— John 14:6. If we do not know him, and he does not know us, and we wait until we face a crisis to call on God, we may be praying to the air. God knows our hearts and our needs before we ever utter a prayer, and he always responds to our prayers if they are rightly presented through Jesus Christ. We may not get the answer we pray for, but God knows best how to respond to our prayers.

Prayer is more than a request for something. If we are familiar with the Bible, we are aware that Jesus prayed to the Father often, usually separating himself from others and praying in private. Prayer is a conduit for communicating to God the Father through God the Son. God is not hard of hearing or inattentive to our prayers; he knows what we need before we ask, and we should never present frivolous prayers. If we pray from the heart, more often than not, the prayer will be short and to the point. I am not convinced God always listens to a prayer from the head, but I am convinced he will always respond to a prayer from the heart.

> And when thou prayest, thou shalt not be as the hypocrites *are*: for they love to pray standing in the synagogues and in the corners of the streets, that they may be seen of men. Verily I say unto you, They have their reward. But thou, when thou prayest, enter into thy closet, and when thou hast shut thy door, pray to thy Father which is in secret; and thy Father which seeth in secret shall reward thee openly. But when ye pray, use not vain repetitions, as the heathen do: for they think that they shall be heard for their much speaking. Be not ye therefore like unto them: for your Father knoweth what things ye have need of, before ye ask him.
> —Matthew 6:5–8

It is important to realize that a relationship with God is a personal relationship, and our prayers should be a secret communication with God. Most people are familiar with what is erroneously referred to as the Lord's Prayer, which begins "Our Father"—the true Lord's Prayer is found in John 17—but how many of us really know who it is that we call Father? A major problem that complicates our prayer life is the lack of patience. God has no restraints of time, and we serve at his pleasure, not ours. When we make our requests to God, and it is his pleasure to grant them, he will decide the best time be it a day or a year from now. Another thing is to keep our prayers simple and to the point.

And he spake this parable unto certain which trusted in themselves that they were righteous, and despised others: Two men went up into the temple to pray; the one a Pharisee, and the other a publican. The Pharisee stood and prayed thus with himself, God, I thank thee, that I am not as other men are, extortioners, unjust, adulterers, or even as this publican. I fast twice in the week, I give tithes of all that I possess. And the publican, standing afar off, would not lift up so much as his eyes unto heaven, but smote upon his breast, saying, God be merciful to me a sinner. I tell you, this man went down to his house justified rather than the other: for every one that exalteth himself shall be abased; and he that humbleth himself shall be exalted.

—Luke 18:9–14

One of the shortest prayers in the Bible—"God, be merciful to me, a sinner!" says all that the tax collector needed to say. God knows what is in our hearts, and no matter the verbiage we use, it is better to keep it short and to the point. God is all knowing and we cannot impress him with eloquent and long-winded verbiage. We can talk to God as loving children to a loving Father and make our requests known to him with a humble heart, confident that he will hear us if we present our prayers in the name of Christ. I will share with you my personal method of prayer. I know it is not necessary, and some may think it is silly, but I am comfortable with it, but you need to develop your own method. I am strong on metaphors, so here it is one: I have what I call an imaginary prayer /blessings basket. I am not comfortable with spontaneous prayers, especially head-prayers. I like to think my prayers through, calling on the Holy Spirit for assistance. Once I am satisfied that my prayers are worthy, I put them in my prayer basket and pass it on to Jesus to be presented to the Father. In return, it is eventually returned to me as a blessings basket. If I am to be in a situation where I may be called on to say a prayer, I always make sure I bring along my prayer basket.

If we have doubt our prayers will be answered, they probably will not be. We must have faith and patience to wait for an answer, and we must accept that sometimes God's answer is no, which always turns out to be for our good.

Communicating with God

> Verily, verily, I say unto you, He that believeth on me, the
> works that I do shall he do also; and greater works than these
> shall he do; because I go unto my Father. And whatsoever ye
> shall ask in my name, that will I do, that the Father may be
> glorified in the Son. If ye shall ask any thing in my name,
> I will do it.
> —John 14:12–14

We cannot have a relationship with someone with whom we never commune. If Jesus is the most important person in our lives, which he should be, we will share everything with him, follow his guidance, and depend on him to lead us on the right path. If we truly know who he is, we will know how to talk to him and, more important, how to listen to him. If we have a specific request to address to the Father, it must be done through Jesus Christ; otherwise, the Father will not respond to our prayer. Christ is our arbiter and we do not choose him, he chooses us. If he does not acknowledge us, neither will the Father. The only prayer God will acknowledge from an unsaved person is referred to as the Sinner's Prayer. Many sinner prayers have been written down but, like all prayers, they must come from the heart. If you have a sincere desire to turn to God, tell him so and open your heart to him and he will draw you to himself no matter what verbiage you may stutter through.

> Likewise the Spirit also helpeth our infirmities: for we know
> not what we should pray for as we ought: but the Spirit itself
> maketh intercession for us with groanings which cannot be
> uttered. And he that searcheth the hearts knoweth what is
> the mind of the Spirit, because he maketh intercession for
> the saints according to the will of God. And we know that
> all things work together for good to them that love God, to
> them who are the called according to his purpose.
> —Romans 8:26–28

We can talk to Jesus from the heart anytime, anywhere, but we should set aside a time every day to pray to the Father—not just when we go to bed after watching six hours of television and then falling asleep. Establish a specific time and place, without any outside interference, that is reserved for communing with God. You may be surprised how quickly it becomes the most important part of your day.

Dedication and Commitment

If you are not a born-again Christian, this is the hour of decision and could very well be your last opportunity to surrender your life to Jesus Christ. He is always ready to receive you, and the only preparation you need is faith. You may say you have things to take care of across the river and then come back to this side, but that is a dangerous thing, the bridge may collapse as you cross it, or you may succumb to the trappings of man's world and abandon any desire to live on this side of the river. No matter what you need to take care of across the river, Christ will make a way for you to deal with it without it being necessary to go back.

> And another of his disciples said unto him, Lord, suffer
> me first to go and bury my father. But Jesus said unto him,
> Follow me; and let the dead bury their dead.
> —Matthew 8:21–22

Theologians have different interpretations about the meaning of these two verses, but I only know about how they speak to me. As harsh as that may appear, it serves to illustrate the level of devotion we must have for Christ and to make him the master of our lives. It is a small sacrifice compared to what he did for us. God has not made it difficult to enter his world, but do not think it will be an easy journey in this sinful world. Compared to living without God in our lives, however, it is a sweet journey.

Titles

One of man's greatest follies is the obsession with titles. Man has a title for everything and seems to be unable to exist without one. Most Americans have become so shallow and without depth to their characters, they adopt identities personified by a title or label without the slightest idea of what it represents. This is certainly prevalent in the world of politics. By no means does simply attaching a label to ourselves or putting a bumper sticker on our cars reveal who we really are. Most people will not know what the label they identify with represents.

A master thief goes door to door in a neighborhood, identifies himself as Mr. Good Guy who is running for political office, gives everyone a hundred-dollar bill, and promises another hundred-dollar bill if they vote for him. Then he moves on to the next house to do the same. Before dark, most of the neighborhood will be bragging about Mr. Good Guy and pledging their support by labeling themselves as a "Goody," and they will rush to the polling place to vote for him. Feeling empowered because they are supporters of a winner and by his promise of another hundred-dollar bill, they awaken in the morning to discover that Mr. Good Guy is a fraud. He has broken into their houses, and not only has he recovered the hundred-dollar bill, he has taken everything in the house of any value. This is a wordy metaphor and seems to be off the subject, but there is a relevant message to be learned. It describes a common practice across the river, but it is not totally absent on this side of the river, even though this side has nothing to do with politics. The prince of thieves is snooping around over here, and he is looking for souls to conquer. Satan is a master deceiver and he is not after your possessions; he is after you.

Simply calling ourselves Christians does not make us so. Proclaiming to be born again does not mean we are. Participation in church activities, including baptism, does not provide salvation. Our Christian life is manifested in the way we live our lives, not by titles or participating in church activities. If we are true Christians at 9:00 a.m., we will be Christian at 9:00 p.m. If we are Christian at home, we will be Christian at work. Christianity is not something to display only when it is comfortable to do so.

> Giving thanks unto the Father, which hath made us meet
> to be partakers of the inheritance of the saints in light Who
> hath delivered us from the power of darkness, and hath
> translated us into the kingdom of his dear Son: In whom
> we have redemption through his blood, even the forgiveness
> of sins ...
> —Colossians 1:12–14

If you are a young person with a perceived long life ahead of you, things of God may not seem important enough to deal with until you get a little gray hair. However, there are graveyards filled with the decaying bodies of young people who once had the same view. A long life is promised to no one; perhaps you choose not to think about it, but dying is the easy part if you are prepared for the life that follows. Whether or not you think about it, hell is a reality and a place you do not want to go. Like King Solomon, who looked back on his life and realized the futility of pursuing the trappings of man's world, you have the opportunity to change your future.

The difference between *thinking* and *knowing* is a chasm as wide as the ocean. God knows if we are fit for his kingdom, but we may only think we are. Each of us is solely responsible for being sure of our salvation. If you are not sure of your salvation, now is the time to evaluate your relationship with Jesus Christ. Superficial Christians—I call them Shakespearean Christians because they *act* as though they are Christians although they do not know Jesus Christ— are Satan's favorite target, and he is devious enough to convince them they are something they are not. If we fiddle away our limited time in front of the television and other forms of entertainment and keep Christ in the shadows, we cannot expect much from our relationship with him.

Faith

God always leaves out an excess of details in the Bible in order to develop our faith, helping us to believe what we cannot see. Faith is not required to believe what is obvious; it takes faith to believe in what is not. It is fashionable to say we believe in God, and almost everyone makes that confession, but many do not know in whom they are confessing to believe in. God is not an old gray-haired grandfather who, with a wink of the eye, pats you on the head and welcomes you to his kingdom. God is the rule-giver and, if we are to be part of his kingdom, we must obey his rules. The same rules and promises apply to everyone. A misunderstanding about God is that he is a loving God who will not allow anyone to go to hell. The only truth in that statement is that God is a loving God. He is certainly that, but he is also a holy God and that means he will not tolerate sin. Sin will be judged, and there are no exceptions. It is not up to God whether we go to hell or not; it is up to us.

> At the ninth hour Jesus cried out with a loud voice, Eloi,
> Eloi, lama sabachthani? which is translated, My God, My
> God, why have thou forsaken Me?
> —Mark 15:34

At that moment, Christ had taken upon himself the sins of the world; through him and only through him, we have a chance of salvation. God the Father had to separate himself from Christ because Christ had taken upon himself the sins of the world, and God cannot have any association with sin. Jesus Christ is the savior of a born-again Christian, and we are covered by his blood. When we sin, if we repent, God will forgive and forget; a repented sin will never be remembered by God. Jesus sacrificed himself on a cross for mankind, and he is the doorkeeper to heaven. Only with his permission are we granted access; there is no back door.

The foundation on which a relationship with Christ must be grounded is faith. Most of us have learned that when we have faith in people, it usually results in disappointment. Even faith in ourselves will not always bring satisfaction. Only when our faith is directed toward God are we assured of positive results. Faith in God is unique in that it never disappoints. Despite man's natural arrogance toward total faith in anything or anyone other than himself, we must not have any doubt when we put our faith in God. A little faith, or occasional faith, is not sufficient for dealing with God's word. If our faith and trust is directed toward God, we can be assured of positive results. God always keeps his word, and he knows what is best for us, even if it is contrary to our own desires. That is the essence of faith. No one can love and care for us more than God does. If we love and trust him to do the right thing for us, we soon will learn the peace and joy that comes from abandoning our will and accepting his because he will never lead us astray.

Sometimes God will lead us in a direction we would not choose to go, but in the end, it turns out to be a great blessing. If we put our trust in him, he is always there to rescue us from going down the wrong path. Satan also can lead us in a direction we would not choose, but that always leads to the wrong path. It is not necessary for you to accept my word that trusting in God will change your life in a way you never imagined, but if you give him the opportunity, you can experience it for yourself.

Again, we must not lose our focus because as the saying goes, "out of sight, out of mind." Satan is a master at diverting people's attention from the things of God, and we must continue to grow in faith to resist him. The sure way to do that is to have God's word in our hearts, not in our heads, by studying the Bible. I would not continue to emphasize how important it is to study the Bible if it were not essential for increasing our faith. Without faith, we cannot grow in our relationship with Christ.

> I beseech you therefore, brethren, by the mercies of God, that ye present your bodies a living sacrifice, holy, acceptable unto God, which is your reasonable service. And be not conformed to this world: but be ye transformed by the renewing of your mind, that ye may prove what is that good, and acceptable, and perfect, will of God. For I say, through the grace given unto me, to every man that is among you, not to think of himself more highly than he ought to think; but to think soberly, according as God hath dealt to every man the measure of faith. For as we have many members in one body, and all members have not the same office: So we, being many, are one body in Christ, and every one members one of another. Having then gifts differing according to the grace that is given to us, whether prophecy, let us prophesy according to the proportion of faith ...
> —Romans 12:1–6

God gives everyone a measure of faith for believing in him, and it rests in the empty place in our souls that is reserved for his spirit. Man can build on that faith and grow in the knowledge of God through the study of his word. On the other hand, he can be consumed by man's world and never allow his faith to mature. As I have previously stated, we cannot advance our knowledge of God without absolute faith and trust in him.

The Road to Salvation

The subject of salvation is what God's word is all about; salvation is a pardon from a death sentence and is granted by the grace and mercy of God. There is no way we can do for ourselves what Christ did for us. We cannot earn it by works or deeds; salvation is freely given by accepting Jesus Christ into our life, abandon a wearisome life in man's world, and devote ourselves to serving him. Our only contribution is faith in him and his promises. It is not through our own good works we are saved, but by the good works of Jesus Christ. We may appear as pious as an old-time Southern preacher may be, but if we think we are without sin in our lives, we do not know what sin is.

> For by grace are ye saved through faith; and that not of yourselves: it is the gift of God: Not of works, lest any man should boast. For we are his workmanship, created in Christ Jesus unto good works, which God hath before ordained that we should walk in them.
> —Ephesians 2:8–10

Attending church, teaching Sunday school, singing in the choir, aiding the needy, being baptized—all of these things are Christian things to do. They will not provide salvation, but they can be a manifestation of salvation. Christ has not made it difficult to become a member of his family, we complicate it ourselves by our own stubbornness and unwillingness to accept the truth of his word.

> But what saith it? The word is nigh thee, even in thy mouth, and in thy heart: that is, the word of faith, which we preach; That if thou shalt confess with thy mouth the Lord Jesus, and shalt believe in thine heart that God hath raised him from the dead, thou shalt be saved. For with the heart man believeth unto righteousness; and with the mouth confession is made unto salvation. For the scripture saith, Whosoever believeth on him shall not be ashamed.
> —Romans 10:8–11

Wherefore, my beloved, as ye have always obeyed, not as in my presence only, but now much more in my absence, work out your own salvation with fear and trembling. For it is God which worketh in you both to will and to do of his good pleasure. Do all things without murmurings and disputings: That ye may be blameless and harmless, the sons of God, without rebuke, in the midst of a crooked and perverse nation, among whom ye shine as lights in the world ...
—Philippians 2:12–15

The above verses contain a phrase that sometimes is overlooked or misunderstood: "work out your own salvation with fear and trembling." Salvation is an ongoing process and is what it means to work out our salvation. The term "work out" comes from the Greek word, *katergazomai*, which means to strive to accomplish our full potential. We cannot provide our own salvation; it is a precious gift from God. In addition, it is not something to be stored away but should be cherished, protected, defended, and put on display in our everyday lives. It is an ongoing process, and we should not reach a point where we sit back with hands in our laps, focused on man's world instead of God's world. We always should strive to glorify him in every endeavor as thanks for his precious gift of salvation, and continue to do so as long as we are on this earth. There are no vacancies in God's world for sinful man. Only those who accept Christ as their savior and are covered by his righteousness are granted access to his world.

Fear and trembling has its own significance; what we should fear is taking our salvation for granted or failing to know what it means. We cannot stamp "saved" on our foreheads and carry on living as usual in man's world. God will pay as much attention to us as we pay to him, and he will not continually pursue us in man's world. Christians are Christ's workers. We are to serve him and be ready to perform whatever he calls on us to do, but we cannot respond to Christ unless we are focused on him and know who he is.

The Failures of American Churches

Everyone seems to have an opinion about why America is in decline, but only a few appear to know the real reason. Moral decline is the rot that is eating away at our Judeo-Christian foundation; if that foundation is destroyed, it will destroy America. As a realist, I find no justification for optimism that the trend of America turning away from God somehow will be reversed.

Can American churches provide a legitimate reason why God will save America? Well, let us see: extermination of an entire generation through abortion; same-sex marriage; gay-rights legislation; the Ten Commandments banned from public places; gays in the military; a child kicked out of school for drawing a cross on a piece of artwork; schoolchildren banned from speaking or writing the name God, Jesus, or Christ; the word Christmas banned; and the most hideous crime of all is for a child to dare to utter a prayer on a public school ground. Allowing the lies and distortions about the Christian heritage of America, which are being taught to our schoolchildren, to go unchallenged—an endless array of sexual deviance, violence, and anti-God programming, brought into millions of living rooms in America through television, and in many homes, children are exposed to it—and that includes the living rooms of many that profess to be Christians. That is what God sees when he looks at America. There is much more that could be included, but it is already enough to draw a conclusion: We do not have much going for us, do we?

There are no shortages of church buildings in America; we see them everywhere, all shapes and sizes. From small churches on a Sunday morning can be heard inspired sounds of singing and praise from a small congregation that knows, loves, and cares about each other. There is what I refer to as "uptown churches," with parishioners so pious and full of themselves, they avoid eye contact with others as they are ushered to their seats of honor, as if they are doing God a favor just by showing up.

The more modern churches are attended by mostly younger adults, who once a week go to get their ears massaged by entertainment and feel-good, noncommittal messages. Not to be left out are the mega churches, with thousands of members who gather once a week and the only people they know are the ones with whom they came. Personalities and entertainment are provided to draw in more people, to raise more money, to build bigger churches, to accommodate more people, to pay more money to—and on it goes. It would be unfair to group more than a few churches in such a category, but one is one too many.

Today, while driving along a rural road in the foothills of Texas, a few miles from the town of New Braunfels, I was attracted by a small church beside the road that would probably seat no more than 10 to 15 people. It was a quaint little church, freshly painted with very bright white paint, and on the roof above the door was a small steeple. I imagined that if the rapture occurred on a Sunday morning during church service, there would probably not be a person remaining in that little church. Conversely, many churches in America today would not miss a member, or even know the rapture had occurred. It was clear that whomever the little white church belongs to, they are obviously proud of it and had enough faithful members to take good care of it.

It brought to mind the dismal conditions of many churches in America today, and I do not mean the condition of the buildings. I visualize inside the little white church a piano or maybe a small organ to lead a spirit-filled congregation in singing the old *inspired hymns* that have brought more people to Christ than the best of preaching. On the other side of the spectrum, are mega churches with a 50-piece orchestra and a two hundred-member choir, with entertainers and celebrities waiting in the wings to entertain a spirit dead congregation with music that is about as inspiring as an earache. Perhaps you do not approve of my assessment, but I feel qualified to make it because during my travels, I have experienced both categories of churches, and many in between. Nevertheless, the size of a church does not matter; it is the relationship the people inside have with the Lord Jesus Christ because that does matter.

There are churches in America today that warrant criticism for abandoning the true Gospel of Christ, and they are subject to his judgment. The point is, attending a church does not replace the necessity for a personal relationship with Christ, and we can have that relationship even if we never set foot in a church. On the other hand, it is possible for a person to be a born-again Christian no matter what church he goes to, but why tempt Satan by going to a church where Jesus Christ is not glorified. What is the point of boarding a church bus that drives you to hell?

The Christian church has nothing to do with buildings or denominations. Christianity is in the heart, and many church buildings are full of Shakespearean Christians. If you ride around many cities on a Sunday morning, you will see more cars in a McDonald's parking lot than in a churchyard. It could be that born again Christians are fed up with man's world infiltrating their church and leave the service, wishing they had not attended. Many Christians are ahead of their church leaders in realizing the expansion of Satan's influence on their fellow members. If church leaders do not soon rededicate themselves to do what God ordained them to do, and if parishioners do not give wholehearted support to their churches, what right do we have to expect God to rescue us from the destruction we are bringing upon ourselves?

> Now the Spirit speaketh expressly, that in the latter times
> some shall depart from the faith, giving heed to seducing
> spirits, and doctrines of devils;
> —1 Timothy 4:1

Churches are Satan's favorite hangout, and he knows better than anyone does how to infiltrate them. I suspect that Satan has more minions snooping around the little church I passed by today than are snooping around some of the mega churches I saw when entering the city of San Antonio. We are warned in the above verse of coming apostasy—"depart from the faith"—and it is a reality in America today. That is why it is important to have a personal relationship with Jesus Christ, who will protect us from being influenced by false teachings. Although church attendance is declining in America, it does not necessarily mean that there is an equal decline in worship. Like the members of the early church, many Christians today gather in private homes, or small churches like I saw today, to worship God, and that is a sign of things to come. As apostasy continues to increase, there will be an increase in the ostracizing and eventual persecution of true Christians in America. Depending on the severity of persecution, it could force the true church underground, as we witness in many places around the world.

This is an appropriate time to readdress the subject of Christianity not being a religion. Before I continue, I should state that I recognize that people who are members of a religious organization may disagree with me, and that is okay. It is normal for any of us to defend our beliefs, regardless of whether they are universally accepted or not, but we should not display animosity toward anyone who disagrees with us. If we are born-again Christians, that does not mean we are members of a religion called born-again Christianity. Some substitute the term "evangelical Christians" when referring to born-again Christians, but that also is just a title. It is not necessary for us to adopt a title so God will know who and what we are; he knows more about us than we know about ourselves.

It is important to clarify that I am not saying we are to isolate ourselves; on the contrary, it is vitally important to fellowship with those who worship the Lord Jesus Christ, no matter the title with which they may choose to identify. There is no substitute for having a personal relationship with Jesus Christ, and no religion is going to ensure that we have that relationship. It is exactly what it suggests: *personal*. People who are members of an organized religion are subject to be led astray, but there is one thing born-again Christians can be assured of: We will never be led astray by Jesus Christ.

If a person is stranded on a deserted island, what religious ritual is going to help him? He probably will realize in short order that nothing is required between man and a relationship with Christ. It did not take long following the first church for man to contaminate it with false doctrines. Under no circumstances would the Jesus Christ that I know tolerate some of the evil that has come from so-called organized Christian religions.

The original Christian church was founded upon the teachings of the person whose name it bears—Jesus Christ, and no other. It has survived for two thousand years and will continue to exist right up to the time when, in a twinkling of an eye, it will be removed from this sinful world. What will be left are all the false religions, which will form a prophesized single and global organized religion to aid the Antichrist. Born-again Christians are looking forward to the great-blessed hope of the rapture of the church, and I am confident that organized religions that are left behind will be pleased to see us go. In the meantime, as born-again Christians, we must be prepared for a time that is coming, when we will experience rejection and even persecution for our beliefs.

> Blessed are ye, when men shall hate you, and when they shall separate you from their company, and shall reproach you, and cast out your name as evil, for the Son of man's sake. Rejoice ye in that day, and leap for joy: for, behold, your reward is great in heaven: for in the like manner did their fathers unto the prophets,
> —Luke 6:22–23

In the days of old, prophets were rejected by most leaders because they were purveyors of the truth. Sinful man does not want to be confronted with the truth, especially when it is a truth of condemnation. There is nothing new under the sun, and today the influence of institutions of organized religion has diminished because they have turned away from God and ignored their mandate to confront man with the truth of God's word. However, there are many born-again Christians in the world, enjoying a personal relationship with Christ; they make up the Christian church. Their numbers may be relatively small, but their influence will continue to flourish by telling the truth of God's word to a spiritually hungry world.

> And unto the angel of the church of the Laodiceans write; These things saith the Amen, the faithful and true witness, the beginning of the creation of God; I know thy works, that thou art neither cold nor hot: I would thou wert cold or hot. So then because thou art lukewarm, and neither cold nor hot, I will spew thee out of my mouth. Because thou sayest, I am rich, and increased with goods, and have need of nothing; and knowest not that thou art wretched, and miserable, and poor, and blind, and naked: I counsel thee to buy of me gold tried in the fire, that thou mayest be rich; and white raiment, that thou mayest be clothed, and that the shame of thy nakedness do not appear; and anoint thine eyes with eyesalve, that thou mayest see. As many as I love, I rebuke and chasten: be zealous therefore, and repent. Behold, I stand at the door, and knock: if any man hear my voice, and open the door, I will come in to him, and will sup with him, and he with me. To him that overcometh will I grant

to sit with me in my throne, even as I also overcame, and am
set down with my Father in his throne. He that hath an ear,
let him hear what the Spirit saith unto the churches.
—Revelation 3:14–22

The above verses are Christ's assessment of one of the Christian churches of the first century as revealed by Christ to the Apostle John—the author of the book of Revelation. We can learn from those verses that there has been little change from then until now. I chose Christ's assessment of the Laodicean Church because it describes many churches in America today. There are six other churches addressed in the first three chapters of Revelation that easily can be compared to churches of today.   The primary reason I chose these verses is to draw attention to these words: "Behold, I stand at the door, and knock: if any man hear my voice, and open the door, I will come in to him, and will sup with him, and he with me." Throughout the Bible, Christ makes this offer, not to groups or assemblies, but to each individual—i.e., any man. Christ deals with us on a personal level, and it is his desire to have a personal relationship with us, but we must open the door. Once we open the doors of our hearts and accept him for whom he is, he will send the Holy Spirit to partnership with us, to guide us in doing his will. We must study his word to show our willingness to learn about him, grow in faith, and mature into a useful Christian so that we may endure the obstacles Satan sets before us, turn away from man's world, and rest upon God's love, grace, and mercy.

Moral issues such as abortion, gay rights, and same-sex marriage are under God's purview and he will deal with them at his chosen time. God does not ignore sin, or sinners, eventually they will be brought to account. To oppose immorality is a Christian obligation, but to fight against them is a fight with Satan and those under his influence. We do not have the power to be victorious in that battle on our own. God would have no difficulty in dealing with this problem if a united church would get on its knees and petition him to act on its behalf. Unfortunately, it seems unlikely that churches in America could come together and unite in one accord to support anything. As previously discussed, we do not have much going for us to justify God's intervention.

> If my people, which are called by my name, shall humble themselves, and pray, and seek my face, and turn from their wicked ways; then will I hear from heaven, and will forgive their sin, and will heal their land.
> —2 Chronicles 7:14

Although God spoke those words to Solomon about the Jewish people, they are just as applicable to Christians today. This is one of the most frequently quoted scriptures by Christians, and like John 3:16, the Bible verse that is perhaps the most quoted, it requires careful consideration. The key phrase in this verse is *If my people*. God does not expect the carnal man either to pray or seek his face for anything or to turn from his wicked ways. In addition, the verse does not refer to some of my people or a few of my people, but my people. This can be accomplished only with a unified brotherhood of believers, which currently does not exist in America or anywhere else. This verse has always been in the Bible, but one would think it had been discovered recently. God is long-suffering and patient, but there is a limit to his patience as the Jews learned in 70AD. For at least the past fifty years, Christians have paid little attention to verses such as this, and all around us there is evidence that God has had enough with rebellious America, just as he did with rebellious Israel.

Jesus is not concerned about our country because he knows what the outcome will be. Nevertheless, he is concerned, about his church; and he wants us to keep focused on him, not on this world. Not one of us can declare himself blameless for what is happening in America, and to think otherwise is self-denial. Jesus Christ is the believers' shepherd, and we are his sheep. If he has to pursue those who have wandered off, we will never be a united flock, which is what Christ wants for his church. In the old days, when a sheep kept wandering off, the shepherd would break one of its legs to keep it safe in the fold. I wonder if the Good Shepherd Jesus is about to break some legs.

Once Saved, Always Saved?

The concept of "once saved, always saved" is characterized by a lack of consensus among the different Christian denominations. Although I am unqualified to give an expert opinion, the fact that there is only one truth must prevail. It serves no purpose to be bogged down in the theology of this subject because there are scriptures in the Bible that, when isolated, support either view, but this is a subject that cannot be satisfied by one or two scriptures. The dangerous thing for any of us to do is to accept any opinion that concerns salvation simply because it is popular to do so. The relevant question is not whether we can lose our salvation, but whether we are truly saved. I suspect that one of Satan's most effective traps to snare people is to cause them to believe they are saved when they are not.

Any book is nothing but a dust collector unless its contents are explored, and exploring the Holy Bible is a fascinating journey when the Holy Spirit is our guide. Without guidance from the Holy Spirit, reading the Bible is like meandering through a forest of strange-looking trees. The Bible is a one-way bridge that separates man's world from God's world. The Bible consists of sixty-six spans constructed by builders under direction of the Holy Spirit. For thousands of years, it has been examined from end to end by doubtful men looking for flaws or imperfections, but it is as sound and perfect as when it was first constructed. The primary reason that only a few people read the Bible is because most people do not know what it is. The Bible is not a novel or a history book; it is a source from which we can learn about the creator of the universe and his plan and purpose for mankind. The Holy Bible is the only reliable source to provide the knowledge of who God is, interpreted through the Holy Spirit.

Here is an example of why it is important to read the entire Bible. Many people accept John 3:16 as the only verse for the basis of salvation: "For God so loved the world, that he gave his only begotten Son, that whosoever believeth in him should not perish, but have everlasting life." Is it enough to proclaim to believe in Jesus? The word "believeth" is taken from the Greek word *pisteuo*, which means to commit or entrust. However, isolating that word does not tell the whole story. If we go to the beginning of chapter 3 of the Gospel of John, we will find the following words:

> There was a man of the Pharisees, named Nicodemus, a ruler
> of the Jews: The same came to Jesus by night, and said unto
> him, Rabbi, we know that thou art a teacher come from

> God: for no man can do these miracles that thou doest, except God be with him. Jesus answered and said unto him, Verily, verily, I say unto thee, Except a man be born again, he cannot see the kingdom of God. Nicodemus saith unto him, How can a man be born when he is old? can he enter the second time into his mother's womb, and be born? Jesus answered, Verily, verily, I say unto thee, Except a man be born of water and of the Spirit, he cannot enter into the kingdom of God.
> —John 3:1–5

Are we to ignore John 3:3: "Verily, verily, I say unto thee, "Except a man be born again, he cannot see the kingdom of God." The word "again" in Greek is *anothen,* taken from the root word *ano,* which means "from above." The carnal man must die and be reborn into the spiritual world of God. We must let go of man's world and all its enticements and trappings and focus on the things of God, and that is the greatest hurdle for man to overcome. I suppose it is why many people skip over John 3:3 and rush to John 3:16. A person committed to serving God will not search through the Bible looking for a verse or two he can accept without vacating his comfort zone. From the mouth of Jesus, we are told in unambiguous words that unless we are born again, we cannot see the kingdom of God.

Words in the Bible apply whether or not we are familiar with them, and it is each person's responsibility to learn the truth of God's word. It is by God's word that we are judged. Many things in man's world beckon the weak in faith, but to believe God's word, we cannot live on both sides of the river. We cannot be half born again; we are either reborn or stillborn. Following are verses from the Bible that support the message of salvation.

> But what saith it? The word is nigh thee, even in thy mouth, and in thy heart: that is, the word of faith, which we preach; That if thou shalt confess with thy mouth the Lord Jesus, and shalt believe in thine heart that God hath raised him from the dead, thou shalt be saved. For with the heart man believeth unto righteousness; and with the mouth confession

is made unto salvation. For the scripture saith, Whosoever believeth on him shall not be ashamed.
—Romans 10:8–11

Not everyone that saith unto me, Lord, Lord, shall enter into the kingdom of heaven; but he that doeth the will of my Father which is in heaven. Many will say to me in that day, Lord, Lord, have we not prophesied in thy name? and in thy name have cast out devils? and in thy name done many wonderful works? And then will I profess unto them, I never knew you: depart from me, ye that work iniquity.
—Matthew 7:21–23

Just as a well balanced diet of meat, fruit and vegetables, is nourishment to the body, a well balanced diet of scripture is nourishment to the soul. John 3:16, is meat, but what about fruit and vegetables, i.e. John 3:3, Romans 8:10-11, and Mathew 7:21-23. The soul can be malnourished just as the body can be. However, there is a distinction, we can over-feed the body, and most people do, but we cannot over-feed the soul, which most people do not. Metaphors can be very helpful in making a point, so we will explore one more before we move on. Suppose you are tasked to write a 500-word essay based on a single word, and, it can be used only once. It would be very difficult if not impossible for most of us to accomplish such a task. However, during our struggle, our Nemesis (goddess of reward and punishment in Greek mythology) awards us with additional words, one at a time; eventually, we will have enough to complete a comprehensible survey. In the King James Bible, God provides us with 774,746 words; the message of salvation is contained in these words and one does not need a high IQ, or a Nemesis, to receive the message. The message of salvation is not freely given to the lazy, it must be sought, either from the pulpit of a church, or the Holy Bible; it is up to you to determine the better source.

Do we get the message from the verses in Matthew, chapter 7? Will we ignore those words as if they apply to someone else? There are many such verses in the Bible, and God put them all there for a reason. There are no meaningless words in the Bible, and they apply to everyone. Are we to be Shakespearean

Christians, confident of our salvation, only to have Christ shoo us away from his sight? God says what he means and means what he says, and we ignore his word at our own peril. It is not easy to be a born-again Christian in this sinful world; if it were, everyone certainly would be one. It requires total faith, commitment, dedication, and obedience to God and to him alone.

We cannot establish a conclusion with a single verse taken in isolation. As we can see from the text cited above, when we put biblical verses together they build upon themselves to broaden the message. The Bible contains verses throughout that culminate in the complete message of salvation. The message of salvation does not start in Mathew; it begins in Genesis. Nowhere in the Bible is ignorance of God's word an acceptable excuse. Some may think I have overemphasized the need to study the Bible, but there is no other way to establish a solid footing with God. I close this subject by encouraging you to adopt the mindset that there is a message in the Bible for each of us individually. There are many words in Bible, but the purpose of the Bible is summed up with very few words: Accept Jesus Christ as the Lord of our life, spend eternity with him in Heaven, or reject him and spend eternity in hell with Satan. That is the simple and relevant message in the Bible, and there are no loopholes or alternatives.

> "This I say then, Walk in the Spirit, and ye shall not the lust of the flesh. For the flesh lusteth against the Spirit, and the Spirit against the flesh: and these are contrary the one to the other: so that ye cannot do the things that ye would.
> —Galatians 5:16–17

These verses from establish a foundation for readdressing the subject of drawing a conclusion based on a verse or two. Without relying on philosophical logic and semantics, we will approach this subject with common sense. Can we comply with John 3:3 and not comply with John 3:16? No, we cannot. Can we comply with John 3:16 and not comply with John 3:3? Yes, we can. This is a simple illustration of how easy it is to go astray by overindulging in dissecting seemingly contradicting verses. As stated, if one has the desire to do so, there are many verses in the Bible to support either viewpoint. However, when we look at the Bible in its entirety, it becomes clear that "once saved, always saved" is a subject that requires a thorough knowledge of the Bible and a close and personal relationship with Christ. It is human nature to choose the more acceptable point of view, but I caution you not to be too eager to dismiss the conclusion that demands more of you. Because this is such a controversial subject, we will address it again later at a more appropriate juncture.

In an attempt to determine the number of born-again Christians in America, I found that the estimates are all over the place. As we are dealing with unreliable information, to make my point, I will use an estimate. As mentioned earlier, approximately 70 percent of Americans claim to be Christians, but less than half that number claim to be born again. Before we attempt to learn from this, we need to set some parameters. I presume the reason a person desires to be a Christian is so he will go to heaven; at least we will move forward on that basis. If we accept the words of Jesus in John 3:3, unless we are born again, we will never get to heaven. That reveals a great problem among those who consider themselves Christians, but are not born again. Either they do not know what a Christian is, or they do not believe the words of Jesus. As stated earlier, Jesus makes things simple. Rebellious and arrogant people complicate the simple.

If there were other ways to gain entry into the kingdom of God, i.e., aside from being born again, Jesus would have told us so. What is the point in being a Christian if it is not to gain entrance into the kingdom of God? I suppose the real problem is misunderstanding what it means to be born again.

> My sheep hear my voice, and I know them, and they follow
> me: and I give unto them eternal life; and they shall never
> perish, and no one shall snatch them out of my hand.
> —John 10:27–28

I believe the answer to the question is contained in these words: "My sheep hear my voice." Do you listen for his voice before you go wandering off on your own? In addition: "and they follow me." Do you follow him in total faith and obedience? Finally, "and no one shall snatch them out of my hand." Jesus protects his flock against would-be thieves; however, there is nothing to prevent a sheep from wandering off on his own.

I am in no way an expert on these matters, but God has given all of us a measure of common sense. Coupled with wisdom from God, I find myself sufficiently able to discern his word. My common sense tells me that those who are truly born again have no desire to be involved in man's world. Nevertheless, if your common sense leads you in a different direction, you are certainly free to draw your own conclusion.

Many Christians, in their apathy, lament about why God does not do something about the mess in which we are. If that describes you, perhaps God is looking down on you, wondering why you do not do something about it. Christians are God's workers, and we have the authority to petition him to bring his power to bear to alter the circumstances that the world now faces. As Christians, we must ask ourselves if we are part of the problem. The answer is, yes, we are. Most Americans either ignore, or fail to realize, the evil influence Satan is having on our country. It gives me no pleasure to make such a statement, but it is time for Christians to face reality. The struggle against Satan is a battle; unfortunately, many Christians have gone AWOL, and those who remain on the front lines must remain vigilant to avoid losing the battle.

The Apostle Paul

When Jesus walked the streets of Jerusalem seeking men to be his disciples, he did not pick learned religious leaders, quite the contrary; he chose a group of mostly uneducated misfits, there was not a MA, or PhD among them, except perhaps Doctor Luke, who was a Physician. God cannot use the proud and arrogant to do his will. God chooses those he knows he can use for his purpose and it is often one that seems to defy logic like Judas. The Apostle Paul is an excellent example of how Jesus chooses the most unlikely person to do his work.

Paul (formerly Saul) was a tent maker by trade but he was also a Pharisee, and probably well educated in Jewish Law. In his role as a Pharisee, he was to search out Christians, arrest and imprison them. We know he witnessed the stoning of Stephen— "And cast *him* out of the city, and stoned *him*: and the witnesses laid down their clothes at a young man's feet, whose name was Saul. And they stoned Stephen, calling upon *God*, and saying, Lord Jesus, receive my spirit." — Acts 7:58-59. Given his role at the time, he probably also witnessed Christ's Crucifixion. After Paul's conversion, he became the commander in chief of many of the men who built the first Christian churches.

> As also the high priest doth bear me witness, and all the estate of the elders: from whom also I received letters unto the brethren, and went to Damascus, to bring them which were there bound unto Jerusalem, for to be punished. And it came to pass, that, as I made my journey, and was come nigh unto Damascus about noon, suddenly there shone from heaven a great light round about me. And I fell unto the ground, and heard a voice saying unto me, Saul, Saul, why persecutest thou me? And I answered, Who art thou, Lord? And he said unto me, I am Jesus of Nazareth, whom thou persecutest....
> —Acts 22:5-8

These verses reveal a great deal about our Lord Jesus Christ. This young man Saul was devoted to his task of arresting Christians, and probably received accolades for a job well done. Having foreknowledge of Paul's future, Jesus, as always, chose the most unlikely character to spread the Gospel.

> ..."And they that were with me saw indeed the light, and were afraid; but they heard not the voice of him that spake to me. And I said, What shall I do, Lord? And the Lord said unto me, Arise, and go into Damascus; and there it shall be told thee of all things which are appointed for thee to do. And when I could not see for the glory of that light, being led by the hand of them that were with me, I came into Damascus. And one Ananias, a devout man according to the law, having a good report of all the Jews which dwelt *there*, Came unto me, and stood, and said unto me, Brother Saul, receive thy sight. And the same hour I looked up upon him. And he said, The God of our fathers hath chosen thee, that thou shouldest know his will, and see that Just One, and shouldest hear the voice of his mouth. For thou shalt be

121

his witness unto all men of what thou hast seen and heard. And now why tarriest thou? arise, and be baptized, and wash away thy sins, calling on the name of the Lord....
—Acts 22:8-16

Can you imagine the trauma Paul must have experienced? He was on his way to Damascus to bring arrested Christians to Jerusalem, thinking he was doing the right thing. A blinding light forced him to fall to the ground, probably from a horse. He was made blind and a voice, that only he could hear, spoke to him. He did not know who spoke to him, but he called him Lord, and must have known from that moment, his life was about to change forever.

..."And it came to pass, that, when I was come again to Jerusalem, even while I prayed in the temple, I was in a trance; And saw him saying unto me, Make haste, and get thee quickly out of Jerusalem: for they will not receive thy testimony concerning me. And I said, Lord, they know that I imprisoned and beat in every synagogue them that believed on thee: And when the blood of thy martyr Stephen was shed, I also was standing by, and consenting unto his death, and kept the raiment of them that slew him. And he said unto me, Depart: for I will send thee far hence unto the Gentiles.
—Acts 22:16–21

While Paul was in the Temple, and in a trance, he saw the resurrected Christ and received his marching orders. We must keep in mind that, at this time, the Disciples of Jesus had been preaching to the Jews and every person that had accepted the Gospel was a Jew. Now, Jesus was sending Paul into the world of Gentiles, and it easy to see why Jesus chose Paul for such a mission.

Of the twenty-seven books in the New Testament, Paul wrote twelve of them: 1 Corinthians, 2 Corinthians, Galatians, Ephesians, Philippians, Colossians, 1 Thessalonians, 2 Thessalonians, 1 Timothy, 2 Timothy, Titus and Philemon. Some scholars believe he also wrote the Book of Hebrews which, if true, would make him the author of almost half of the books in the New Testament. His writings reveal the tremendous challenges involved in the growth of the early church. Paul was beaten, stoned, shipwrecked, snake-bitten, imprisoned, and eventually executed by Rome because of his love and devotion to the early church. Paul's life demonstrates the power of Christ as manifested in a single individual that he trusts to do his will. Not everyone can be another Paul, but there is potential in everyone, and God chooses people according to their abilities. Helping a neighbor in need, comforting the suffering, praying for the sick, doing good deeds anytime the opportunity arises—all these things are God's will and are things anyone can do.

> Therefore whosoever heareth these sayings of mine, and doeth them, I will liken him unto a wise man, which built his house upon a rock: And the rain descended, and the floods came, and the winds blew, and beat upon that house; and it fell not: for it was founded upon a rock. And every one that heareth these sayings of mine, and doeth them not, shall be likened unto a foolish man, which built his house upon the sand: And the rain descended, and the floods came, and the winds blew, and beat upon that house; and it fell: and great was the fall of it.
> —Matthew 7:24–27

How can we do the will of God unless we know what his will is? We cannot learn it from the television and may or may not learn it in church. There is only one reliable source and, by now, you should know what it is! Again, I remind you that at the time Mathew wrote these verses, the New Testament did not exist, but today we have God's word in writing, and we have no excuse for not availing ourselves to its guidance.

> I am come a light into the world, that whosoever believeth on me should not abide in darkness. And if any man hear my words, and believe not, I judge him not: for I came not to judge the world, but to save the world. He that rejecteth me, and receiveth not my words, hath one that judgeth him: the word that I have spoken, the same shall judge him in the last day. For I have not spoken of myself; but the Father which

sent me, he gave me a commandment, what I should say, and what I should speak. And I know that his commandment is life everlasting: whatsoever I speak therefore, even as the Father said unto me, so I speak.

—John 12:46–50

The Book of Life

From the very beginning, the Bible predicts a day of judgment for everyone. Although most people ignore it, no one will escape Judgment Day.

For the Father judgeth no man, but hath committed all judgment unto the Son: That all men should honour the Son, even as they honour the Father. He that honoureth not the Son honoureth not the Father which hath sent him. Verily, verily, I say unto you, He that heareth my word, and believeth on him that sent me, hath everlasting life, and shall not come into condemnation; but is passed from death unto life. Verily, verily, I say unto you, The hour is coming, and now is, when the dead shall hear the voice of the Son of God: and they that hear shall live. For as the Father hath life in himself; so hath he given to the Son to have life in himself; And hath given him authority to execute judgment also, because he is the Son of man. Marvel not at this: for the hour is coming, in the which all that are in the graves shall hear his voice, And shall come forth; they that have done good, unto the resurrection of life; and they that have done evil, unto the resurrection of damnation. I can of mine own self do nothing: as I hear, I judge: and my judgment is just; because I seek not mine own will, but the will of the Father which hath sent me.

—John 5:22–30

Only those cloaked in the righteousness of Christ are in the book of life. They are judged not at the great white throne but at the judgment seat of Christ, not into condemnation but according to their service and obedience to him, which will determine their heavenly reward.

> And I saw a great white throne, and him that sat on it, from whose face the earth and the heaven fled away; and there was found no place for them. And I saw the dead, small and great, stand before God; and the books were opened: and another book was opened, which is the book of life: and the dead were judged out of those things which were written in the books, according to their works.
> —Revelation 20:11–12

Those who reject Jesus Christ are not in the book of life, their judgment will come at the great white throne, there will be no defense, no appeal and only judgment and sentence, there is only one sentence:

> And the sea gave up the dead which were in it; and death and hell delivered up the dead which were in them: and they were judged every man according to their works. And death and hell were cast into the lake of fire. This is the second death. And whosoever was not found written in the book of life was cast into the lake of fire.
> —Revelation 20:13–15

Every word, deed, thought, and action is recorded in God's book of remembrance. No detail will be overlooked and, as the record is revealed, every detail will be recalled when God unlocks the subconscious mind where all things are stored. Imagine what it will be like when you are confronted with all the things you have long forgotten, and you realize you had the opportunity to avoid eternity in hell. There are no second chances.

The Last Days

Anyone with knowledge of the Bible can easily discern that we are living in the last days—a unique time in human history—and time is drawing short. The truth of God's word is coming to fruition, and those who reject Jesus Christ will not be judged by man's laws, but by the word of God. Changes are coming, and they will come very quickly. Life is a gamble for gamblers, and only a foolish person would gamble with his soul.

The Rapture of the Church

> Now learn a parable of the fig tree; When her branch is yet
> tender, and putteth forth leaves, ye know that summer is
> near: So ye in like manner, when ye shall see these things
> come to pass, know that it is nigh, even at the doors. Verily
> I say unto you, that this generation shall not pass, till all
> these things be done. Heaven and earth shall pass away: but
> my words shall not pass away. But of that day and that hour
> knoweth no man, no, not the angels which are in heaven,
> neither the Son, but the Father. Take ye heed, watch and
> pray: for ye know not when the time is. For the Son of man
> is as a man taking a far journey, who left his house, and gave
> authority to his servants, and to every man his work, and
> commanded the porter to watch. Watch ye therefore: for ye
> know not when the master of the house cometh, at even, or
> at midnight, or at the cockcrowing, or in the morning: Lest
> coming suddenly he find you sleeping. And what I say unto
> you I say unto all, Watch.
> —Mark 13:28–37

I have spent the better part of a morning looking for a needle in a haystack. I was trying to determine the demographics of Jews in the world. What I found was a haystack of opinions and statics, but totally devoid of a consensus. In the course of doing research for this book, I discovered that most information is nothing but recycled opinions taken from a haystack of opinions. Somewhere in the haystack is a needle of truth, however, no rational person would actually look for a needle in a haystack. Statisticians are like historians, neither can be totally trusted. We are awash in information, unfortunately, most of it is unreliable and that includes statistics compiled by the government. It all depends on whose Ox is being gored, and who is doing the goring. Why this information is important, is found in the following verses:

> "And in that day there shall be a root of Jesse, which shall
> stand for an ensign of the people; to it shall the Gentiles seek:
> and his rest shall be glorious. And it shall come to pass in
> that day, *that* the Lord shall set his hand again the second

time to recover the remnant of his people, which shall be left, from Assyria, and from Egypt, and from Pathros, and from Cush, and from Elam, and from Shinar, and from Hamath, and from the islands of the sea. And he shall set up an ensign for the nations, and shall assemble the outcasts of Israel, and gather together the dispersed of Judah from the four corners of the earth."

—Isaiah 11:10-12

When Isaiah says "*in that day*", he is referring to the distant future—"And in that day there shall be a root of Jesse, which shall stand for an ensign of the people; to it shall the Gentiles seek: and his rest shall be glorious."—The ensign the Gentiles seek is none other than the Lord Jesus Christ. In the past twenty years, the organization, "On Wings of Eagles," led by Rabbi Yael Eckstein, and supported by the "International Fellowship of Christians and Jews," has brought multitudes of impoverished Jews from countries like Russia and Ethiopia, to Israel—over a million, from Russia alone. Currently, the number of Jews returning to Israel is only a trickle, but that will change—"The Lord shall set his hand again the second time to recover the remnant of his people. The first time, God rescued them from Egypt. During the first gathering, as seen in Genesis, many of the people rebelled against God for bringing them out o Egypt. The result was God marched them around in the desert for forty years, until the rebellious ones died off. Although it is not clear, I believe, the next time, for whatever reason, Jews will be eager to return to Israel.

Could it be that the world's economical situation will go through a drastic change from what it is today? Perhaps, Israel will become the wealthiest country in the world. As I learned from stumbling around in the *Haystack* this morning, some believe that there are more Jews living in America than in Israel. However, there are those that believe the opposite. In any case, there are millions of Jews living in America. I have previously shared my opinion that America's economy will collapse and, will not have a significant role in the world, *in that day.* I am sure God has it all worked out; God said he will gather his people from the four corners of the earth and bring them to Israel. Whatever means God uses to accomplish the return of his people to Israel—it *will* happen!

"I found Israel like grapes in the wilderness; I saw your fathers as the firstripe in the fig tree at her first time: *but* they went to Baalpeor, and separated themselves unto *that* shame; and *their* abominations were according as they loved."
— Hosea 9:10

In many places in the Bible, the fig tree, symbolically, represents Israel, as in the above verse. With that in mind, the following verses, sends a clear message.

"And he spake to them a parable; Behold the fig tree, and all the trees; When they now shoot forth, ye see and know of your own selves that summer is now nigh at hand. So likewise ye, when ye see these things come to pass, know ye that the kingdom of God is nigh at hand."
—Luke 21:29-31

There are numerous signs and warnings in the Bible about the approaching end-time, but God keeps the precise moment secret for a reason: We are always to be ready to ensure that we are not caught unaware. If we continue to watch for the rapture, it will keep us focused on him and not on the things of the world. The rapture of the church could occur before you finish this book, or years from now your grandchildren could be saying the same thing. The Father alone knows the time, and when he determines its time, it will happen quicker than we can say the word "rapture."

But of that day and hour knoweth no man, no, not the angels of heaven, but my Father only. But as the days of Noe were, so shall also the coming of the Son of man be. For as in the days that were before the flood they were eating and drinking, marrying and giving in marriage, until the day that Noe entered into the ark, And knew not until the flood came, and took them all away; so shall also the coming of the Son of man be. Then shall two be in the field; the one shall be taken, and the other left. Two women shall be grinding at the mill; the one shall be taken, and the other

left. Watch therefore: for ye know not what hour your Lord
doth come.
—Matthew 24:36–42

Those words should be warning enough that we should be ready for the
appearance of Christ in the clouds during the rapture of his church. It will
happen in the twinkling of an eye, and there will be no time for those who
are not already prepared. We are destined to leave this earth someday, and
whether we are *caught up* in the rapture or by physical death, our destination
will be the same. If we die in our sins, we will dwell forever with the master of
sin in hell. If we are cloaked with the righteousness of Christ, we will forever
be with him in his kingdom, regardless of how we get there. However, even
though the great-blessed hope (the rapture) is the expectation of born-again
Christians, it does not give us leave to hibernate and be inactive. As long as
the rapture is delayed, we are to continue doing God's will.

The difficulty in deciphering God's timetable is a subject worth exploring.
Time is an earthly venture that no one can define, but we do know it never
stops—at least, it has not in recent history.

> Then spake Joshua to the LORD in the day when the LORD
> delivered up the Amorites before the children of Israel, and
> he said in the sight of Israel, Sun, stand thou still upon
> Gibeon; and thou, Moon, in the valley of Ajalon. And the
> sun stood still, and the moon stayed, until the people had
> avenged themselves upon their enemies. Is not this written
> in the book of Jasher? So the sun stood still in the midst
> of heaven, and hasted not to go down about a whole day.
> And there was no day like that before it or after it, that the
> LORD hearkened unto the voice of a man: for the LORD
> fought for Israel.
> —Joshua 10:12–14

As fantastic as it sounds, God created the universe, including time, and is
capable of manipulating it any way he chooses. Time is an unsolved mystery
that man is unable to comprehend. God held the sun in position for a day; if

he can stop the motion of the sun to fight for Israel, imagine what he could do for us if we made ourselves worthy of his intervention. God is going to fight for Israel again in the last battle on this earth, and God is gathering his people back to Israel to facilitate that great battle. Satan is a mortal enemy to the Jews, and he has battled God for their souls from the beginning. If you do not believe God can hold back the movement of the sun, if you miss the rapture of the church and are not convinced of God's power by that event, and you survive long enough, you will witness God doing things much more fantastic than holding the sun in place.

Anti-Semitism is the work of Satan that has plagued the Jews throughout their history; Satan's influence caused the Jews to rebel against God repeatedly. Jews are returning to Israel to prepare for the millennium of peace, but first they, along with those left behind during the rapture, will have to suffer through the great tribulation. To illustrate the power of Satan, especially during his last show of strength, many will continue to worship him right up to the end and willingly will follow him into the pits of hell.

> And I saw an angel come down from heaven, having the key of the bottomless pit and a great chain in his hand. And he laid hold on the dragon, that old serpent, which is the Devil, and Satan, and bound him a thousand years, And cast him into the bottomless pit, and shut him up, and set a seal upon him, that he should deceive the nations no more, till the thousand years should be fulfilled: and after that he must be loosed a little season.
> —Revelation 20:1–3

Something to think about is during the millennium, when Satan will be bound for a thousand years, for the first time ever, there will be real peace on earth. Even so, at the end of the millennium (the thousand years of the earthly reign of Christ) Satan will be let loose temporarily and there will be those who join him to rebel against Christ. If you are doubtful that man would be so stupid as to reject Christ during the millennium, remember that man rejects him now in spite of all the warnings of what is coming. This demonstrates the power Satan has over mankind; without the power of Jesus Christ, man is at Satan's mercy. Satan is not, as many people think, a little red man with a forked tail stirring coals in hell. Satan has never been in hell; it will not be his abode until after the millennium, at which time, he will finally be cast into hell along with his worshipers when God's final judgment is brought to rebellious and sinful man.

As you ponder these events, where do you stand? Things mysterious and fantastic in man's eyes are ho-hum to God. Not only is God capable of stopping time, he is going to do away with time all together, the incomprehensible thing we call eternity: no beginning and no ending. God has always existed, and his kingdom shall never end, but our finite minds cannot comprehend such a thing because we are under restraints of time with a beginning and an end.

Unless we are born-again Christians with faith and trust in God, the reality of the current situation in America is depressing and difficult to handle. Remember, nothing happens on the earth that is not according to God's plan. Regardless of the situation, God always looks after the faithful. God does not want us to suffer but he will allow our faith to be tested so it will continue to mature.

> This know also, that in the last days perilous times shall come. For men shall be lovers of their own selves, covetous, boasters, proud, blasphemers, disobedient to parents, unthankful, unholy, Without natural affection, trucebreakers, false accusers, incontinent, fierce, despisers of those that are good, Traitors, heady, highminded, lovers of pleasures more than lovers of God; Having a form of godliness, but denying the power thereof: from such turn away.
> —2 Timothy 3:1–5

Is there a better description for the conditions of the world today? You may think those conditions have always existed in America and they have, but they were not as common and widespread as they are today. All around us, we can identify the reality of what was predicted for the last days, and this is only one of many warnings and signs of the coming end-time. There is truth and purpose in all of God's words, and we ignore them at our own peril.

There is a very significant message in these verses, although it is easy to overlook and requires further study: "from such turn away." One would assume that it is natural to turn away from such things, but perhaps there is more depth to the warning. The world is on a slippery slope, like a torrent rushing through a canyon, and more and more people are being caught in the deluge. We must cling to the higher ground through our faith and trust in Jesus Christ, and reach out a hand to any who desires to be saved. Nevertheless, we must not allow ourselves to be dragged into the torrent and swept away with the lost.

We are witnessing the first time in America's history that a serious effort is underway to remove any reference to God from our society. Such a thing would have been unimaginable fifty or sixty years ago. The anti-God factions may succeed in kicking God out of America, but they cannot kick him out of the hearts of those who love and trust him. We are warned to come to this side of the river, remain here, and to let go of man's degenerate world, which is headed toward disaster. We must not be complacent; it is time to evaluate or reevaluate our relationship with Jesus Christ, and we must do it now. We must not be too comfortable with our own assessment of our relationship with Christ, but pray and study his word to show ourselves approved.

Good People?

Americans suffer from an inherent arrogance that at times causes us to think more highly of ourselves than we should. America was under God's protection for more than two hundred years, but this generation has decided it does not need God's protection anymore and will go on without him.

> And a certain ruler asked him, saying, Good Master, what shall I do to inherit eternal life? And Jesus said unto him, Why callest thou me good? none is good, save one, that is, God. Thou knowest the commandments, Do not commit adultery, Do not kill, Do not steal, Do not bear false witness, Honour thy father and thy mother. And he said, All these have I kept from my youth up. Now when Jesus heard these things, he said unto him, Yet lackest thou one thing: sell all that thou hast, and distribute unto the poor, and thou shalt

have treasure in heaven: and come, follow me. And when he
heard this, he was very sorrowful: for he was very rich.
—Luke 18:18–23

This ruler said that he obeyed the commandments and assumed it would
qualify him as a good person. He was in the eyes of man but not in the eyes
of God. We may be enlightened by thinking of ourselves as good people, but
in the sight of God, none of us is good. It is man's sinful and wanting nature
that prevents him from being good in the eyes of God, and that is further
evidence that we need Jesus Christ to cover our failings. It does not mean that
we should not do good deeds; that is something we should always strive to do.
It is humbling to admit that we are not good people, but that is exactly what
we need to do if we intend to find favor with God. We must not rely on our
own opinions but seek the wisdom of God's word. Jesus said no one is good
except God, and that is what he means, no matter how difficult it is for some
to accept. If we look at mankind through the eyes of God, it will be difficult
to disagree with the words of Jesus.

A question that is often asked is why bad things happen to good people. We
have learned from the words of Jesus that none of us is good. However, I
will propose a question; answer it and you will answer both questions: why
do good things happen to bad people? The real answer to the question is
extremely revealing. God has given us a free will to make our own choices,
so why do *we* allow bad things to happen to good people? Most bad things
that happen to us are self-induced, and if we think about it honestly, there are
probably events in our life when we could have prevented a bad thing from
happening, not only to ourselves but also to someone else.

God does not want bad things to happen to us, but he will not stop us from
doing bad things to ourselves if we reject his guidance. Sinful human nature
causes many to blame others, including God, rather than themselves for the
bad things that happen. If we rely solely on ourselves, misery is sure to follow.
If a person chooses to enter into a risky or dangerous situation that results in
something bad occurring, should he blame God for allowing it to happen? It
is easy to indulge in such pondering, but true faith will keep us constantly in

contact with the spirit of God, which will guide our way. We have nothing to fear from anything in this world, except to die in our sins.

Accidents happen, and are we any less likely to be a victim of an accident than anyone else is? Death is part of living, and it is one thing—inherited from Adam—that we all have in common. As previously mentioned, we begin to die the minute we are born. Like all living things, we are in constant deterioration, and none is assured longevity. Unfortunately, many people voluntarily embrace a lifestyle that is sure to hasten their demise, and God cannot be blamed for that.

God did not bring death and sickness to the earth; we can thank Satan for that. God loves us all the same and, as previously stated, he has no favorites. The only way we can be special to God is to accept his son as our Lord and Master. We cannot comprehend the love God has for the human race and none of us are worthy of his love. Even though it is a mystery, it is nevertheless real.

On Whom Can We Depend?

We can witness the world over the trouble mankind brings to himself when depending only on his own perceived wisdom. We are all God's creation and his love and promises are available to each of us. It is God's desire that we depend on him and his guidance because he knows our propensity to make bad decisions that complicate our life. God offers each of us the opportunity to have peace and contentment in our life by depending on him and being a member of his family.

> That ye may be the children of your Father which is in heaven: for he maketh his sun to rise on the evil and on the good, and sendeth rain on the just and on the unjust.
> —Matthew 5:45

Like all human beings, Christians are bound to this earth and subject to the curses that Adam and Eve brought unto us all. Man cannot escape the storms of life that affect everyone, but we also can enjoy the warmth of the rising sun. What sets Christians apart is the opportunity to bask in the sunlight of the glory of Jesus Christ at all times. When the storms approach, we have a shelter, provided by our heavenly Father that delivers us from fear and anxiety. God's world is a world of hope and promise provided by one who never lies, deceives, or fails to keep his promises. God will not allow his children to go hungry or naked, but we must have faith that he will do what he promises and put total trust in him. God promises to provide for our needs, not our wants, and if we trust him, he always will make a way for us to have what we need.

There is a lot of talk today about hope and faith, and they are a cure-all if properly applied. To whom should we direct our hope and faith? Having hope and faith within ourselves has not spared us from a path to destruction, and anyone who puts his faith and hope in the government deserves the ultimate result. There is only one in whom we can have hope and faith, one in whom we can be assured of positive results, now and forever. Since time began, Almighty God has been, and continues to be, the only one worthy of our faith, hope, and trust.

God knows our hearts, and we cannot fool him by pretending. I do not know the origin of the popular saying that God helps those who help themselves, but I have never found it in the Bible. I suppose we could balance it by saying God will not help those who will not help themselves, but that is not in the Bible either. If we are members of God's family and need help, God will provide, but it is an insult to the goodness of God to expect him, or anyone else, to do for us what we are able to do for ourselves.

> Rejoice in the Lord always: and again I say, Rejoice. Let your moderation be known unto all men. The Lord is at hand. Be careful for nothing; but in everything by prayer and supplication with thanksgiving let your requests be made known unto God. And the peace of God, which passeth all understanding, shall keep your hearts and minds through Christ Jesus. Finally, brethren, whatsoever things are true, whatsoever things are honest, whatsoever things are just, whatsoever things are pure, whatsoever things are lovely, whatsoever things are of good report; if there be any virtue, and if there be any praise, think on these things. Those

things, which ye have both learned, and received, and heard, and seen in me, do: and the God of peace shall be with you.

—Philippians 4:4–9

These words of the Apostle Paul are as relevant today as they were two thousand years ago: "the God of peace shall be with you." How sad it is that most people never experience real peace but are beaten down by the trials of this life. Any peace aside from that provided by a relationship with Jesus Christ is short-lived and sporadic. Christians are not exempt from the same trials and troubles that affect everyone else. Nevertheless, we have a partner who is willing to take on our troubles so that we may continue in peace through his strength, comforted by the Holy Spirit. I am aware of the difficulty some may have in accepting what they have never experienced, but God is anxiously waiting to reveal himself to anyone with a true desire to know him.

The Inevitability of Sinning

I have mentioned the ignorance and arrogance of man many times in this book; if one observes the human race from God's perspective, is there any doubt that they exist? If we accept that life extends beyond our time on earth, we must conclude that we need God in our lives. Whether we accept it or not, there is a heaven and a hell, and our eternal souls will advance to one or the other.

Brethren, if a man be overtaken in a fault, ye which are spiritual, restore such an one in the spirit of meekness; considering thyself, lest thou also be tempted. Bear ye one another's burdens, and so fulfil the law of Christ. For if a man think himself to be something, when he is nothing, he deceiveth himself. But let every man prove his own work, and then shall he have rejoicing in himself alone, and not in another. For every man shall bear his own burden. Let him that is taught in the word communicate unto him that teacheth in all good things. Be not deceived; God is not mocked: for whatsoever a man soweth, that shall he also reap. For he that soweth to his flesh shall of the flesh reap

corruption; but he that soweth to the Spirit shall of the Spirit reap life everlasting. And let us not be weary in well doing: for in due season we shall reap, if we faint not. As we have therefore opportunity, let us do good unto all *men*, especially unto them who are of the household of faith.
—Galatians 6:1–10

God blessed each of us with life and an instruction manual on what to do with it; if we ignore those instructions, our lives will eventually fall apart. There are no perfect people on this earth, and as human beings, none of us are exempt from looking back with regret at some choices we have made. That, however, is life. God did not create man to live apart from him, and sometimes he will lead us in a direction that we have no control over and it always turns out for the best. If we live for God, we will have him as our shield and guide; but if we live for Satan, we will serve a master of destruction.

God is well aware of our sinful natures and the struggle we endure living in a sinful world, but if we turn to him and repent of our sins he will forgive and forget our sins. Sin is not what man says it is but what God says it is. In God's eyes, sin is sin and not parsed in degrees or effects. In God's eyes, lying is no less sinful than murder, and that is proof enough that we cannot live in this sinful world without sinning. Jesus Christ loved us enough to cover our sins by shedding his blood. When we sin, we must recognize it as sin and bring it before him in repentance. In no way can we continue to live in man's world and repeatedly expect God to accept our repentance for the same sin.

Total Commitment

Whosoever therefore shall confess me before men, him will I confess also before my Father which is in heaven. But whosoever shall deny me before men, him will I also deny before my Father which is in heaven. Think not that I am come to send peace on earth: I came not to send peace, but a sword. For I am come to set a man at variance against his father, and the daughter against her mother, and the daughter in law against her mother in law. And a man's foes shall be they of his own household. He that loveth father

or mother more than me is not worthy of me: and he that
loveth son or daughter more than me is not worthy of me.
And he that taketh not his cross, and followeth after me, is
not worthy of me. He that findeth his life shall lose it: and
he that loseth his life for my sake shall find it.
—Matthew 10:32–39

These verses are direct, personal, and easy to skip over, but dismissing them
will not erase them. Jesus' message is relevant to us today, and it is a simple
message: Jesus is first in our lives, or he is last. If anyone thinks of Jesus as
meek and passive, read those verses again. Jesus is indeed the savior of the
world, but in these verses, he reminds us that we shall be judged according to
his word. If, following him, it causes conflict with members of our own family,
we still must choose to follow him. We must make such a commitment if we
are to have a relationship with Jesus. This type of commitment separates the
wheat from the chaff.

The Volunteer Army

There are no obsolete verses in the Bible, and after thousands of years, God
has not found it necessary to make any revisions. Life is a constant struggle
of one degree or another, but the struggle is not without, it is within. When
we become born-again Christians, we voluntarily join an army, God's army.
Like any army, we are in a war, not with other men but with Satan. We
cannot benefit God's army if we remain hunkered down in the comfort of
a foxhole. Satan does not go on furlough and does not lack sophisticated
weaponry; he has a well-equipped force, well trained, and motivated. Christ
is our commander, and he has the power to assure ultimate victory, which will
result in eternal life. The battle is a daily struggle with no lull in the fighting
until the battle it is won.

For I am now ready to be offered, and the time of my
departure is at hand.
I have fought a good fight, I have finished my course, I have
kept the faith:
Henceforth there is laid up for me a crown of righteousness,
which the Lord, the righteous judge, shall give me at that

day: and not to me only, but unto all them also that love his
appearing.
—2 Timothy 4:6–8

Those are the words of the Apostle Paul near his end; take note of his confidence
in the reward that awaits him after death. His confidence was manifested by
the promises of God; he fought a good fight and finished his course in God's
army, never losing faith in God's promises. These words are a reminder to all
of us that we also can partake of the same promises. Are we keeping the faith
and wearing the full armor of God to fight the good fight? Are we staying on
course, listening to God's voice and following him?

God Knows Our Circumstances

We are all individuals with unique personalities and quirks, and God deals
with us personally. We do not have the same abilities and understanding; God
knows our circumstances. God makes it possible for us to accomplish his goals
for our lives, if we have faith to trust him to do what he promised. He is the
only protection we have against the influence of Satan and his sinful world.

We learn from scripture that man repeatedly makes a mess of his life when
left to his own devices. Even Christians sometimes mess up their lives, but
we have a master fixer who will rescue us from our own failures. Life is hard
sometimes, and Christians are not exempt. It is not easy being a Christian in
America today, and it is only going to get more difficult. In some countries,
professing Christians can lose their lives, and we should pray for God's
protection for those people because a similar situation could come to America.
We can witness today a trend toward a distain for Christians, not only in
America but even more so in other countries. Still, that comes as no surprise
to those familiar with the Bible.

> If the world hate you, ye know that it hated me before it
> hated you. If ye were of the world, the world would love his
> own: but because ye are not of the world, but I have chosen
> you out of the world, therefore the world hateth you.
> —John 15:18–19

How fortunate we are to live in a country where we are free to openly worship Jesus Christ, but make no mistake, things are changing. We are not yet put to the test Christians in some parts of the world have been, but the future for Christians in America involves the separation of the chaff from the wheat. The day is coming when it will cost something to be a practicing Christian in America, and our faith will be tested like never before. In case you have not noticed, and many have not, Christians have been under attack in America for fifty years, and we can expect the attacks to intensify. *Will the real Christians please stand up!* What will you do if confronted with that demand? Will you eagerly jump to your feet or sink down in your seat like a coward in the hope that no one will notice you? Only you can answer that question, and you need to answer it today. Does this verse describe you? "but because ye are not of the world, but I have chosen you out of the world." If you are a truly born-again Christian, it does; and you can expect and accept that the world *will* hate you. This verse reminds us, once again, that we cannot live on both sides of the river.

The Future of America and the World

Life across the river is one of constant turmoil and change, but the spiritual life that exists on this side is constant and unchanging. In other words, God does not change, his word does not change, and his truth does not change. If we adopt that as a mindset, it will be clear that spiritual things and worldly things cannot be intermingled. Another important fact is that the people across the river cannot choose, with any certainty, their own destiny because they are controlled by sinful, untrustworthy, and deceiving man. On this side of the river, we choose our own destiny because we can be sure of the results of the choices we make.

The future is laid out for us, and it is clear, unambiguous, and unchanging; therefore, we know exactly what to expect. The controlling power here is the spirit of God; through a relationship with Jesus Christ as our guide and counselor, we can live the kind of lives unavailable to those across the river.

> Then said Jesus to those Jews which believed on him, If ye continue in my word, then are ye my disciples indeed; And

ye shall know the truth, and the truth shall make you free.
—John 8:31–32

America the Ugly

> Wherefore God also gave them up to uncleanness through the lusts of their own hearts, to dishonour their own bodies between themselves: Who changed the truth of God into a lie, and worshipped and served the creature more than the Creator, who is blessed forever. Amen. For this cause God gave them up unto vile affections: for even their women did change the natural use into that which is against nature: And likewise also the men, leaving the natural use of the woman, burned in their lust one toward another; men with men working that which is unseemly, and receiving in themselves that recompence of their error which was meet. And even as they did not like to retain God in *their* knowledge, God gave them over to a reprobate mind, to do those things which are not convenient; Being filled with all unrighteousness, fornication, wickedness, covetousness, maliciousness; full of envy, murder, debate, deceit, malignity; whisperers, Backbiters, haters of God, despiteful, proud, boasters, inventors of evil things, disobedient to parents, Without understanding, covenant breakers, without natural affection, implacable, unmerciful: Who knowing the judgment of God, that they which commit such things are worthy of death, not only do the same, but have pleasure in them that do them.
> —Romans 1:24–32

There is no better source other than the above verses to describe the current conditions in America across the river, and most of the world. Man, because of his sinful nature, continues to rebel against God by giving into his own selfish desires, oblivious to the consequences. "Who knowing the judgment of God, that they which commit such things are worthy of death, not only do the same, but have pleasure in them that do them." Anyone who calls himself a Christian and condones or supports "they which commit such things" shares the same guilt and is himself worthy of death. We cannot avoid God's judgment if we condone evil anymore than if we commit evil.

> For by him were all things created, that are in heaven, and that are in earth, visible and invisible, whether they be thrones, or dominions, or principalities, or powers: all things were created by him, and for him ...
> —Colossians 1:16

The above verse is short, but it is too important to be dealt with lightly, so before we continue, read it again. Those words are the key to how America got to its current state in such a short period. It is not necessary to devote any more time on *what* is going on in America so we will address the *why*. Nothing occurs on earth that is not the pure will of God, according to his plan and purpose. God has control over the powers on this earth and chooses who wields those powers. Man has no power to do anything that is contrary to God's purpose for mankind. Barak Obama is president of the United States of America because it is part of God's plan.

Is America in the Bible?

Our future is preordained, and God uses all he has created in the universe to facilitate his plan and it is difficult to ignore the signs that we are entering the end-time. Almost every event prophesized in the Bible has occurred exactly as predicted, and there are only a few things left to occur. The next big event is the rapture of the church.

As previously, discussed, any link between America and places in the Bible is pure speculation; if the United States is mentioned in the Bible, it is not made clear. Some have speculated that one possibility is that America is the rebirth of ancient Babylon, and there are certain similarities. The mystery of the new Babylon is not made clear in the Bible, and that gives birth to speculation. There are, however, Bible scriptures that may exclude the ancient city of Babylon from being the new Babylon.

> For in one hour so great riches is come to nought. And every shipmaster, and all the company in ships, and sailors, and

as many as trade by sea, stood afar off, And cried when they
saw the smoke of her burning, saying, What city is like unto
this great city!
—Revelation 18:17–18

The distance from ancient city of Babylon to the nearest commercial shipping lane—the Persian Gulf—is approximately three hundred miles. Even if a nuclear bomb exploded where old Babylon is now located, it could not be seen from the Persian Gulf. If we take the Bible literally, and there is no other way to take it, the new Babylon must be a coastal city, or very close to a coastline, and a major commercial trading center. Maybe less than a dozen cities in the world meet those criteria. Several are along or near the coastlines of the United States (i.e., New York City, Miami, Los Angeles, and Seattle). However, we do know the centralized world power will come from the rebirth of the old Roman Empire. However, it does not necessarily mean it will be in Europe. Now, with that information, you are free to speculate to your heart's content.

If one chooses to name an American city as the new Babylon, it would be difficult indeed to find scriptures in the Bible that contradict that choice. There are certainly many reasons to connect America with descriptions of the new Babylon; even so, it is nothing more than speculation. Personally, I do not believe America will have any significant role in the end-time because we are now, or are soon to be, under God's judgment. Only time will tell. Wherever the new Babylon is, it will be destroyed in an hour—"For in one hour"—and unless God uses some other means, it will probably be the result of nuclear weapons. We saw in chapter 1 how America can be destroyed in one hour, and that certainly is attention getting. That adds to the speculator's notebook, but to ensure I do not forget, I will offer some advice. Do not rely on man's opinions, including my opinions. If there is such a thing as an expert on the Bible, it certainly is not me. Study, study, study the Bible for yourself, and allow the Holy Spirit to reveal the truth to you—if it is God's will for you to know. God has not revealed the mystery of Babylon to me, so I certainly cannot reveal it to you.

If God wanted us to know where the new Babylon will be, he would have told us. The fact that he did not tell us is why there is so much speculation. I am not convinced it would be of any benefit to us if we did know. If we suspect America is the new Babylon, how would it be any different if we knew for sure? What would we do about it?

> "And Babylon, the glory of kingdoms, the beauty of the Chaldees' excellency, shall be as when God overthrew Sodom and Gomorrah. It shall never be inhabited, neither shall it be dwelt in from generation to generation: neither shall the Arabian pitch tent there; neither shall the shepherds make their fold there. But wild beasts of the desert shall lie there; and their houses shall be full of doleful creatures; and owls shall dwell there, and satyrs shall dance there. And the wild beasts of the islands shall cry in their desolate houses, and dragons in *their* pleasant palaces: and her time *is* near to come, and her days shall not be prolonged."
> —Isaiah 13:19-22

Here we see another reason the old city of Babylon will not be rebuilt—"It shall never be inhabited, neither shall it be dwelt in from generation to generation." Except for a wall or two left by the attempt by Saddam Hussein, to rebuild the city of Babylon, there is nothing there today but rubble. Moreover, it has been that way for over two thousand years.

"And the woman was arrayed in purple and scarlet colour, and decked with gold and precious stones and pearls, having a golden cup in her hand full of abominations and filthiness of her fornication: And upon her forehead *was* a name written, MYSTERY, BABYLON THE GREAT, THE MOTHER OF HARLOTS AND ABOMINATIONS OF THE EARTH. And I saw the woman drunken with the blood of the saints, and with the blood of the martyrs of Jesus: and when I saw her, I wondered with great admiration." — Revelation 17:4-6

Whatever, or whomever, mystery Babylon is, while the merchants of the world morn its destruction, God's people will have reason to rejoice—in Heaven.

"Rejoice over her, *thou* heaven, and *ye* holy apostles and
prophets; for God hath avenged you on her."
—Revelation 18:20

The mystery Babylon may not be a city! That possibility adds to the
woodpile of speculations. Could the woman arrayed in purple and scarlet
be an anti-Christian religion? There are no contradictions in the Bible, only
misunderstandings by its readers. "And the woman was arrayed in purple and
scarlet colour, and decked with gold and precious stones and pearls, having a
golden cup in her hand full of abominations and filthiness of her fornication."
Some people connect those words to the Roman Catholic Church. I do
not share that view, because during the tribulation, all false religions will
intermingle into a new global religion under control of the Antichrist. After
the rapture of the Christian church, all religions left behind will make up
the global false religion—The Mother Of Harlots. The mystery Babylon,
continues to be a mystery to me, so, I will leave it to others to figure it out.

America's moral decay can be traced back at least a hundred years and it
seemed to accelerate under progressive leaders like Woodrow Wilson.
However, the progressive agenda of President Wilson left its mark long after
he left office. Some of the like-minded radicals who have always existed in
America were emboldened by having a president who shared their views.
When the Eighteenth Amendment, banning alcohol, was enacted in 1920,
it provided opportunities for the underground criminal elements, who were
motivated by greed and corruption to openly challenge laws, especially in
Chicago. Bootleggers amassed so much money, it gave them the power to
intimidate or pay off any official who stood in their way. Bootlegging exposed
the most notorious criminal in American history, Al Capone, and gave rise to
the Mafia, which spread its illegal activities into every major city in America.
The "live for self, anything goes" element spawned during that era consumed
the city of Chicago and created a cesspool of government corruption that
continues to plague that city today. Now the Chicago style of politics is
controlling national politics, and it does not take a genius to realize that it is
bad for America. The circumstances today are quite different from in Wilson
or Roosevelt's time. No subsequent administration, if there is one, will be
capable of undoing the damage the current administration has already, and

will continue to perpetrate. America has accumulated massive unrepented sins over the past hundred years that brings us to this present day of retribution.

To whom much is given, much is required. God always keeps a watchful eye on America, and he brought the country back to its senses with the Great Depression in 1929. The overstated failures of Republican President Hoover were blamed for the Great Depression, and he certainly deserves part of the blame, especially his policy of raising taxes. However, his failures were overshadowed by the disastrous agenda of his successor, President Roosevelt, which most Americans did not realize until long after his death. I was not around during President Hoover's time but assuming that the liberal press overstates the failures of any conservative president and understates the failures of a liberal president, Hoover was probably vilified more than he deserved. President Hoover was a Quaker, and most of the press probably did not have a clue what a Quaker is, but it sounds religious and that was justification enough to vilify Hoover. President Nixon was also a Quaker, and Liberals, especially the liberal press, hated him long before we ever heard of Watergate. The same distain hurled toward a president who is not shy about proclaiming his faith in God was directed toward Presidents Bush and Reagan who publically proclaimed their faith in God. That was like dumping hot coals on the heads of the liberal press.

The Rise of American Power

In biblical days, the world's economic and political power was concentrated in Babylon (in modern Iraq) and remained in the Middle East until it migrated toward Europe, where it remained there for hundreds of years.

When the oil fields in Texas and Oklahoma, and the great American industrial machine, created a magnet that began to draw economical power across the Atlantic from Europe, it put the United States on a path to economical and military supremacy. Wealth, personal and national, brings with it the greed, jealousy, envy, corruption, and self-indulgence that first were introduced to mankind when Cain killed his brother Abel.

> And the LORD said unto Cain, Why art thou wroth? and
> why is thy countenance fallen? If thou doest well, shalt thou

not be accepted? and if thou does not do well, sin lieth at the door. And unto thee shall be his desire, and thou shalt rule over him. And Cain talked with Abel his brother: and it came to pass, when they were in the field, that Cain rose up against Abel his brother, and slew him."
—Genesis 4:6–8

Did America Do Well?

Do you think America did well? "If thou does not do well, sin lieth at the door." America began its transition from producing to consuming in the 1960s when Japan and Germany began to flood the country with cheaper cars and other cheap commodities, which brought about a slow deterioration of America's economic power. Billions of dollars were dumped in the pit in Vietnam, a debacle from which we never recovered. The perceived economic growth in the 1990s was a myth supported on a foundation of credit. Personal debt began to grow, and greed motivated providers of credit to encourage consumers not to spend—spend—spend but to charge—charge—charge. The federal and state governments became caught up in the same madness when tax revenue could no longer support social programs, and they too began to turn to credit. There is always a payday someday, and the payday has arrived; unfortunately, America is bankrupt and has been left to the mercy of its creditors. The same people who got us into this mess are the same people chosen to get us out of it. How stupid is that! Our folly has spread to most of the industrialized nations, and the world's economy is on the brink of collapse. Some of us are not at all surprised by these events because it is straight out of the Bible.

As the result of our folly, God shifted the economic power back to the Middle East, giving that area a stranglehold on other parts of the world through the control of oil supplies. Those of us who were around in the 1970s remember when the price of gasoline went from forty cents to a dollar a gallon overnight. Our government foolishly prevents exploiting our own resources and it has resulted in making us slaves to the world's despots, a trap from which there is no escape.

The Lights Are about to Come on

I do not want to appear arrogant, but unless you accept that God's providence created this great country and unless you are familiar with the Bible, you will have little understanding of what is transpiring in America or the world. If you have a clear understanding of world events, and what is ahead, you are indeed enlightened and among the minority.

There is much speculation today about the coming of a one-world government and a one-world religion. These things are coming; however, they will not come to fruition until the tribulation period—after the rapture of the Christian church. From that perspective, we can explore the entities left on the earth to develop a global government and a global religion. It does not require much imagination to recognize that the United Nations is already in place to facilitate a global government, but what about a global religion. For decades, speculators have seen elements of the Catholic Church as the foundation of the coming global church. However, today, there is emerging a new player—Islam. Whatever constitutes a global government and religion, they will be controlled by the Antichrist. Whether remnants of the Catholic Church, Islam, or a new type of religion will be involved, I will leave it to speculators to determine—if they can.

The United States and countries in Europe and elsewhere in the world are at the brink of economic collapse, and the only hope for survival is a centralized controlling authority that will end the sovereignty of individual countries and their ability to manage their own affairs. The prophecy is materializing right before our eyes; it is unimaginable that such a thing could happen so quickly, but throughout the Bible, there are examples of where God might have taken a long time to implement parts of his plan, however, he declines to call a community organizer for advice and will act at his own chosen time.

I mentioned previously that America started on the road to bankruptcy in the early 1960s, but Americans were so used to living in the dark, they paid little attention to the dimming of the lights. Today, we are deep into bankruptcy, and the lights of exposure are beginning to intensify, revealing the truth that America's economic power is an illusion. After the party, someone always has to pay the fiddler, and that someone is we.

To put it in perspective, do you own outright the house you live in, the car you drive, or your house full of stuff? The answer is probably no, and that is the state of our country today. If you fail to pay for all the stuff you easily and conveniently purchased with credit cards, what you assumed was yours can be repossessed by the rightful owner. America is in a similar situation today. We will never be able to pay our bills, and someone is going to demand we turn over what rightly belongs to him. One needs only to observe the current housing market to see the results of government involvement in free enterprise, lenders greed, and borrowers stupidity.

It is clear to me that only the power of Satan's influence could bring about the chaos overtaking the world today, especially America, and God is allowing it to happen because America has turned its back on him. It is undeniable that Americas' economic situation cannot be sustained when we are faced with the forthcoming day of reckoning. The massive debt this administration has, and continues to accumulate, far exceeds our ability to deal with it. The eventual collapse of our economy is a foregone conclusion.

It is obvious that practically nothing forecast by the president has materialized as predicted and only the very naïve would believe future forecasts would produce a different result. The government knows this; it is probably the reason the president is on television every day trying to distract the gullible from knowing the truth, and he will continue to do so until after the upcoming elections. After that, reality will spring forth like a Jack-in-the-Box, followed by shock and awe. How many lies does it take to get people's attention? Evidently, there is no limit.

To get back to the point, and I apologize for drifting back to the morass, there must be something other than our economic collapse to account for America not mentioned in the Bible. From the first time, monetary value was given to a coin, or rock, or whatever it was, he who had the largest bagful inherited power commensurate with the size of the bag. When our moneybag shrinks, so will our military power and here comes the scary part. Unless you are among the group of Americans who do not have a clue, it should be obvious that there are forces in this world that will never give up their quest to bring America to its knees. It is much easier to kick a person when he is down than when he is holding a gun in your face. No country can maintain a strong military without the funds to support it, and someday, we will be in that situation. No country can maintain power in the perilous times in which we live without a strong military.

To quote a statement made by the former prime minister of the United Kingdom, Margaret Thatcher, "The trouble with Socialism is that eventually you run out of other people's money." Compare the level of intelligence reflected in that statement to statements coming from the White House where they believe other people's money is theirs for the taking. I suppose it would be too much to expect our naïve president to understand that if you take money from hardworking people to give to those who do not work at all, eventually both groups will become destitute.

God's Intervention

If we trace back through our history, God's intervention is apparent throughout. Our Founding Fathers were chosen and put in place by God to build and develop the greatest form of government the world has ever known. Our founders and the majority of the population glorified God and looked to him for guidance and in return, God heaped his blessings on the birth of this great nation. However, we cannot ignore the fact that many times God has chastised America for turning away from him. The Vietnam War is a good example; God will never sanction an unjust war. The majority of American people fail to learn from his warnings and continue to make the same mistakes repeatedly.

We were victorious in the Revolutionary War because God intervened to ensure that America would rise as a beacon to the rest of the world, revealing, not our great power, but his great power. George Washington survived that war, despite having horses shot out from under him and many bullet holes in his clothing because God had plans for him to spearhead the development of this great country. Nothing, including bullets, can prevent God's plans from succeeding, and no one understood that better than George Washington did.

According to a program aired on the history channel on April 9, 2010, titled: "First invasion: the War of 1812," the British set fire to Washington, D.C, and were on the brink of taking control of America. As the flames made rubble of the Capitol and other buildings, seemingly from nowhere, a great storm swept across the area with violent winds and torrential rain that not only doused the flames, but also routed the British Army, killing more troops than had been lost in the fighting. It turned the tides of the battle, and eventually the British gave up the fight. You may see this as a coincident, but I believe the British left licking their wounds, after being smitten by Almighty God. What God did *for* America is about to be done *to* America because we are no longer under his protection.

The Civil War was a just war because it put an end to the tyranny of slavery, and it united our country to become what God had ordained. Germany lost World War I, but there were no winners, only hundreds of thousands deprived of life. America was victorious in World War II because it helped to end to Adolph Hitler's demonic plans to destroy the Jewish race and conquer the world. World War II was the only war in modern times we can claim to have won; it is also the last war we will ever win. The Korean War has not yet been won because it continues and is becoming more dangerous; the future of the wars in Iraq and Afghanistan will end the same way.

Among the most despicable people on the planet are politicians who send people into battle without an absolute resolve to win and commit everything at their disposal to support those given the task to be victorious. More importantly, it must be a just war. The senseless debacle in Vietnam is a perfect example of how not to fight a war. This generation has long forgotten the fifty thousand–plus "political fodder" human beings who lost their lives and the tens of thousands maimed and crippled in Vietnam. If America survives to see another generation, they will not remember the political fodder being sacrificed today in Iraq and Afghanistan. Unless our leadership accepts that there is evil in this world, and forces that would love to see an end to America's power, America has won its last battle. We will win neither the war in Afghanistan nor the war against al-Qaeda—not because we cannot but because this liberal government has no desire to defeat our enemies. In fact, the government is in denial; it does not believe that we have enemies. The murders and chaos across our southern borders in Mexico are like a poisonous fog that is slowly drifting into our mainland. Evil people have existed in this world since Adam and Eve and it would be foolish to think there are less evil people in the world today. It is easier for al-Qaeda or the Taliban to cross the border between America and Mexico than it is for them to cross the border between Afghanistan and Pakistan, so what sense does it make to send thousands of our young people halfway around the world to defend the border in Afghanistan when our own borders are unprotected?

Bureaucracy: government marked by specialization of functions under fixed rules and a hierarchy of authority; *also*: an unwieldy administrative system burdened with excessive complexity and lack of flexibility. (Merriam Webster's Dictionary) I will allow that definition from the dictionary to speak for itself. We could drastically reduce the amount of money spent, and wasted, by the country's largest Bureaucracy—the Defense Department—if we would confine the mission of the military to self defense rather than sending troops all over the world sticking our nose in other countries' business. We have enough enemies here in America without going all over the world looking for more. Our major threat is not from a great world power like Russia, but from demented people like al-Qaeda and Ahmadinejad. If you think these type of people will just go away, you are greatly mistaken; they have been at war with the world for hundreds of years and they are not going away, they are not afraid of America, or any other country.

People who die on the front lines of the military are real people not movie actors, they have families and love ones that care about them and they are mostly young with young families. We should never sacrifice their lives for political reasons, but unfortunately, it is part of our history to do so, as we did in World War I, Vietnam, and are now doing in Afghanistan. Fighting al-Qaeda is like swatting flies, kill as many as you can, but they will keep coming and like flies, they seem to appear from nowhere. America is bankrupt and our enemies know it, all they need to do is keep poking us in the eye until we destroy ourselves.

War is a terrible and devastating undertaking, but the purpose of war is to kill your enemies before they kill you. It was a disastrous mistake to get involved in a war in Afghanistan; Al-Qaeda is not a country with borders; their operatives are scattered all over the world, including America, and they will never give up the fight or be completely defeated. Our Defense Department claims that its strategy is to run al-Qaeda out of Afghanistan; a more sensible strategy would be to run them out of America before they succeed in killing millions of our citizens. That should be the primary role of the military; defend our own borders. Another giant dysfunctional Bureaucracy in our government is Homeland Security, I am at a loss to know whose homeland they are trying to secure. We will view 9/11 as a minor incident compared to what is likely to come to America if our government does not wake up and face reality. What foolish people we have in our government today. However, let us not forget who has ultimate control over world events.

God always gives signs and warnings to prepare us for the future, but they go unnoticed except by those who are looking for them. A problem with Americans, and I suppose the rest of the world, is that unless the consequences are immediate, we think we can get away with ignoring God. The evidence of his harsh dealings with countries that have rejected him is plain to see the world over. God would have to be a liar to allow America to escape his wrath, and all one needs to do is study the Bible and world history to see how God deals with nations. God will not be mocked; his word is true, and when he says he will do something, you can count on it. God is clearly a God of love, but he is also a judge, and no country has ever escaped punishment for rejecting him or for anti-Semitism. Because of the many blessings God has bestowed on America, we probably will receive a double dose of his wrath for turning its back on him.

When the Jews blessed God, he blessed them, and when they rejected him, he rejected them. That has happened many times throughout their history. In 70 AD, his patience ran out and Jerusalem's city and temple were destroyed, just as Jesus predicted. The Jewish people were deprived of the foundation of their existence and remained homeless for almost two thousand years, until God restored them to their land in 1948. If God deals with his own chosen people that way, what chance does America have to escape his judgment.

And when he was come near, he beheld the city, and wept over it, Saying, If thou hadst known, even thou, at least in this thy day, the things which belong unto thy peace! but now they are hid from thine eyes. For the days shall come upon thee, that thine enemies shall cast a trench about thee, and compass thee round, and keep thee in on every side, And shall lay thee even with the ground, and thy children within thee; and they shall not leave in thee one stone upon another; because thou knewest not the time of thy visitation.
—Luke 19:41–44

If you have access to a copy of "The Complete Works of Josephus," translated by William Whiston, go to chapter 2 of book 5. Here he gives an eyewitness account of the destruction of Jerusalem and the temple in 70 AD. You will discover that it occurred exactly as Jesus predicted. You can order a copy of this book from eBay, or if you have a Kindle reader, Kindle has a copy, published Jan 6, 2008. Flavius Josephus was a Jewish historian, and his work is a fascinating book to read. It is, however, not for casual reading. If you have any doubt of the power of God's wrath, reading this account will remove it. The Roman emperor Titus and his mighty army was God's choice to initiate his wrath against his people, and he could just as easy choose someone like Ahmadinejad to do the same to America.

The threat to the United States from Iran, as discussed previously, is a real possibility, particularly if this administration fails to continue America's support for Israel. If God chooses to allow Iran to attack America as the source of his wrath, nothing Americans can do will stop it. Whether God chooses Iran to perpetrate his punishment on America, or some other means, anyone familiar with the Bible will know that unless America turns back to God, it will happen. Unlike what many people think, America no longer has favor with God, and it will not be judged by a different standard than anyone else. God's judgment on America will be swift, exact, and devastating for those who are not prepared. America has reached its day of reckoning, and God has put the current administration in place to fulfill his wrath. God has known from the beginning that America would not be a major player in the end-time, and that is why the United States of America is not clearly mentioned in the Bible. If America is in the Bible, the only reference to it is its destruction.

Ignored Warnings

Why people choose to ignore warnings is a mystery. I suppose there are many reasons, but none of them makes good sense. Warnings are given for a reason, and there are consequences if they are ignored.

> For as in the days that were before the flood they were eating and drinking, marrying and giving in marriage, until the day that Noe entered into the ark, And knew not until the flood came, and took them all away; so shall also the coming of the Son of man be. Then shall two be in the field; the one shall be taken, and the other left. Two women shall be grinding at the mill; the one shall be taken, and the other left. Watch therefore: for ye know not what hour your Lord doth come. But know this, that if the goodman of the house had known in what watch the thief would come, he would have watched, and would not have suffered his house to be broken up. Therefore be ye also ready: for in such an hour as ye think not the Son of man cometh.
> —Matthew 24:38–44

While Noe (Noah), was building the ark, rather than pitching in and helping, the people laughed and scoffed at him; that is, until the ark was finished, and God shut the door to the Ark. In a very short time, scoffers were wiped from the face of the earth amid screams of fear and hopelessness. It is estimated that it took Noah more than a hundred years to build the ark; thus, the people had ample warning of what was to come, but they ignored the warnings and considered Noah some kind of religious kook. Once God closes the door against those who reject him, it will not be reopened, and that is a clear warning to this generation that is rejecting him. I hope you will heed this warning; the ark is almost finished, and the dark rain clouds are beginning to form. When God shuts the door, all who are outside will perish.

God has been patient with man for thousands of years, and the phrase, "behold, I come quickly" often is misinterpreted as suggesting that Jesus warned he would come soon. That is not what he is saying. If he comes next week, next year, or in the next millennium, when he acts it will be very quick. In other words, for almost two thousand years, some have been looking for the coming of Christ to rapture his church but because he has not yet come; many are lured into believing he never will. God has a different timetable than we do, what to us is a year, to God it is like a thousand years, and what we know as a thousand years, is only a year to God. In other words, God has no restraints of time. I suppose to God, the universe was created a year ago, or maybe yesterday.

Are you not at times amazed how quickly time appears to go by? There are still twenty-four hours in a day, but it seems that as soon as a new week or month begins, before we know it, we are at its end. We are so occupied with keeping up with the hustle and bustle of modern life that we have to hurry to beat the clock. In truth, we may waste several hours a day in front of the television or computer, oblivious to the reality of what is transpiring in the world.

People's jobs seem to occupy the majority of their thoughts, interrupted only by short periods of mindless distractions as they rush toward another day of the same. There is nothing wrong with devotion to a job, but if the job is the most important part of your life, your family is to be pitied. Many fathers and mothers come home from work after stopping by day care and are aggravated by their little ones, whom they scarcely know, bidding for their attention. The result of this lifestyle is frustration from trying to cope with the stress it produces. Could you have imagined only a few months ago that America would be changed to become what it is today? Things have happened so fast no one has any idea what the outcome will be; that is, no one but those familiar with God's word. The fact is, the conditions occurring in America today have not happened as quickly as you might think; they have been building for decades, and those of us paying attention saw it coming a long time ago.

America has had its problems in the past, but because God has blessed us, we have survived. For those who lived through the ten years between 1945 and 1955 can agree that it was America's greatest decade in recent history. If

America has ever been a moral nation, it was during that period, and God poured out his blessings on our country like never before. One of the major reasons was America's support for Israel, and it is probably the primary reason he is withholding his wrath from us today. Keep your eyes on Israel; if America abandons support for that country, batten down the hatches because a storm is coming. Anyone expounding that view today is mocked by the anti-Israel, anti-American mainstream press, but woe to anyone who mocks God.

> And the LORD God of their fathers sent to them by his messengers, rising up betimes, and sending; because he had compassion on his people, and on his dwelling place: But they mocked the messengers of God, and despised his words, and misused his prophets, until the wrath of the LORD arose against his people, till there was no remedy. here fore he brought upon them the king of the Chaldees, who slew their young men with the sword in the house of their sanctuary, and had no compassion upon young man or maiden, old man, or him that stooped for age: he gave them all into his hand.
> —2 Chronicles 36:15–17

The same God who sent the Chaldees to perpetrate his wrath against his own chosen people is the same God controlling events in the world today. If you think this is all Old Testament stuff, look at recent history. Germany, Italy, United Kingdom, France, Greece, and Turkey are examples of how God raises and brings down empires. Each of these countries had its day in the sun and are dotted with relics of great majestic Christian churches and cathedrals that demonstrates the importance of serving God in their past. Today, however, those churches and cathedrals are nothing more than tourist attractions because God has been kicked out of most of Europe. On April 6, 2009, at a conference in Turkey, President Obama made this statement: "One of the great strengths of the United States is … we have a very large Christian population—we do not consider ourselves a Christian nation or a Jewish nation or a Muslim nation. We consider ourselves a nation of citizens who are bound by ideals and a set of values." I agree, America is not a Christian nation, but I totally disagree with where he spoke these words. Moreover, I disagree that he has the right to say them. He has no right to declare what the citizens of this country consider themselves. I have no right to do so either. We have the right to decide for ourselves in such matters. The President was right about one thing: we are bound by a set of ideas and a set of values. The question is, what ideas and what values? We certainly are not bound by moral values. Perhaps there have been periods in our history when we were bound by moral values, but not today. If there is such a thing as a Christian nation on this earth—if we consider it a nation—it is the Christian church, which has no borders. no buildings and is ruled by a single authority—Jesus Christ. Moral principles are the adhesive that binds every society, and history teaches us that if the adhesive loses its strength, the society crumbles.

Israel is, and always has been, God's focal point, and throughout its history, this tiny piece of land has been embroiled in chaos and trouble that continues even today. The city of Jerusalem, where Jesus walked during his short time on this earth, once was referred to as the City of Peace, but it has witnessed very little peace, and many are confused by that contradiction. Very soon, however, that contradiction will be resolved. Jesus Christ will return to the place from which he departed this earth almost two thousand years ago and bring peace, not only to Jerusalem but also to the entire world, that will last a thousand years. Not only will there be Christian nations, there will be a Christian world.

Any nation that ignores the fact that the land of Israel is protected by Almighty God will be the recipient of his wrath, and America is facing that truth today. Over the past few years, there has been a gradual shift away from a favorable attitude toward Israel and never more so than with this current administration. For many years, the only reason Liberals feigned to support Israel was due to the millions of Jews who defy logic and continue to vote for them. However, God is not fooled by pretense; he knows what is in the heart of man. While it is unnoticed by most people, God's wrath is already at work in America today. Katrina, 9/11, severe floods and tornados, and terrorism are warnings to America but they go unheeded. These warnings will continue with more severity until they can no longer be ignored. You may ask what could be worse than what is being experienced today, but believe me, unless the people of America wake up, far worse things are headed our way.

God allowed this current government to take control of America to facilitate our downfall, and unfounded optimism cannot alter reality. There is no logic or common sense to be made of the actions of this administration except by those familiar with how God deals with nations. When this administration joins the rest of the world and turns its back on Israel, which is inevitable because the Bible predicts the entire world will turn against Israel in the end-time, Jewish people will be faced with the reality that the only true friends they have in the world are born-again Christians. Whether or not Jewish people acknowledge it, Christians will continue to support Israel with funds and prayers because it is in our hearts to do so.

> Now the LORD had said unto Abram, Get thee out of thy country, and from thy kindred, and from thy fathers house, unto a land that I will shew thee: And I will make of thee a great nation, and I will bless thee, and make thy name great; and thou shalt be a blessing: And I will bless them that bless thee, and curse him that curseth thee: and in thee shall all families of the earth be blessed.
> —Genesis 12:1–3

America's Moral Decline

Not all of God's people reside in America, quite the contrary. Christianity is increasing in other parts of the world, including China and many countries in Africa, but it is in decline in America. According to the *American Religious Identification Survey* (ARIS), published in 2008: from 1990 to 2008, the number of Americans identified as Christians declined 10.2 percent, from 86.2 percent to 76 percent. Liberalism, cults, false religions, and false teachings have infested America with an anti-Christian sentiment that is spreading into every corner of our society, including many churches. I have already lamented to how it is impossible to get a consensus on anything, especially in matters of faith. To support my conclusion, following is a sample of what I discovered is the fastest growing religion in America. Take note, the fastest-growing *religion*—singular—Christianity, Islam, Scientology, and Wicca (Witchcraft). They cannot all be right, but they can all be wrong. The point is does it really matter who is right and who is wrong? A survey is not required to identify reality; speculations are always nullified by reality. No one involved with

Christianity in America today will need a survey to recognize its decline. The ARIS survey covered a period from 1990 to 2008. My personal observations, and I am sure many others, recognized that Christianity in America was in trouble long before 1990.

I do not have permission to quote it, but in 1963, Dr. Martin Luther King Jr., in *his Strength of Love* speech, recognized that America was headed in the wrong direction morally. In his wisdom, Dr. King understood that churches were failing to stand for what is morally right, and, he was right. Where were church leaders in 1962 when prayer in public schools was banned? Where were church leaders in 1973 when abortion was legalized? Where are church leaders today with the courage to unite and stand against the growing influence of an anti-God and anti-America radicals in our government and the mainstream press? Where are the church leaders who stand in protest against our children being taught in public schools that homosexuality is an acceptable or even preferred lifestyle? Where are the church leaders who stand against Satan's efforts to remove any reference of God from our country?

Churches in America today have no spiritual authority to affect anything in our government. They have voluntarily shackled themselves to the government because of the tax exemption for religious organizations even though they are not required to do so. In America today, you can create a society that worships a cabbage head, call it a church, and qualify for tax-exempt status. Being obligated to the government for any reason is not something a church, or a Christian, should be.

> Then went the Pharisees, and took counsel how they might entangle him in his talk. And they sent out unto him their disciples with the Herodians, saying, Master, we know that thou art true, and teachest the way of God in truth, neither carest thou for any man: for thou regardest not the person of men. Tell us therefore, What thinkest thou? Is it lawful to give tribute unto Caesar, or not? But Jesus perceived their wickedness, and said, Why tempt ye me, ye hypocrites? Shew me the tribute money. And they brought unto him a penny. And he saith unto them, Whose is this image and

superscription? They say unto him, Caesar's. Then saith he
unto them, Render therefore unto Caesar the things which
are Caesar's; and unto God the things that are God's.
—Matthew 22:15–21

If people give money to churches only because they can claim the exemption
on their tax returns, churches would be better off without their money. In
fact, only a few churchgoers give substantial amounts anyway. If a church has
faithful tithers, the loss of the tax exemption would have little effect, other
than maybe clean the house. Do you believe God would allow a true faithful
church to fail because it broke the chains of bondage to the government by
refusing tax-exempt status?

It is an essential duty of any ministry to send missionaries to other parts of the
world to spread God's word, and churches spend millions of dollars for that
purpose when half of their own congregations are unsaved and hell bound.
Perhaps it is time for other countries to send missionaries here to help us get
back on the right path.

Our moral decline is being accelerated by much of this godless generation.
Millions of Americans love the heritage of our country and are sick at heart
over what is transpiring, but reality must be confronted. It saddens me to say
so, but it needs to be said: the majority of people who are now awakening and
paying attention to what is taking place were silent and inattentive when they
could have prevented our demise—not through politics but by acknowledging
the one who controls world events. We have had fifty years of clear and
obvious warnings of changes coming to our country, changes that will lead
to our downfall, but who was paying attention? I will admit, although I
suspected it was coming, I paid little attention to it until Bill Clinton was
elected president; for me, that was the writing on the wall. Can we expect God
to continue to be patient with us forever? God has sounded his clarion call,
and I do not expect he will sound it again, only to be ignored again.

Politics is the oxygen that sustains Liberals, and they believe everything can be
solved through negotiations, wheeling and dealing, and deception because it
is all they know how to do. Politics is a fantasyland and politicians, especially

liberal Socialists, are among the most ignorant of the human race. They cannot deal with the real world and, because of their unbridled power, create their own reality, which is contrary to the wishes of the majority of normal people. Liberalism has infected every segment of our society, including the government, churches, schools, and probably the military, and if it continues unchecked, we cannot survive as a nation. Socialism and Communism are universally known failures; they have never produced anything but death and misery to the inhabitants of countries where they are tried.

There is however, an upside to what is in our future. It will cause many Shakespearean Christians to reevaluate their relationships with Jesus Christ, and the coming hard times will cause many to turn to God because that usually occurs when people are forced to take their eyes off the world and focus on him. Unfortunately, many will be defiant right up to the end, and others will take the "wait and see" attitude, but Jesus will come without any warning other than what is clearly predicted in the Bible. No one knows when the rapture will occur, and we should not give up on living for God while waiting for him to take us out of this sinful world. Without doubt, there are many signs that point toward the coming of the rapture very soon. We learn from the Bible that God allows it to rain on the just and unjust alike, the question is, how long will God allow rain to fall on the righteous before he takes them into perpetual sunlight?

God's Judgment on America

Those of us familiar with the Bible clearly realize that there is no way America will escape God's wrath; to do so would invalidate the entire Bible. God has always punished disobedient people, and it is foolish to think he will show any special consideration to America. People are so wrapped up in politics and blaming each other for our ills, they fail to realize the real reason America is faltering: for fifty years, we have abused God's patience, and the day of reckoning is upon us. To those to whom much has been given, much will be required, and because the many blessings God has bestowed on America are ignored by this generation, the retribution will be devastating.

> Thus saith the LORD; Stand in the court of the LORD'S
> house, and speak unto all the cities of Judah, which come to

worship in the LORD'S house, all the words that I command thee to speak unto them; diminish not a word: If so be they will hearken, and turn every man from his evil way, that I may repent me of the evil, which I purpose to do unto them because of the evil of their doings. And thou shalt say unto them, Thus saith the LORD; If ye will not hearken to me, to walk in my law, which I have set before you, To hearken to the words of my servants the prophets, whom I sent unto you, both rising up early, and sending them, but ye have not hearkened; Then will I make this house like Shiloh, and will make this city a curse to all the nations of the earth.
—Jeremiah 26:2–6

Although the Prophet Jeremiah was speaking to the Jews of Judah thousands of years ago, his message is just as relevant to us today. Jeremiah was not talking to the world; he was talking to his people. Today Jesus is telling Christians through his word to wake up and turn away from the things of this world and toward him. When God decides that it is time to act, he will do so very quickly; the demise of America could take years or it could happen in months, weeks, or even in a flash as we discussed in chapter 1.

History is replete with societies that have brought about their own ruin by underestimating the threat from their enemies. King Nebuchadnezzar is a good example.

All this came upon the king Nebuchadnezzar. At the end of twelve months he walked in the palace of the kingdom of Babylon. The king spake, and said, Is not this great Babylon, that I have built for the house of the kingdom by the might of my power, and for the honour of my majesty? While the word was in the king's mouth, there fell a voice from heaven, saying, O king Nebuchadnezzar, to thee it is spoken; The kingdom is departed from thee. And they shall drive thee from men, and thy dwelling shall be with the beasts of the field: they shall make thee to eat grass as oxen, and seven times shall pass over thee, until thou know that the most High ruleth in the kingdom of men, and giveth it to whomsoever he will. The same hour was the thing fulfilled upon Nebuchadnezzar: and he was driven from men, and did eat grass as oxen, and his body was wet with the dew of heaven, till his hairs were grown like eagles' feathers, and his nails like birds' claws.

—Daniel 4:28–33

Here we see God's wrath at work upon an arrogant man. Nebuchadnezzar took credit for the greatness of Babylon and placed himself above anything else, without any remorse for what he did to the Jews he had enslaved. God remembered, and in an hour, the mighty king was made insane and banished to the wilderness to live as an animal for seven years. After seven years of forging around in the dirt for his subsistence, Nebuchadnezzar came to realize that God controls the affairs of man, and there are consequences to ignoring that fact. Once Nebuchadnezzar came to his senses, he acknowledged God's sovereignty over mankind and repented, and his kingdom was restored to him.

In 539 BC, after the death of King Nebuchadnezzar, Belshazzar became the ruler of ancient Babylon, the most powerful country in the world at the time; Belshazzar had the same sense of false security as our president. The great city Babylon was a wonder of the ancient world and the Greek historian Herodotus gives a detailed description in, *The Histories*. (Translated into English, by G.C. Macaulay, M.A. ,in 2008.) However, for this discussion, we will concentrate on the great wall that was around the city. According to book 1, paragraph 178 of *The Histories*, written during the fifth century BC, the outer wall was 50 royal cubits wide (85 feet), 200 royal cubits high (335 feet), and encircled the city with a total length of 480 furlongs (56 miles). Although these exact measurements cannot be verified by archeologists, no one questions it was a formidable fortress. While Belshazzar was at a banquet drinking with his friends, a message appeared on a wall for all to see:

Belshazzar the king made a great feast to a thousand of his lords, and drank wine before the thousand. Belshazzar, whiles he tasted the wine, commanded to bring the golden and silver

vessels which his father Nebuchadnezzar had taken out of
the temple which was in Jerusalem; that the king, and his
princes, his wives, and his concubines, might drink therein.
Then they brought the golden vessels that were taken out
of the temple of the house of God which was at Jerusalem;
and the king, and his princes, his wives, and his concubines,
drank in them. They drank wine, and praised the gods of
gold, and of silver, of brass, of iron, of wood, and of stone. In
the same hour came forth fingers of a man's hand, and wrote
over against the candlestick upon the plaister of the wall of
the king's palace: and the king saw the part of the hand that
wrote. Then the king's countenance was changed, and his
thoughts troubled him, so that the joints of his loins were
loosed, and his knees smote one against another.
—Daniel 5:1–6

Although the writing on the wall scared him sober, Belshazzar was confident
the great walls made it impossible for any enemy to enter the city. Belshazzar
was an idiot, but his enemy Cyrus the king of Persia (Iran), had a secret
weapon: his own intelligence. While he was outside the city with his army
scratching his head trying to figure how to breach the great walls, a voice
whispered to him, "block the channel" (my words). Herodotus wrote that
Cyrus diverted the Euphrates River, which is not very feasible. Many believe
it was a channel diverted from the great river Euphrates that ran under the
walls and through the center of the city. While old Belshazzar was partying
with his labor bosses and political hacks, Cyrus blocked the channel. When
the water level dropped, his army marched under the walls via the dried-up
channel and captured the city. —The Histories, book 1, paragraph 190.

If there was indeed a voice whispering to Cyrus, where did it come from?
First, we will explore why Babylon was taken from Belshazzar. Who was
Belshazzar? Many historians believe he was the grandson of Nebuchadnezzar.
The book of Daniel refers to him as the son of Nebuchadnezzar, but in the old
tradition that could mean son, grandson, or great-grandson. Nebuchadnezzar
is credited with building Babylon into the world's greatest empire, and exactly

who Belshazzar is does not matter for the purpose of our discussion. I prefer to believe Daniel rather than a historian.

Back to Belshazzar's last banquet; scattered about the great banquet hall were cups, plates, and goblets made of pure gold and silver, which were being filled with alcohol and slobbered over by gluttonous fat cats. These golden utensils were sacred items that had been taken from the Jewish Temple in Jerusalem seventy years earlier when King Nebuchadnezzar destroyed it and took the Jews captive and brought them to Babylon. That is how the Prophet Daniel came to be in Babylon.

> Then was the part of the hand sent from him; and this writing was written. And this is the writing that was written, MENE, MENE, TEKEL, UPHARSIN. This is the interpretation of the thing: MENE; God hath numbered thy kingdom, and finished it. TEKEL; Thou art weighed in the balances, and art found wanting. PERES; Thy kingdom is divided, and given to the Medes and Persians. Then commanded Belshazzar, and they clothed Daniel with scarlet, and put a chain of gold about his neck, and made a proclamation concerning him, that he should be the third ruler in the kingdom. In that night was Belshazzar the king of the Chaldeans slain. And Darius the Median took the kingdom, being about threescore and two years old.
> —Daniel 5:24–31

Within hours of the appearance of the writing on the wall, Belshazzar was dead and his kingdom lost to King Darius. Evidently, Belshazzar failed to learn from the experience of Nebuchadnezzar—namely, that defying God brings with it severe punishment. In the case of Belshazzar, it cost him his life. Historians differ in their understandings of the identity of Darius and Cyrus. Like the fictitious Frick and Frack, who is Frick, and who is Frack? Some say it was Cyrus who became the ruler of Babylon, some say it was Darius. Others say it was both, first Cyrus, followed by Darius. Not to be outdone, some proclaim the opposite. I have more faith in Daniel and the Bible than I do in historians. Daniel says it was Darius, and that is good enough for me.

History does indeed repeat itself. Belshazzar's ignorance has been repeated through the ages by men who fail to see the "writing on the wall." If you have any doubt of the danger President Obama has created for America, for the sake of you and your family, wake up and educate yourself about what is going on, not only America, but also the rest in the world. We are living in perilous times, and by now, you should be aware that our current administration is ill equipped to deal with it. Prepare to deal with it yourself because you will get very little help from the government. I do not believe it is any more difficult for Ahmadinejad to launch a nuclear-tipped missile over America than it was for Cyrus to breach the walls of mighty Babylon. If it is in God's will for America to be brought down, you can be assured he will make it happen. There are no easy solutions in preparing for what is coming to America, but you will have to do the best you can for you and your family.

Shakespearean Christians

The majority of Americans call themselves Christians, but common sense dictates that there is no way our country could be taken over by anti-God, abortion-supporting politicians without the support of many people who identify themselves as Christian. Christianity is not a mere title; it is a declaration of a separation from man's world, and a personal relationship with Jesus Christ. Our children would not be denied the mere mention of the name Jesus in our schools if the masses who call themselves Christians did not facilitate the success of the American Civil Liberties Union (ACLU), and liberal Socialism. Enablers share the same guilt and responsibility as the ones being enabled.

If you consider yourself a Christian and support a politician, through voting or finances, who is—among other godless things, in favor of abortion, gay rights, or same sex marriage, I recommend you read the Bible and learn for yourself how you will be judged for doing that—I pause here to stress a very important subject. As Christians, we should constantly perform a self-test, to evaluate our relationship with Christ. I know of no better subject, except perhaps abortion, to determine if we have the spirit of Christ living in us than our attitude toward homosexuality. Homosexuality is an abomination to God, and as Christians, we cannot view it otherwise. As Christians, we should never accept that which God does not accept. Furthermore, as God has compassion for all sinners, which includes all of us, we should do the same. Where would any of us be without compassion from a loving God? We will all be judged, and rendering judgment on others, is not for us to do. All people are God's creation, and, he loves all of his creation the same. Nevertheless, it does not mean anyone will escape reaping what he sows. I do not understand the homosexual lifestyle, but it was not created this century. It brought destruction to Sodom and Gomorra thousands of years ago and the following verses expose the first case of wheeling and dealing in the Bible. Abraham is attempting to persuade God not to destroy Sodom and Gomorra:

> And Abraham drew near, and said, Wilt thou also destroy the righteous with the wicked? Peradventure there be fifty righteous within the city: wilt thou also destroy and not spare the place for the fifty righteous that *are* therein? That be far from thee to do after this manner, to slay the righteous with the wicked: and that the righteous should be as the wicked, that be far from thee: Shall not the Judge of all the earth do right? And the LORD said, If I find in Sodom fifty righteous within the city, then I will spare all the place for their sakes. And Abraham answered and said, Behold now, I have taken upon me to speak unto the Lord, which *am but* dust and ashes: Peradventure there shall lack five of the fifty righteous: wilt thou destroy all the city for *lack of* five? And he said, If I find there forty and five, I will not destroy *it*. And he spake unto him yet again, and said, Peradventure there shall be forty found there. And he said, I will not do *it* for forty's sake. And he said *unto him*, Oh let not the Lord be angry, and I will speak: Peradventure there shall thirty be found there. And he said, I will not do *it*, if I find thirty there. And he said, Behold now, I have taken upon me to speak unto the Lord: Peradventure there shall be twenty found there. And he said, I will not destroy *it* for twenty's sake. And he said, Oh let not the Lord be angry, and I will speak yet but this once: Peradventure ten shall be found there. And he said, I will not destroy *it* for ten's sake. And

the LORD went his way, as soon as he had left communing
with Abraham: and Abraham returned unto his place.
— Genesis 18:23-33

That is a wonderful passage. Abraham is trying to bargain with God, and, it
demonstrates the affection they had for each other. Abraham was careful not
to overstep his bounds, but, at the same time, he was nudging God a little.
Of course, from the onset, God knew Abraham would not find ten righteous
people. Sodom and Gomorra had brought God's wrath upon themselves, and
after God sent Angels to rescue Abraham's Nephew—Lot, and his family, he
erased Sodom and Gomorra from the face of the Earth. God will not tolerate
wickedness. Sodom and Gomorra did not get away with it, and, neither will
America. While we are thinking about Abraham, if you are a mystery seeker,
the following two verses describe one of the greatest mystery in the Bible.

And Melchizedek king of Salem brought forth bread and
wine: and he *was* the priest of the most high God. And he
blessed him, and said, Blessed *be* Abram of the most high
God, possessor of heaven and earth: And blessed be the
most high God, which hath delivered thine enemies into thy
hand. And he gave him tithes of all.
— Genesis 14:18-20

The identity of Melchizedek is indeed a mystery. Throughout the book of
Genesis, characters are identified, and, their families. Nowhere in the Bible is
Melchizedek identified, other than to say, he was the King of Salem (present
day, Jerusalem)—and the priest of the most high God—Who made him king
of Salem? How did he become the priest of the most high God? To deepen
the mystery, why did Abraham (formally Abram) pay tithes to Melchizedek?
There are many theories, born by those more qualified than I am. I confess,
I do not know, but I will continue to explore the mystery, as I have for thirty
years. I do however have my own theory who this man could be, but it would
only add to my already stack of speculations, so, I will keep it to myself.

Christian principles are meaningless unless they are defended and
uncompromised. We cannot justify abandoning our Christian principles to

support the lesser of two evils among politicians. God is going to decide who rules America; he also is going to decide our fate based on our adherence to his word. Republican politicians fail to realize that without the support of true Christians, they will not regain power. Moreover, they are not going to get support from Christians unless they share their Christian principles. I will leave you with a serious matter to ponder: Do not jeopardize your relationship with God by becoming overly involved in politics and ignoring his word.

I remind you of the words of Jesus, which were spoken to Nicodemus: "Except a man be born again, he cannot see the kingdom of God." —John 3:3. Every word in the Bible screams out that it is impossible to divide our loyalty and obedience between God and man. The extent of our involvement in man's world depends on the situation. We cannot avoid being affected by worldly things, but we can make a decision about how they influence our lives. God has never, nor will he ever, turn a blind eye to sin, and he has made it clear through his word, what sin is.

Christianity is not a democracy or a representative republic; it is a dictatorship, and we do not have the privilege to debate the rules set forth by God the dictator. Even if we did, everything God does is perfect, fair, and just; there is no way to improve on his actions. Unlike earthly dictators, God is a benevolent and fair dictator, and living under his rule and reign provides the only means for man to have peace in his life while living on this earth.

> For they that are after the flesh do mind the things of the flesh; but they that are after the Spirit the things of the Spirit. For to be carnally minded is death; but to be spiritually minded is life and peace. Because the carnal mind is enmity against God: for it is not subject to the law of God, neither indeed can be. So then they that are in the flesh cannot please God. But ye are not in the flesh, but in the Spirit, if so be that the Spirit of God dwell in you. Now if any man have not the Spirit of Christ, he is none of his.
> —Romans 8:5–9

Do you have Christ on your mind when you wake up in the morning? Do you call on him to help get you through the rough spots of your everyday life? Do you rely on his guidance when faced with making decisions? The answers to those questions can determine whether we have the spirit of God in us. "Now if any man have not the Spirit of Christ, he is none of his." There are many ways for Christians to perform a self-test to keep check on our relationship with Christ. Following is an example: Suppose you enter the voting booth, and before you pull the lever or push a button, you ask yourself, would Jesus vote for this person. If you are a born-again Christian, that will be a consideration. The test comes when we must make a decision based on our conclusion about whether Jesus would make the same choice we wish to make. If you conclude, Jesus would not vote for the person you wish to vote for, what will you do. I will leave you to wrestle with that question as a means of testing yourself.

A Christian often is referred to as a follower of Christ, but Christianity is much more than that. It is arrogant to think we can imitate Jesus Christ. We have no power in ourselves, but if we are in him and he is in us, we are one with him and he is revealed through us. It is an awesome responsibility to be in partnership with the ruler of the universe and, before we present ourselves as such, we should be prepared to accept the responsibility. The reason many people are turned off by Christians is due to the behavior and actions of some—I call them Shakespearean Christians—who act as though they are something they are not: "Having a form of godliness, but denying the power thereof." —2 Timothy 3:5. Jesus Christ is not our buddy, or old pal, Christ is the ruler of the universe, and to forget that truth, is to forget who he is.

Satan at Work

The proclamation that America is the most powerful country in the world was a fact until about twenty to thirty years ago, but now our once-dominant economic power is a myth. Our military power is also diminishing due to misuse; we spend billions of dollars we cannot afford and waste the lives of thousands of America's best in wars we are not committed to win. America deploys thousands of our military people throughout the world to defend the borders of other countries, such as South Korea, but refuses to protect our own borders. That is insane. We cannot, or will not, guard our own borders and our dysfunctional immigration department is clueless about the number of our enemies that have come here illegally. If there is any effort to solve that problem, it is a well-kept secret. Everyone seems to focus on illegal Mexicans in our country, but they demonstrate very little concern for the number of potential enemies who have crossed our borders illegally. There are evil forces crouching in the shadows all over this country, but they will be ignored until another 9/11.   Only the supernatural influence of Satan could account for the upheaval now taking place in America and the world. For those familiar with God's word it is a clear as crystal what is taking place, and why. No one yet has come up with a more logical explanation for the chaos that is overtaking the whole world. It is all so surreal and unnatural, no other explanation makes any sense. For all who are looking for the Great Blessed Hope, keep watching and be prepared because our redemption is drawing nigh. God is giving sufficient warning to give everyone a chance to get prepared for the coming rains. When God shuts the door to those who have rejected him, they are lost.

Now Is the Time to Prepare

The time is at hand when we need to evaluate and reevaluate our relationship with Jesus Christ to ensure we are prepared for the rapture, or death, whichever comes first. If we are prepared for the rapture, we are also prepared for heaven and the mode of transportation to get us to heaven does not matter. In either event, we shall be with our Lord Jesus Christ and no longer concerned with man's world. What a comfort that is to contemplate. If any of you think this is all a fairytale, before you reject it outright, turn off your television, read the Bible, and learn the truth for yourself.

> The Lord is not slack concerning his promise, as some men count slackness; but is longsuffering to us-ward, not willing that any should perish, but that all should come to repentance.
> —2 Peter 3:9

We can count on those comforting words, but God has been longsuffering for a very long time. His plan has a conclusion, and it is staring us in the face. God could have ended this old world a long time ago, but he has given sufficient warning to all who are paying attention, and we are living in a unique time in the history of the world. Of course, you will never hear such talk from any politician and certainly not the press; unfortunately, you will not hear it in many churches either.

Everyone is aware that life on this earth will end, but most people choose to ignore it and live as if they will be the exception. Graveyards are filled with young people who thought they would live to a ripe old age. I had a younger brother with a bright future ahead of him who lost his life in a car accident a couple of weeks before his twenty-first birthday: although he is no longer here, I know what kind of person he would be if he were alive today. Those thoughts comfort me when I think about him. Tomorrow is promised to no one, and death is just around the corner for all of us. Our eternal souls will forever live somewhere, and that somewhere can be one of only two destinations. Reality always will defeat fantasy, but fantasy will never defeat reality. People are living in a fantasyland across the river and, sadly, some on this side are living in a fantasyland as well.

United We May Survive, Divided We Perish

As promised, there is hope, and it is time to explore it. What needs to be realized is that the opposition against this current administration is not against Obama, or any politician; our battle is against ourselves. We are a divided and polarized country, not only politically and socially, but also spiritually. We are in a civil war between ideologies and ethics. Ethics are stamped on the human heart by God, but guidance from the heart can be overpowered by guidance from a degenerate mind. The war is not a universal war, but a personal battle within us. The battle will be won when good triumphs over evil in our personal lives, regardless of the outcome of the war. Satan is the enemy, and I can assure you that we do not have the power to defeat him without Jesus Christ.

It will take a miracle to undo what has been done to America. We cannot perform miracles, but God can and does. If true Christians would separate themselves from the things of this world—forget about e-mail and concentrate on Knee-mail, pray constantly, and petition God to deliver us—miraculous things could happen. We not only would win the battle, we also would win the war. It would save our country and prove finally to those who are ignorant of him, who is in control of this earth. The power of the US government, or any other government, is impotent against the power of God.

You do not have to wait for someone to form a prayer committee; it took the faith of only one man for God to part the Red Sea, and God suspended time for a whole day to deliver his people from their enemies. My friends, he created the entire universe with a word; he is a God of miracles. Do not doubt for a minute that he could undo the mess we have made of this country very quickly. America itself is one of God's miracles, and he certainly would not turn his back on us if we had not turned our back on him.

> Again I say unto you, That if two of you shall agree on earth as touching anything that they shall ask, it shall be done for them of my Father which is in Heaven. For where two or three are gathered together in my name, there am I in the midst of them.
> —Matthew 18:19–20

God is our judge, but he is also a God of mercy and forgiveness. If we came to him in humble repentance as a united church and begged for his pardon, he would act. God knows sinful man is not going to turn to him, but Jesus Christ cares about his sheep and will protect them if they obey him. We must give God a reason to act on our behalf, in other words, we must first take action before we can expect God to take action.

One only has to look at the rest of the world to realize the uniqueness of America. The United States is set apart from the rest of the world because of the Judeo-Christian foundation on which it was established. World history is an open book that demonstrates the folly of countries that turned away from God to pursue their own selfish interests, and America today is on the brink of joining the has-beens if we fail to turn back to God.

At the same time I confess that there is a possibility America can be saved by God's intervention, I also confess that my personal feeling is that we have passed the point where God is willing to intervene in cleaning up the mess we have made. It is not a question of *if* God can save America, but *will* he. I have previously concluded we do not have much going for us in that regard. In addition, it is obvious from his word we are approaching the end-time. If we can agree, the end will come some day, why not now!

Walking with Jesus

If we have Christ in us, we should not attempt to lead him, but allow him to lead us and not burden him with hours fiddled away in front of a television. Christ is on the move, and unless we keep up with him, he soon will be out of sight and out of mind. The popular cliché, "What would Jesus do," is a question we should be asking many times a day. We always should strive to rise to the unattainable level of Christ, not try to bring him down to our level. Jesus Christ is the ruler of the universe and the master of all, and it should humble us to know that we can have a personal relationship with him. We cannot yet go to where he is, but he can come to where we are.

It is essential to have a personal relationship with Christ, but on his terms, not ours. Familiarity breeds contempt, and we should never lose sight of who Christ is. Believers are his sheep, and sheep follow their shepherd because they trust him and are obedient to his guidance. If you look at a herd of sheep, they all look the same, but a good shepherd recognizes his sheep and has names for each of them. He deals with them as individuals and not as a herd. If you put a hundred sheep in a field without a shepherd and one sheep begins to wander off, the other ninety-nine will follow. Man is the same way.

> Let as many servants as are under the yoke count their own masters worthy of all honour, that the name of God and his doctrine be not blasphemed. And they that have believing masters, let them not despise them, because they are brethren; but rather do them service, because they are faithful and beloved, partakers of the benefit. These things teach and exhort. If any man teach otherwise, and consent not to wholesome words, even the words of our Lord Jesus Christ, and to the doctrine which is according to godliness; He is proud, knowing nothing, but doting about questions and strifes of words, whereof cometh envy, strife, railings,

evil surmisings, Perverse disputings of men of corrupt minds, and destitute of the truth, supposing that gain is godliness: from such withdraw thyself.
—1 Timothy 6:1–5

One cannot transverse a muddy swamp and come out with clean feet; neither can one associate with sinful man without being influenced by it: "from such withdraw thyself." Those should be our watchwords, and we should avoid associating with those things that influence us away from the will of God. If you die in your sins, you may have long ago forgotten the things God will remind you of when you stand before him in judgment with your knees knocking together. It will be too late for remorse, and none of those people you associated with will help you because they will be in line behind you with their knees knocking. It is not always easy to be a born-again Christian today, but it was not easy for Christ to do what he did for us, and we should always strive to do what we can for him.

Then cometh Jesus with them unto a place called Gethsemane, and saith unto the disciples, Sit ye here, while I go and pray yonder. And he took with him Peter and the two sons of Zebedee, and began to be sorrowful and very heavy. Then saith he unto them, My soul is exceeding sorrowful, even unto death: tarry ye here, and watch with me. And he went a little further, and fell on his face, and prayed, saying, O my Father, if it be possible, let this cup pass from me: nevertheless not as I will, but as thou wilt. And he cometh unto the disciples, and findeth them asleep, and saith unto Peter, What, could ye not watch with me one hour? Watch and pray, that ye enter not into temptation: the spirit indeed is willing, but the flesh is weak. He went away again the second time, and prayed, saying, O my Father, if this cup may not pass away from me, except I drink it, thy will be done. And he came and found them asleep again: for their eyes were heavy. And he left them, and went away again, and prayed the third time, saying the same words.
—Matthew 26:36–44

It is beyond heartbreaking to contemplate what Jesus went through that night in the garden of Gethsemane. While he was sweating blood over the knowledge of every detail of what lay ahead of him, his disciples slept. However, you see they did not know what Jesus knew; they had been with him in person for three years without really knowing who he was. There are many Christians today in the same situation; they participate in all the Christian activities every time the doors of their churches open and may do so for their entire lives without ever knowing the real Jesus.

If we love him for what he did for us, we should, in our spirit, join him in that garden on our knees and share in his agony; share the pain of his scourging, bleed with him on the cross, then join him at the tomb and rejoice at his resurrection. Finally, we should engross ourselves in God's word and learn all we are able to about the one who paid the price for our salvation. That is what Christianity is all about; it is a serious matter and is not to be obscured by mingling it with worldly things.

The above verses from Mathew 16:36-44 can be used to support a subject previously discussed: the matter of repeating prayers. Jesus made the same prayer to the Father three times, and at that point, Jesus was alone and subject to man's evil. The only comfort for him was at the feet of his Father, who by the way also knew what his son was facing. When he returned to find the disciples sleeping, the only comfort to his agony was to return to the Father. He repeated his prayer three times, and if his captors had not arrived when they did, he probably would have repeated it again. Everyone has or will face a situation when there is no one in man's world to offer comfort to his agony. A Christian has Christ to go to and bow at his feet for comfort, love, and understanding. If it is his will for us to suffer to test our faith, we can endure it because we can rest assured that he will help us through it and a brighter day will come. The point is where does an unsaved person or a Shakespearean Christian go to find relief for their agony?

> Rejoice in the Lord alway: and again I say, Rejoice. Let your moderation be known unto all men. The Lord is at hand. Be careful for nothing; but in every thing by prayer and supplication with thanksgiving let your requests be made

177

known unto God. And the peace of God, which passeth all
understanding, shall keep your hearts and minds through
Christ Jesus.
—Philippians 4:4–7

Hope and Promise

God's world is a world of hope and promise that offers a sheltered abode for
anyone who accepts him. It is difficult indeed to understand why anyone would
choose to ignore the opportunity to abandon the bleakness of man's world and
bask in the sunlight of Jesus Christ. People are hurting and suffering, unaware
of the relief that is only a prayer away. Christians have failed miserably in
spreading the word of salvation to a lost world. There are churches today like
the Laodicean church depicted in Revelation 3:14–22. They have put a veil
around themselves to separate from the true Christian church, and they are
on the increase. It only demonstrates the great influence Satan has on every
aspect of American life.

Having the spirit of Christ in us will provide a gentle spirit as we climb the
ladder of life and are content to be the last to climb the ladder. Give up a bus
seat to someone standing; sit in the middle of seat of a crowded car; greet
everyone with a genuine smile. These are examples that are the opposite of our
normal carnal inclinations, but when we have Christ in us, our inclinations
will change from an "I want" person to an "I want to help" person. Such
change in our lives is a manifestation of the peace and contentment that God
promises, which defies human understanding. It is one of God's greatest
blessings and exceeds anything this world may provide. I offer a simple self-
test, to help you understand that you can, with very little effort, affect other
peoples' lives. The next time you are around other people, give a genuine smile
to every person you pass. Not everyone will return your smile, but you may
be amazed that most will. There are a lot of sad hurting people in this world,
and for some, a simple smile from a stranger, can lift their spirit.

We are each unique individuals, but we are all God's creations and are worthy
to be treated as such. Having a gentle spirit does not mean we are to accept
abuse from other people, but the way we act usually will determine how we
are treated. If we elbow our way to the head of a line, it will certainly offend

someone. However, if we step aside to allow someone to go ahead, we will make a friend rather than a potential enemy. Simple things in life often can have the greatest impact. While it is human nature to wish for a simple life, it is also human nature to complicate the simple.

> These six things doth the LORD hate: yea, seven are an abomination unto him: A proud look, a lying tongue, and hands that shed innocent blood, An heart that deviseth wicked imaginations, feet that be swift in running to mischief, A false witness that speaketh lies, and he that soweth discord among brethren.
> —Proverbs 6:16–19

God has the right to hate, but we are not given the same privilege. "Hate the sin but love the sinner" is a cliché that is not found in the Bible, but it may be inferred. We are to love everyone for *who* they are, God's creation, but nothing in God's word compel us to love *what* they are. It would be hypocritical to deny distain for the actions of some, such as the damage being done to America by very misguided people, who display nothing but hatred for this great country and all things Christian. We should have compassion and pity for any human being who lives apart from God.

Satan's Temptations

The closer we are to God, the more temptations Satan will put in our path. Satan has no reason to tempt the lost—they are already conquered—but he is in a battle with Christ for the souls of man. He has no chance to defeat Christ, but he can defeat us if he can isolate us from Christ's protection.

> Blessed is the man that endureth temptation: for when he is tried, he shall receive the crown of life, which the Lord hath promised to them that love him.
> —James 1:12

Satan uses temptation to look for any weakness in our faith, and the more we resist his temptation, the easier it becomes. Satan never gives up on those he has not conquered, and we must guard against his devious ways and face them head on. I discovered a long time ago that resisting Satan's temptations is a daily struggle; he never gives up, and we must not either.

> I wrote unto you in an epistle not to company with fornicators: Yet not altogether with the fornicators of this world, or with the covetous, or extortioners, or with idolaters; for then must ye needs go out of the world. But now I have written unto you not to keep company, if any man that is called a brother be a fornicator, or covetous, or an idolater, or a railer, or a drunkard, or an extortioner; with such an one no not to eat. For what have I to do to judge them also that are without? do not ye judge them that are within? But them that are without God judgeth. Therefore put away from among yourselves that wicked person.
> —1 Corinthians 5:9–13

How many Christians, and churches, are willing to adhere to those verses today? Are we to ignore those who damage the church because it would eject too many members? God will judge the world because the world does not know him or his word, but the church is judged by the adherence to his word. If you get nothing else from this book, realize that the scriptures in the Bible are not empty words. They are the words of God, and each is a message to believers. Whether you read them or not, they are still there and have meaning for how we are to live. Know the truth, and the truth will make you free; and the Bible is the only source for verifying the truth. If a church leader leads you astray, he will face his judgment, but you will be no less guilty for not knowing the truth. As previously stated, Christianity is not a religion; it is an individual relationship with Christ and, if you know nothing else, know him.

> If ye then be risen with Christ, seek those things which are above, where Christ sitteth on the right hand of God. Set your affection on things above, not on things on the earth. For ye are dead, and your life is hid with Christ in God. When Christ, who is our life, shall appear, then shall ye also appear with him in glory. Mortify therefore your members which are upon the earth; fornication, uncleanness,

inordinate affection, evil concupiscence, and covetousness, which is idolatry: For which things' sake the wrath of God cometh on the children of disobedience: In the which ye also walked some time, when ye lived in them. But now ye also put off all these; anger, wrath, malice, blasphemy, filthy communication out of your mouth. Lie not one to another, seeing that ye have put off the old man with his deeds; And have put on the new man, which is renewed in knowledge after the image of him that created him: Where there is neither Greek nor Jew, circumcision nor uncircumcision, Barbarian, Scythian, bond nor free: but Christ is all, and in all.

—Colossians 3:1–11

Covetousness and Idolatry

There are two subjects to deal with before we go further that are the most damaging, not just to the carnal man, but to Christians as well: idolatry and covetousness. It is easy to disregard them by misinterpreting what they mean. There are various definitions, but to keep things simple I will reduce them to the most basic interpretation. Are you envious of the new car your neighbor just bought or the big house your rich brother-in-law bought for your sister? I could go on and on with examples, but you get the point. We can flip the coin over to see another side: Did you buy a newer car or bigger house or bigger this or that just to empress your friends and neighbors. It is pride and covetousness, both of which God hates.

Most people think of an idol as some carved statute of ancient Rome or Greece. However, unless you have been lost in the wilderness for the past sixty years, you have in your home, the most cherished idol the world has ever known—television. God will not play a secondary role to sinful man; God must be first in our lives because it is the only position he will honor. The biggest threat to modern man's spiritual wellbeing is a desire for stuff. Most people are fanatically driven by the desire for more earthly stuff and are only comfortable when they are surrounded with more and more. It makes it difficult to concentrate on anything else, especially God. America has set itself up for all the earthly things people cherish to be taken away, to force them to focus away from earthly things and toward God.

Give yourself a little evaluation: Go through your house and mentally pick out everything you really need and put it in one room. Put all the things you want but do not really need in the other rooms. I predict that the want pile will be larger than the need pile. It is not necessity that drives us to fill our lives with stuff; it is pride, vanity, and a wanting nature. It creates obstacles between God and ourselves; the fewer things of man's world we have in our lives, the more we can focus on God.

> And if thine eye offend thee, pluck it out: it is better for thee
> to enter into the kingdom of God with one eye, than having
> two eyes to be cast into hell fire: Where their worm dieth
> not, and the fire is not quenched.
> —Mark 9:47–48

Food that goes in the mouth goes to the stomach, is processed, and provides nourishment to the body. We can become sick or even die from what we put in our mouths. Similarly, what goes through the eye goes to the brain, processed, and guides our life: garbage in, garbage out. Television produces more garbage than all the restaurants in the world combined, and if you think it does not influence your life, you are kidding yourself. If you disagree with me, I offer you a challenge if you have the willpower: Abstain from watching television for just one week and expose yourself to the real world, and you will realize the hideous nature of television and your addiction to it.

I am not implying you should get rid of your television if it does not interfere with your walk with God, and that is possible if you are vigilant about what you watch. However, if it interferes with your spiritual life, and I can assure you it will unless you manage what you and your family are exposed to, you need to pull the plug. If you have any doubt that watching television is an addiction, pull the plug and see how little time passes before you plug it back in. The television is not addictive, but what is on the screen and is absorbed by the brain that influences our lives. Millions of people, some of them Christians, could instantly name at least six or seven winners of *American Idol* or the same number of NFL players. However, they could not name more than four disciples of Jesus if their lives depended on it, and it very well could.

The Great Commandment

> Then one of them, which was a lawyer, asked him a question, tempting him, and saying, Master, which *is* the great commandment in the law? Jesus said unto him, Thou shalt love the Lord thy God with all thy heart, and with all thy soul, and with all thy mind. This is the first and great commandment. And the second is like unto it, Thou shalt love thy neighbour as thyself. On these two commandments hang all the law and the prophets.
> —Matthew 22:35–40

The first and great commandment—"Thou shalt love the Lord thy God with all thy heart, and with all thy soul, and with all thy mind"—is perhaps the most violated of God's commandments. There is no substitute for this commandment; if we love God with heart, mind, and soul, there will be no period in our lives when we are not thinking of him and are fully aware of his presence. For most people, if they think of God at all, it is usually the last resort after all else fails. God is not an entity on standby waiting for us to focus on him when we feel like it; we may not be focused on him, but there is not a millisecond that he is not focused on us. The second commandment is "Thou shalt love thy neighbour as thyself." These two commandments are not just part of the law of the Old Testament but are handed down by Jesus Christ and are applicable to everyone.

Pray for America and Israel

I believe my feelings for America are shared by most of you, but never forget that God is in control. Those of us who have him in our lives need not be concerned about what happens to America; however, for the sake of our children and grandchildren, and for ourselves, we should be prepared to call on God to save our great country, if it is his will. There is no other way to reverse the direction this country is heading except for our God of mercy and forgiveness to intervene. However, we must not get so involved in what is going on in America that we neglect to secure our relationship with Christ; after all, we cannot help the country if we fail to help ourselves.

If you are a born-again Christian or Jewish, do not let a day pass that you do not pray for America and for Israel. Our fates are closely linked, and our survival is dependent not on the government but on the will of Almighty God. Our current government officials have abandoned our Judeo-Christian heritage, and they appear to be about to abandon Israel; they do not care about either country. God will take care of those who love him and, if we make ourselves worthy, we will witness his mighty power at work in our lands. For anyone that does not have a personal relationship with him, he is only a prayer away; all you have to do is open your heart and mind to him, and he will change your life forever.

Narrow Is the Way

There is nothing across the river that can compare to becoming a child of God and, I must repeat, we cannot live on both sides of the river; we must let go of one or the other. If you cannot let go of man's world, it is a rebuke against God to pretend to live in his world when your heart is somewhere else. It will not be an easy decision for some to make, but do not have any fear. If this side of the river is your choice, there are plenty of people over here to walk with you, love you, and welcome you into their family.

> Therefore all things whatsoever ye would that men should do to you, do ye even so to them: for this is the law and the prophets. Enter ye in at the strait gate: for wide is the gate, and broad is the way, that leadeth to destruction, and many there be which go in thereat: Because strait is the gate, and narrow is the way, which leadeth unto life, and few there be that find it.
> —Matthew 7:12–14

The words in the above verses transcend any lack of intelligence in revealing one of the most profound passages in scripture. The road leading from the bridge on this side of the river is narrow with an unknown length, but at its end is the promise of salvation—"few there be that find it." Any other road leads to destruction: "many there be which go in thereat." It would be frivolous to speculate on how many "a few" represents, but we do know that a few is the opposite of many and can deduce that only a few of the earth's inhabitants will enter the kingdom of God. Are you among the few? I certainly hope so; those who remain on the straight and narrow road and focused on the Great Blessed Hope will receive their reward for perseverance.

> And as it was in the days of Noe, so shall it be also in the days of the Son of man. They did eat, they drank, they married wives, they were given in marriage, until the day that Noe entered into the ark, and the flood came, and destroyed them all. Likewise also as it was in the days of Lot; they did eat, they drank, they bought, they sold, they planted, they builded; But the same day that Lot went out of Sodom it rained fire and brimstone from heaven, and destroyed them all. Even thus shall it be in the day when the Son of man is revealed.
> —Luke 17:26–30

The above verses aroused a curiosity in me I could not ignore without seeking something other than what is obvious. Today we eat, drink, marry, build, buy, sell, and plant, and there is nothing wrong with that. The problem in Noah's day people were living strictly in man's world and took no interest in the old man who was building some sort of floating device because he believed the world was going to be covered with water. "And as it was in the days of Noe, so shall it be also in the days of the Son of man." We know that only eight people were saved during the flood, and it would be interesting to know how many people were on the earth at the time so I began research to see if perhaps it could be known. After hours of research to determine when the great flood occurred and what the world's population was at the time, I realized it was fruitless to try to obtain any consensus from the so-called experts. Their opinions varied by thousands of years as to the date of the flood, and from less than a million to over a billion people alive at the time.

Since it was all speculation anyway, I did discover some statistics I could accept; I refer you to an article: *The Date of Noah's Flood,* published in 1981.

Based on what appears to be the result of thorough research by Dr. J. Osgood, I estimated the year of the flood as approximately 2304 BC. If you have access to the internet, enter the name, Dr. J. Osgood, in your URL address window. Scroll down to the bottom of the page to find Dr. Osgood's article. Using that date and information from the *Atlas of World Population History* (Viking, 1978) by Colin McEvedy and Richard Jones, I estimated the world population at the time of the flood was approximately 23 million people. These statistics do not mean much until we compare them to what we do know: only eight people were saved from the flood. Even if there were only a million people on earth at the time of the flood, for each one saved, 125,000 were lost. If we accept the figure of 23 million people, for each one saved, 2,875,000 were lost.

Assuming God would not destroy righteous people, common sense dictates that if there were a billion people on earth at the time of the flood, they could not all know about Noah's ark. CNN did not exist then. It is, however, reasonable to assume that a million people, or even 23 million people, could have learned about Noah's efforts to build an ark since he worked on it for more than a hundred years. Using the same ratio of people saved to those lost during the flood, if the rapture occurred today, only 53,600 people worldwide would be caught up in it. That is a ridiculously low number, and it may be equally ridiculous to consider it as anything other than wild speculation, but I am not willing to dismiss it outright either. It certainly falls within the realm of the few referred to by Jesus. Given the direction the world is heading today, unless the rapture occurs soon, such a low number may not seem so ridiculous. If you are a statistics seeker, visit the website: www.religioustolerance.org/worldrel.htm. However, I advise you to view all statistics with skepticism. According to the *World Christian Encyclopedia*, 2002, almost 2 billion people worldwide claim to be Christians, but I do not consider it any more ridiculous to believe that only 53,600 will be taken up in the rapture than to believe 2 billion will. Here is the relevant question: if you knew that only 53,600 people would be caught up in the rapture of the church, how would it change your life? I dare say you probably would be more focused on this side of the river. The important thing is whether there are a few thousand, or a couple billion caught up in the rapture, it has no relevance unless we are among the few.

Is the world any less wicked today than it was in the days of Noah or Lot? Are people today paying any more attention to warnings from God than they did in the days of Noah? Does God have any less reason to destroy the world today than he did in the days of Noah? I will leave you to answer those questions for yourself; my answer is a resounding no! I do not arrive at my conclusion based on statistics but on observations. My observations of the world around me leads me to believe there are millions of people in the world who do not understand what a Christian is, even though they proclaim to be one. When it comes to being a born-again Christian, ignorance abounds, and only those seeking the path to the kingdom of God will find it..

Again, I will delve into speculation to make another point. During the hundred-plus years it took Noah to build the ark, is it unreasonable to believe that at least some of the people adopted the wait-and-see attitude, much as people are doing today. In other words, if it did indeed begin to rain, then the skeptics would climb aboard the ark.

> And they that went in, went in male and female of all flesh,
> as God had commanded him: and the LORD shut him in.
> —Genesis 7:16

After all was aboard that was going aboard, the door to the ark was shut, not by Noah, but by God.

> And it came to pass after seven days, that the waters of the
> flood were upon the earth.
> —Genesis 7:10

Why did God delay the beginning of the rain for seven days? Perhaps the answer is found in the following verse.

> The Lord is not slack concerning his promise, as some
> men count slackness; but is longsuffering to us-ward, not
> willing that any should perish, but that all should come to
> repentance.
> —2 Peter 3:9

There is no evidence that during the seven days that God delayed the rain that anyone attempted to gain entry into the ark. Although the Bible does not say so, I suspect you will agree there were probably many people trying without success to cling onto the sides of the ark as the water began to rise, begging Noah to let them enter the Ark. Nevertheless, God had shut the door to the ark, and they were not to be reopened once the rain began. The rebellious world is facing the same situation today; evidence of the coming rains is everywhere, but just as in the days of Noah, few are aware of it.

The Great Blessed Hope

The nourishment for the soul of a Christian is the promise of the rapture of the church, and it has been so for almost two thousand years. Anyone familiar with God's word can discern that we are the generation to witness the Great Blessed Hope fulfilled.

> But I would not have you to be ignorant, brethren, concerning them which are asleep, that ye sorrow not, even as others which have no hope. For if we believe that Jesus died and rose again, even so them also which sleep in Jesus will God bring with him. For this we say unto you by the word of the Lord, that we which are alive and remain unto the coming of the Lord shall not prevent them which are asleep. For the Lord himself shall descend from Heaven with a shout, with the voice of the archangel, and with the trump of God: and the dead in Christ shall rise first: Then we which are alive and remain shall be caught up together with them in the clouds, to meet the Lord in the air: and so shall we ever be with the Lord. Wherefore comfort one another with these words.
> —1 Thessalonians 4:13–18

I will take an aside here to address one of the frivolous things that sinful man cannot avoid pouncing on as if he has discovered something to discredit the Bible, and that is the word "rapture." It is true the word rapture does not appear in the Bible and neither does the word Bible. The Greek word *harpazo* used in the original New Testament transcripts means "caught up" or "snatched away," and it is translated that way in our English Bible, as in the above verses. The Latin Vulgate translates the Greek word *harpazo* into the Latin word *rapio*, and from that word, we get the commonly used English word "rapture." It is beyond the scope of this book to explore all things that will come to the earth after the rapture of the church. If we are true born-again Christians we need not be concerned because we will be taken out of this world before the tribulation period begins.

> "that we which are alive and remain unto the coming of the Lord shall not prevent them which are asleep. For the Lord himself shall descend from Heaven with a shout, with the voice of the archangel, and with the trump of God: and the dead in Christ shall rise first: Then we which are alive and remain shall be caught up together with them in the clouds, to meet the Lord in the air: and so shall we ever be with the Lord. Wherefore comfort one another with these words."

That is the Great Blessed Hope for a Christian, and we are to live for, look for, and prepare for that coming event. However, it does not give us leave to sit with our hands in our laps, staring at the ceiling. We are to carry on with doing the work of spreading the Gospel of Jesus Christ to an unsaved world so that everyone within it also may share the Great Blessed Hope.

While doing research to determine how many professing Christians are in America, I was dumbfounded by the diversity of statistics and opinions. However, as before, I have pieced together the best estimate from the hodgepodge of statistics to further the discussion about the apparent confusion about what is a Christian. An estimated 173 million American adults claim the title of Christian, but only about 47 million claim to be born again. If the purpose of being a Christian is anything other than partaking of the promise of spending eternity in the kingdom of God, then what is the purpose?

I do not claim to know everything in the Bible, but I have failed to identify what could be classified as a non-born again Christian. If those statics are anywhere near being accurate, they beg for an answer to this question: Is there some other way to gain entry into the kingdom of God aside from being born again? Evidently, there is great confusion about what a Christian is, especially a born-again Christian. Perhaps I am the one who is confused, but I can only rely on God's word for the truth. My understanding is that being a Christian means having a *personal* relationship with Jesus Christ—not a sometime relationship but an everlasting, day-by-day, ever-conscious awareness of his presence and a reliance on him to guide our lives.

> And be not conformed to this world: but be ye transformed
> by the renewing of your mind, that ye may prove what *is* that
> good, and acceptable, and perfect, will of God.
> —Romans 12:2

Many of us have read these words many times: "prove what is that good, and acceptable, and perfect, will of God." However, do they have any impact? Do our daily lives genuinely prove we have the spirit of God living in us, or is it all play-acting?

I have previously mentioned that there are people who spend their lives reading and studying the Bible without ever coming to the knowledge of Jesus Christ, and the following verses bear it out:

> But I have greater witness than that of John: for the works
> which the Father hath given me to finish, the same works
> that I do, bear witness of me, that the Father hath sent me.
> And the Father himself, which hath sent me, hath borne
> witness of me. Ye have neither heard his voice at any time,
> nor seen his shape. And ye have not his word abiding in
> you: for whom he hath sent, him ye believe not. Search the
> scriptures; for in them ye think ye have eternal life: and they
> are they which testify of me. And ye will not come to me,
> that ye might have life. I receive not honour from men. But
> I know you, that ye have not the love of God in you. I am
> come in my Father's name, and ye receive me not: if another
> shall come in his own name, him ye will receive. How can
> ye believe, which receive honour one of another, and seek
> not the honour that cometh from God only?

—John 5:36–44

If we are not predisposed to find Jesus Christ in the Bible, then we search in vain. "Search the scriptures; for in them ye think ye have eternal life" is a strange and confusing statement until it is carefully analyzed. What scripture is referred to here? Obviously, it is the Old Testament; the New Testament did not exist yet. People looked to the law for salvation, not realizing the source of salvation is revealed throughout the Bible in the person of Jesus Christ—The Messiah. People at that time did not realize it, and majority of people today share the same ignorance. When Jesus said we must be born again, it was not a mere suggestion; no corruptible thing will ever be allowed in the kingdom of God. Search the scriptures as you might, there are no loopholes or alternatives to salvation other than through Jesus Christ. Only then, after we shed the corruption of the carnal man, can we be reborn through his spirit.

The New Man

> There is therefore now no condemnation to them which are in Christ Jesus, who walk not after the flesh, but after the Spirit. For the law of the Spirit of life in Christ Jesus hath made me free from the law of sin and death. For what the law could not do, in that it was weak through the flesh, God sending his own Son in the likeness of sinful flesh, and for sin, condemned sin in the flesh: That the righteousness of the law might be fulfilled in us, who walk not after the flesh, but after the Spirit. For they that are after the flesh do mind the things of the flesh; but they that are after the Spirit the things of the Spirit. For to be carnally minded is death; but to be spiritually minded is life and peace. Because the carnal mind is enmity against God: for it is not subject to the law of God, neither indeed can be. So then they that are in the flesh cannot please God. But ye are not in the flesh, but in the Spirit, if so be that the Spirit of God dwell in you. Now if any man have not the Spirit of Christ, he is none of his.
> —Romans 8:1–9

But now ye also put off all these; anger, wrath, malice, blasphemy, filthy communication out of your mouth. Lie not one to another, seeing that ye have put off the old man with his deeds; And have put on the new man, which is renewed in knowledge after the image of him that created him: Where there is neither Greek nor Jew, circumcision nor uncircumcision, Barbarian, Scythian, bond nor free: but Christ is all, and in all.
—Colossians 3:8–11

As obedient children, not fashioning yourselves according to the former lusts in your ignorance: But as he which hath called you is holy, so be ye holy in all manner of conversation; Because it is written, Be ye holy; for I am holy. And if ye call on the Father, who without respect of persons judgeth according to every man's work, pass the time of your sojourning here in fear: Forasmuch as ye know that ye were not redeemed with corruptible things, as silver and gold, from your vain conversation received by tradition from your fathers;
—1 Peter 1:14–18

But sanctify the Lord God in your hearts: and be ready always to give an answer to every man that asketh you a reason of the hope that is in you with meekness and fear:
—1 Peter 3:15

These verses give a glimpse of what it means to be born again.

The Tribulation Period

The tribulation begins after the rapture, when Christ will remove his church from the earth in order to deliver it from the coming troubles. I would like to refer you to the back cover of this book. In my remarks there, I said there was a mystery hidden in the metaphor and it would be revealed along our journey. I warned that the bridge across the river could collapse and from that, we will solve the mystery. The bridge *will* collapse, and it represents the rapture of the church, after which, there will be no passage across the river. Those undecided that remained on the bridge represent those that have died unsaved. Those living on the sunny side of the river will be caught away in the rapture, and those on the other side of the river will face the Antichrist and the great tribulation period.

> Now we beseech you, brethren, by the coming of our Lord Jesus Christ, and by our gathering together unto him, That ye be not soon shaken in mind, or be troubled, neither by spirit, nor by word, nor by letter as from us, as that the day of Christ is at hand. "Who opposeth and exalteth himself above all that is called God, or that is worshipped; so that he as God sitteth in the temple of God, shewing himself that he is God. Remember ye not, that, when I was yet with you, I told you these things? And now ye know what withholdeth that he might be revealed in his time. For the mystery of iniquity doth already work: only he who now letteth will let, until he be taken out of the way. And then shall that Wicked be revealed, whom the Lord shall consume with the spirit of his mouth, and shall destroy with the brightness of his coming: Even him, whose coming is after the working of Satan with all power and signs and lying wonders, And with all deceivableness of unrighteousness in them that perish; because they received not the love of the truth, that they might be saved. And for this cause God shall send them strong delusion, that they should believe a lie: That they all might be damned who believed not the truth, but had pleasure in unrighteousness. But we are bound to give thanks always to God for you, brethren beloved of the Lord, because God hath from the beginning chosen you to salvation through sanctification of the Spirit and belief of the truth: Whereunto he called you by our gospel, to the obtaining of the glory of our Lord Jesus Christ. Therefore, brethren, stand fast, and hold the traditions which ye have been taught, whether by word, or our epistle. Now our Lord Jesus Christ himself, and God, even our Father, which hath

loved us, and hath given us everlasting consolation and good
hope through grace, Comfort your hearts, and establish you
in every good word and work.
—2 Thessalonians 2:1–17

Sometime after the church is removed from the earth, the Antichrist will be revealed: "Who opposeth and exalteth himself above all that is called God, or that is worshipped; so that he as God sitteth in the temple of God, shewing himself that he is God." You may be curious to know how the Antichrist will appear seemingly from nowhere, but he could very well be walking the earth today but he will not be revealed until after the rapture: "only he who now letteth will let, until he be taken out of the way. And then shall that Wicked be revealed..." This is a curious statement, but it refers to the Holy Spirit: "he who now letteth will let ..." Today the power of Satan is restrained by the Holy Spirit, who restricts Satan's power. At the rapture: the Holy Spirit will be taken out of the way for a while, and Satan no longer will be restrained by him, "until he be taken out of the way." The Antichrist will be revealed, and the full force of the unrestrained power of Satan will be released upon the earth's inhabitants.

During the first half of the tribulation, the Antichrist will present himself as a peacemaker, convince the world that he has solutions for all man's troubles, and gain control over all the earth. There will be a global government and false global religion supporting the Antichrist, and together they will deceive the world. The Antichrist will make a covenant with Israel to bring peace to that country, but after three and a half years, he will break that covenant. This will be Satan's moment; since his existence, he has looked forward to this time when he would be set free to implement his demonic agenda. People will believe the lies and deceptions of the Antichrist until the end of the first three and a half years, when his true nature will be revealed.

In almost every generation, there are people who try to identify the Antichrist as some great leader of their time. Some today identify President Obama as the Antichrist, but that cannot be, for many reasons. Although President Obama is good at deceiving people and making promises that will never materialize, he is sorely lacking in leadership abilities, something at which the

Antichrist will excel. In addition, the Antichrist will not be revealed until after the rapture of the church. In the beginning, the Antichrist will mesmerize the world with his lies and deceptions and convince them that only he has the solutions to all of man's problems. He will have the ability to perform wonders that will convince them of his abilities. He will have an answer for everything, including a logical reason for explaining away the rapture of the church. People will be completely under his influence and control, becoming comfortable in the perceived peace and stability he will bring to the world. Once he has entrapped the people, death and destruction will follow during the last three and half years.

If you are among those who do not believe in the rapture of the church, but if it occurs, then you will turn to God, that is a very dangerous thing for you to do for many reasons:

> "And with all deceivableness of unrighteousness in them that perish; because they received not the love of the truth, that they might be saved. And for this cause God shall send them strong delusion, that they should believe a lie: That they all might be damned who believed not the truth, but had pleasure in unrighteousness."

If a person rejects God outright before the rapture of the church, he will be under a strong delusion that causes him to believe a lie and reject God again after the rapture. This subject is debated by the learned and unlearned alike. You can adopt whatever opinion you wish and find those who will agree with you and those who disagree. I learned a long time ago that if we overcomplicate God's word, it will interfere with our learning. There is only one relevant point to make from these scriptures: You do not want to be on the earth after the rapture of the church.

If we are true born-again Christians, secure in our salvation, we are prepared for heaven whether we go there by way of physical death or the rapture. That is the bottom line of the entire Bible. No book, movie, TV program, or any other form of communication can begin to describe the terrible devastation that will come to this earth during the last three and half years of the great tribulation, so concentrate on how to avoid it rather than on the details of something you do not want to experience. That is the reason Christ will remove his church before these terrible events begin, and he invites you to come along.

The extent of the wrath of God poured out on this earth during the tribulation is explained in the book of Revelation and is too enormous to cover in this book, but we can explore a few items:

> And there were voices, and thunders, and lightnings; and there was a great earthquake, such as was not since men were upon the earth, so mighty an earthquake, and so great. And the great city was divided into three parts, and the cities of the nations fell: and great Babylon came in remembrance before God, to give unto her the cup of the wine of the fierceness of his wrath. And every island fled away, and the mountains were not found. And there fell upon men a great hail out of heaven, every stone about the weight of a talent: and men blasphemed God because of the plague of the hail; for the plague thereof was exceeding great.
> —Revelation 16:18–21

The National Geographic News reported in 2003 that the largest hailstone ever recorded in America was found in Aurora, Nebraska, on June 22, 2003; it measured seven inches in diameter and weighed less than two pounds. The hailstones referenced in the above verses weigh a talent; the weight of a Greek talent is fifty-six pounds. Just imagine the damage such hailstones would do.

> And there went out another horse that was red: and power was given to him that sat thereon to take peace from the earth, and that they should kill one another: and there was given unto him a great sword.
> —Revelation 6:4

The peace the Antichrist brings to the earth will be short-lived (three and a half years); the red horse represents war; the nations will be at war against each other, and many will die; but it does not end there.

> And when he had opened the third seal, I heard the third beast say, Come and see. And I beheld, and lo a black horse; and he that sat on him had a pair of balances in his hand. And I heard a voice in the midst of the four beasts say, A measure of wheat for a penny, and three measures of barley for a penny; and see thou hurt not the oil and the wine.
> —Revelation 6:5–7

The black horse represents famine, and it will be worldwide; any available food will be so expensive the average person will do a day's work for a loaf of bread. Many will die of starvation, but much more death will come:

> And when he had opened the fourth seal, I heard the voice of the fourth beast say, Come and see. And I looked, and behold a pale horse: and his name that sat on him was Death, and Hell followed with him. And power was given unto them over the fourth part of the earth, to kill with sword, and with hunger, and with death, and with the beasts of the earth.
> —Revelation 6:7–8

The rider of the pale horse represents pestilence that will kill a fourth of the world's population; excluding the number of people removed in the rapture and those who will have already died, an even greater number will die under this plague. We could go on, but perhaps we have covered enough to convince you that being on this earth during the great tribulation is something you do not want to experience.

> And after these things I saw four angels standing on the four corners of the earth, holding the four winds of the earth, that the wind should not blow on the earth, nor on the sea, nor on any tree. And I saw another angel ascending from the

east, having the seal of the living God: and he cried with a
loud voice to the four angels, to whom it was given to hurt
the earth and the sea, Saying, Hurt not the earth, neither the
sea, nor the trees, till we have sealed the servants of our God
in their foreheads. And I heard the number of them which
were sealed: and there were sealed an hundred and forty and
four thousand of all the tribes of the children of Israel.
—Revelation 7:1–4

If one studies Jewish history, it is clear that only God's protection has
prevented the total annihilation of the Jewish race. Here we see where God
seals (protects) 144,000 Jews—12,000 from each of the twelve tribes—to
survive the tribulation and preach the Gospel, and many people will be
saved. It is not possible for a true Christian to be an anti-Semite, and when
Christians are removed in the rapture, no one will be left to give support to
Jews. Anti-Semitism will dominate the world, and all nations will not only
turn against the Jews but also encourage their annihilation.

Then they will deliver you to tribulation, and will kill you,
and you will be hated by all nations because of My name.
At that time many will fall away and will betray one another
and hate one another. Many false prophets will arise and
will mislead many. Because lawlessness is increased, most
people's love will grow cold. But the one who endures to the
end, he will be saved. This gospel of the kingdom shall be
preached in the whole world as a testimony to all the nations,
and then the end will come.
—Matthew 24:9–14

Jesus is referring to the Jews that are on the earth during the tribulation
period.

After this I beheld, and, lo, a great multitude, which no man
could number, of all nations, and kindreds, and people,
and tongues, stood before the throne, and before the Lamb,
clothed with white robes, and palms in their hands; And

cried with a loud voice, saying, Salvation to our God which
sitteth upon the throne, and unto the Lamb. "And all the
angels stood round about the throne, and about the elders
and the four beasts, and fell before the throne on their faces,
and worshipped God, Saying, Amen: Blessing, and glory,
and wisdom, and thanksgiving, and honour, and power, and
might, be unto our God forever and ever. Amen.
—Revelation 7:9–12

Remember a few pages back I speculated that there would not be nearly as
many people taken up in the rapture as many think. Consider this: "After
this I beheld, and, lo, a great multitude, which no man could number, of all
nations, and kindreds, and people, and tongues, stood before the throne, and
before the Lamb." The question is who makes up this multitude of people?
If a hundred theologians were tasked to answer that question, the result
probably would be at least eighty different answers. My research has failed
to find a definitive answer to that question, but I have my own theory; keep
in mind it is only speculation. Remember these words from 2 Thessalonians:
"And for this cause God shall send them strong delusion, that they should
believe a lie: That they all might be damned who believed not the truth, but
had pleasure in unrighteousness." I believe the people referred to here are
those who rejected Jesus Chris before the rapture of the church; and after the
rapture, Jesus will send a strong illusion that causes them to believe a lie from
the Antichrist and continue to reject Jesus. So, if we exclude all who reject
Christ before the rapture, all born-again Christians caught up in the rapture,
and those who hear the Gospel for the first time—who is left to accept Christ
during the great tribulation? I think we can agree that God will not condemn
those who have never heard the Gospel or do not know of Jesus Christ. Given
worldwide evangelism today, I do not believe there are great multitudes who
have never heard about Jesus Christ. I have referred many times to what I call
Shakespearean Christians, and it is my belief that they will miss the rapture
and make up the bulk of the great multitude that will become born again
during the great tribulation.

Shakespearean Christians are those who have not rejected Jesus Christ outright
but have not lived for him either and will not be taken in the rapture. They

may accept John 3:16 but fail to live according to John 3:3 by being born again. Where we fit in this scenario depends on our understanding of what it means to be born again. I think it is clear that unless we are born again, we will miss the rapture. The subject is far too serious to be taken lightly; we are free today to choose to live for Jesus or not. During the great tribulation period, to choose Jesus and reject the Antichrist probably will cost you your life. For those who accept the mark of the beast, and pledge their allegiance to the Antichrist, there will be no chance to reverse their decision, and they will be condemned to hell.

This brings up another topic: the subject of "once saved, always saved." For at least the past fifteen years, I have been troubled by the fact that many Christian churches adhere to this doctrine; personally, I cannot accept it. We have previously discussed the fact that there are verses that support either point of view, but taken as a whole from throughout the Bible, it does not appear to be consistent with the theme of salvation: "narrow is the way, which leadeth unto life, and few there be that find it." —Mathew 7:14. Statements such as this, coupled with others, should not be ignored: "But the one who endures to the end, he will be saved."—Mathew 24:13. What are we to endure to the end if we cannot lose our salvation? "after this I beheld, and, lo, a great multitude, which no man could number, of all nations, and kindreds, and people, and tongues, stood before the throne, and before the Lamb, clothed with white robes, and palms in their hands;" —Revelation 7:9. Will this multitude include those who believe once saved, always saved? I do not know, but it is possible. Do you really think because we profess John 3:16, Satan will add us to a list of untouchables? However, I believe the relevant question is not whether we can lose our salvation, but whether we are truly saved—"My sheep hear my voice, and I know them, and they follow me: and I give unto them eternal life; and they shall never perish, and no one shall snatch them out of my hand." —John 10:27. This verse is often quoted to support the belief of once saved, always saved. Let us look at the crucial elements: "they follow me" and "no one shall snatch them out of my hand." What if we fail to follow him, remove ourselves from his fold, and wander off into man's world? I have previously written that *we* cannot stamp "Saved" on our forehead and continue to live in man's world.

However, when Christ determines we are saved *he* will stamp "Saved" on our forehead, which means we belong to him and, "no one shall snatch them out of my hand." Therefore, we must strive daily toward receiving that stamp of approval and never arrive at the point where *we* think we have achieved it. I am sure many will disagree with the opinion presented here, but it is what I believe and before you dismiss it outright, I hope you will give it careful consideration.

I am not qualified to offer a theological debate on the subject of once saved, always saved, and I do not attempt to persuade you to accept my point of view. We are talking about our eternal destiny, and it would be foolish not to give the subject the attention it deserves. It is ultimately between you and God; I will share with you how I deal with the subject, and let it go at that. I would rather believe it is possible to lose our salvation and be wrong than believe we cannot lose our salvation and be wrong. My conclusion is to thank God for my salvation and to try to live my life as if I can lose it.

There is no book in the Bible that is debated more often by the learned and unlearned alike than the book of Revelation, but it is not as mysterious as many think. However, it does require preparation if it is to be clearly understood. One, who does not understand the preceding sixty-five books of the Bible will not understand the book of Revelation. If you are familiar with all of the other books in the Bible and allow the book of Revelation to speak for itself, it is not difficult to understand. The book of Revelation was written primarily for the Jews, and they have the background to understand it. The Christian church is not mentioned after chapter 3, because the church will not be on the earth because it will be caught away in the rapture. If you plan to be here following the rapture of the church, you should familiarize yourself with the book of Revelation to understand what is in store for you.

When the Antichrist comes upon the scene, there will be no doubt who he is. We have a perfect example, even though it is a miniscule one, of how the Antichrist will gain control of the world. Does it not border on miraculous, the speed at which this current administration has fundamentally changed the United States of America? President Obama's agenda—if brought to fruition, will do more damage to this country than did FDR, Herbert Hoover,

Richard Nixon, Jimmy Carter, Bill Clinton, and George Bush, combined. If this current administration accomplishes what it has planned for us, it will take many more than a dozen years to recover. Millions are captivated by the president, without any idea of his agenda. However, those of us not living in a fantasy world will survive. I receive no pleasure from harshly criticizing our President. For seventy years, this beloved country has been my home, and now it is being taken from my children and grandchildren. Not only is it our right to criticize our leaders, when warranted, it is our obligation to do so. My passion for America has driven me off course, but I will not retract what I have written, but I will get back on course.

If we consider the above paragraph, and, multiply it by a hundred, it will give some idea of the effect the Antichrist will have on this world. He will display supernatural powers and intelligence not seen on this earth since Jesus ascended into heaven. He will convince people that he is, in fact, God.

Many are deceived by America's current administration, and if you can so easily be deceived by such a group of amateurs, what chance will you have to resist the influence of the Antichrist? When he does gain power, he will bring unimaginable destruction to the inhabitants of the earth.

> For then shall be great tribulation, such as was not since the beginning of the world to this time, no, nor ever shall be. And except those days should be shortened, there should no flesh be saved: but for the elect's sake those days shall be shortened.
> —Matthew 24:21–22

Mark of the Beast

> And I beheld another beast coming up out of the earth; and he had two horns like a lamb, and he spake as a dragon. And he exerciseth all the power of the first beast before him, and causeth the earth and them which dwell therein to worship the first beast, whose deadly wound was healed. And he doeth great wonders, so that he maketh fire come down from heaven on the earth in the sight of men, And deceiveth them

that dwell on the earth by the means of those miracles which he had power to do in the sight of the beast; saying to them that dwell on the earth, that they should make an image to the beast, which had the wound by a sword, and did live. And he had power to give life unto the image of the beast, that the image of the beast should both speak, and cause that as many as would not worship the image of the beast should be killed. And he causeth all, both small and great, rich and poor, free and bond, to receive a mark in their right hand, or in their foreheads: And that no man might buy or sell, save he that had the mark, or the name of the beast, or the number of his name.

—Revelation 13:11–17

Is that the kind of life to which you want to be exposed? There always has been evil in the world, and we can witness it around us today. However, it is nothing compared to the evil Satan brings to the earth after the rapture of the church when the restraints of the Holy Spirit are removed. People alive today have the opportunity to accept Jesus Christ as the Lord of their life; yet most people reject him. If people refuse to accept Jesus today, who expects that they will accept him during the tribulation, when it will probably cost them their lives to do so?

The Second Coming of Christ

The Second Coming of Christ is not to be confused with the rapture of the church. At his second coming, Christ will return to the earth with his saints to defeat Satan and his followers, end the tribulation period, and establish a millennium of peace on the earth.

And I saw heaven opened, and behold a white horse; and he that sat upon him was called Faithful and True, and in righteousness he doth judge and make war. His eyes were as a flame of fire, and on his head were many crowns; and he had a name written, that no man knew, but he himself. And he was clothed with a vesture dipped in blood: and his name is called The Word of God. And the armies which were

in heaven followed him upon white horses, clothed in fine linen, white and clean. And out of his mouth goeth a sharp sword, that with it he should smite the nations: and he shall rule them with a rod of iron: and he treadeth the winepress of the fierceness and wrath of Almighty God. And he hath on his vesture and on his thigh a name written, KING OF KINGS, AND LORD OF LORDS.
—Revelation 19:11–16

This subject is far too complex to address here, but we can take a cursory look at it. No program can begin to depict the terrible events to take place during the last three and a half years of the great tribulation period. It will be Satan's last stand and, unrestrained by the Holy Spirit, he will bring the full force of his demonic evil upon the earth's inhabitants. God restrains Satan today because of his love for his church; when the church is removed in the rapture, Satan will no longer be restrained and will be free to bring the full force of his demonic agenda to those who are left behind. If you are a born-again Christian taken up in the rapture, you will be a member of the army of our Lord Jesus: "And the armies which were in heaven followed him upon white horses, clothed in fine linen, white and clean." Is it not exciting to think of returning to the earth as a member of the army of Jesus Christ to defeat Satan and his followers?

The world will be controlled by a one-world government, and there is already talk of organizing such a government due to the world's failing economies. During the great tribulation period, the Antichrist will be all-powerful and a total dictator, martyrdom will be the only alternative to bowing in total allegiance to his demands. The earth will be shaken to its core by a worldwide earthquake; changes in the heavens will occur, affecting the moon and sun. A great number of the world's population will die from disease and famine. All the countries of the world will focus their anger against Israel, and a war that will end all wars will occur at a tiny spot in Israel called Megiddo, where many great wars of the past have been fought."For I will gather all nations against Jerusalem to battle; and the city shall be taken, and the houses rifled, and the women ravished; and half of the city shall go forth into captivity, and the residue of the people shall not be cut off from the city." —Zechariah.

14:2. "And it shall come to pass in that day, *that* I will seek to destroy all the nations that come against Jerusalem." —Zechariah. 12:9. These events will culminate in the end of man's sinful existence. As the lord Jesus Christ promised, he will return to this earth, and man will learn firsthand the real power that rules this universe.

If we study prophecy, not from the present toward the future, but beginning at the end, as predicted in the Bible, and working backward, we will not have to go far before we arrive at the present day. The time gap between the present and the rapture of the church is known only to God, but it could be much shorter, or longer, than we think. The next major event to occur in God's final plan is the rapture of the church. I believe God has preordained a specific number of people to be saved; God knows who will be saved, and when that number is reached, the rapture will occur. God has been counting for a very long time and I believe the tally is about to be complete.

The tribulation will last only seven years, and many things have to occur before the Antichrist is revealed. The Bible is silent about a precise time lapse between the rapture of the church and the beginning of the tribulation. However, the Bible does not preclude the possibility that preparation for the coming tribulation could begin before the rapture of the church. The purpose of the rapture is for Christ to remove his church before things get so bad he will not want his church to be here. How bad things have to be before we see the rapture, is up to the Father.

It is not difficult to see the possibility that the world is being prepared for the coming tribulation. The question is who has the power to bring about a global power shift? The countries of the world are divided into two categories: consumers, and producers. Unfortunately, America is in the consumer category. Saudi Arabia has been, and continues to be, the world's largest producer of oil. Oil produces wealth for some countries, and takes wealth from other countries. According to an article by Hubert B. Herring, published in the New York Times on September 17, 2006, during a period of six months in 2006, Russia produced more oil than Saudi Arabia. It does not take a Harvard graduate to understand that the gain of wealth equals a gain in power. Conversely, a loss of wealth results in a loss of power. It does not require a Harvard education to realize where America fits in that scenario. Remember, I mentioned before that the cold war with Russia has not yet been won, and it never will be. Based on Russia's role in the battle of Armageddon, we will not be a major player.

An increase in Russia's wealth, and power, may not seem significant, until you explore the following verses from the Bible:

> And the word of the LORD came unto me, saying, Son of man, set thy face against Gog, the land of Magog, the chief prince of Meshech and Tubal, and prophesy against him, And say, Thus saith the Lord GOD; Behold, I *am* against thee, O Gog, the chief prince of Meshech and Tubal: And I will turn thee back, and put hooks into thy jaws, and I will bring thee forth, and all thine army, horses and horsemen, all of them clothed with all sorts *of armour, even* a great company *with* bucklers and shields, all of them handling swords: Persia, Ethiopia, and Libya with them; all of them with shield and helmet: Gomer, and all his bands; the house of Togarmah of the north quarters, and all his bands: *and* many people with thee. Be thou prepared, and prepare for thyself, thou, and all thy company that are assembled unto thee, and be thou a guard unto them. After many days thou shalt be visited: in the latter years thou shalt come into the land *that is* brought back from the sword, *and is* gathered out of many people, against the mountains of Israel, which have been always waste: but it is brought forth out of the nations, and they shall dwell safely all of them. Thou shalt ascend and come like a storm, thou shalt be like a cloud to cover the land, thou, and all thy bands, and many people with thee. Thus saith the Lord GOD; It shall also come to pass, *that* at the same time shall things come into thy mind, and thou shalt think an evil thought: And thou shalt say, I will go up to the land of unwalled villages; I will go to them that are at rest, that dwell safely, all of them dwelling without walls, and having neither bars nor gates, To take

a spoil, and to take a prey; to turn thine hand upon the desolate places *that are now* inhabited, and upon the people *that are* gathered out of the nations, which have gotten cattle and goods, that dwell in the midst of the land. Sheba, and Dedan, and the merchants of Tarshish, with all the young lions thereof, shall say unto thee, Art thou come to take a spoil? hast thou gathered thy company to take a prey? to carry away silver and gold, to take away cattle and goods, to take a great spoil?
—Ezekiel 38:1-13

Those words are not a lot of gobble-the-gook. It is a prediction of the coming final battle, a battle called Armageddon. "And he gathered them together into a place called in the Hebrew tongue Armageddon." —Revelation 16:16. This battle will take place during the great tribulation period. We are familiar with the countries, Ethiopia and Libya, but what about the other strange sounding names. Magog=Russia; Meshech and Tubal, Togarmah =Turkey; Persia=Iran; and Gomer=Germany. Russia will spearhead a vast army that will cover the land of Israel like a storm cloud. "And I will turn thee back, and put hooks into thy jaws, and I will bring thee forth," God will bring these countries to Israel to be destroyed. What God will use as a hook, is greed. Will oil be discovered in Israel to draw the greedy to that land? Some people think so. However, if oil is discovered, God put it there for his people, along with an abundance of natural resources, hidden in, and below, the salty waters of the Dead Sea—God's bait for the greedy.

"Therefore, son of man, prophesy and say unto Gog, Thus saith the Lord GOD; In that day when my people of Israel dwelleth safely, shalt thou not know *it?* And thou shalt come from thy place out of the north parts, thou, and many people with thee, all of them riding upon horses, a great company, and a mighty army: And thou shalt come up against my people of Israel, as a cloud to cover the land; it shall be in the latter days, and I will bring thee against my land, that the heathen may know me, when I shall be sanctified in thee, O Gog, before their eyes. Thus saith the Lord GOD; *Art* thou

he of whom I have spoken in old time by my servants the prophets of Israel, which prophesied in those days *many* years that I would bring thee against them? And it shall come to pass at the same time when Gog shall come against the land of Israel, saith the Lord GOD, *that* my fury shall come up in my face. For in my jealousy *and* in the fire of my wrath have I spoken, Surely in that day there shall be a great shaking in the land of Israel; So that the fishes of the sea, and the fowls of the heaven, and the beasts of the field, and all creeping things that creep upon the earth, and all the men that *are* upon the face of the earth, shall shake at my presence, and the mountains shall be thrown down, and the steep places shall fall, and every wall shall fall to the ground. And I will call for a sword against him throughout all my mountains, saith the Lord GOD: every man's sword shall be against his brother. And I will plead against him with pestilence and with blood; and I will rain upon him, and upon his bands, and upon the many people that *are* with him, an overflowing rain, and great hailstones, fire, and brimstone. Thus will I magnify myself, and sanctify myself; and I will be known in the eyes of many nations, and they shall know that I *am* the LORD."
—Ezekiel 38:14-23

There is an interesting passage in the above verses—"and many people with thee, all of them riding upon horses,"—I must admit, I am puzzled by those words. I am not puzzled by the fact that a modern army will be riding horses—the Bible says they will, and I accept it as fact. My question is what will occur between now and the time of the invasion, to require them to ride horses.

I hold onto my understanding of his word that is revealed to me, but I will not try to convince you to accept my opinion; I prefer you get it directly from him, and if you study his word, the truth will be revealed to you. Continue to study and pray and build your faith, and God will reveal his word according to your ability to understand. A lot of time and devotion was given by more than forty authors to write the Bible, and a lot of time and devotion is required to understand it.

Personal Responsibility

There is a subject difficult to write about without sounding judgmental. However, it needs to be addressed. Worldly enticements are having a profound effect on many American churches, and it is time we Christians face the problem. First, we must evaluate our personal circumstances. If you are not comfortable with your relationship with Jesus Christ, then it is time to do something about it. If you attend a church where the truth of God's word is not being taught and Jesus Christ is not glorified, find another church. If the Holy Spirit causes you to feel uncomfortable around old friends, find new friends. If you are not into studying God's word, it is time to start. Tough times are coming, and refusal to think about them will not delay them. God has a finger on the pulse of this world, and he knows what is ahead. I believe that soon Jesus is going to remove his church from this world, and you do not want to be among many who will be shocked to discover they have been left behind.

The rapture of the church is the hope of every Christian, but none of us may live to witness it. Only truly born-again Christians will see the kingdom of God, whether by the rapture or by death; that is a fact straight from the mouth of Jesus and, to be honest, there may not be as many truly born-again Christians on this planet as we might think. The greatest period for the church occurred at its beginning in the first century, and except for a rise here and there, it has been going downhill every since. However, a loving God is reaching out today to gather all who will, to come to him before it is too late. God has infinite patience and desires that everyone turns to him, but after thousands of years, the human race is farther away from God than ever before, especially in America. However, the coming economical problems, not only in America but also throughout the world, will cause many to turn to God, as is usually the case. Although we cannot know the exact time of the end, there is one thing we can be sure of: it will come exactly as the Bible predicts, so why not now!

Our twentieth president, James Garfield, said, "The truth will set you free, but first it will make you miserable." He was right about that if he was referring to man's truth, and it is the reason people resist facing the truth. Since he was a pastor, perhaps President Garfield should have added, knowing God's truth will make you free and keep you free, with hope and promise, not misery. Arrogant man does not want to know the truth unless it supports his views, and if it does not, he will reject it. I do not know if the following words have been previously spoken; but if not, I will coin them here: *Even when the truth is pursued, many that find it will wish they had not looked for it.*

It is my prayer that I have convinced you of the seriousness of the subject of salvation. Everything that is happening in the world today is predicted in the Bible, and the next prediction to be fulfilled is the rapture of the church. Everything is coming together for the climax of the end of time, and it is coming very soon. If you have not already, get your focus away from this world and turn to God and you can have the peace and joy of being a member of his family.

In the event you are left with the impression that living a Christian life is easy in this sinful world, there are a few things to realize. We are all born with a sinful nature, and as long as we are on this earth, we will have to deal with it. Even the most devout Christian occasionally will find himself appearing on a Shakespearean stage or doing things that are more pleasing to Satan than to Christ. It is better to die in battle than to be conquered without a fight. Jesus Christ is the only hope man has to defeat Satan from conquering his soul, and taking on the full armor of God is the only hope for mankind. I have mentioned many times that Christianity is an individual relationship with Jesus Christ, but it is important to fellowship with other Christians so that we may strengthen and encourage each other in our walk with God. That has never been more important than it is today.

A Reality Check

Reality is what happens when most people are looking the other way. As Americans, we have a hard reality to face, our country is dying; our former glory never will be recaptured. If you think I am a defeatist, you are dead wrong; my faith, hope, and trust is in Almighty God and, no matter the future of America, I have a bright and glorious future to which to look forward. Whatever God has in store for America, it will be fair, just, and deserved. America has spat in his eye, and now we are being held to account.

The Hour of Decision

Throughout our lives, we are faced with decisions, but there is no decision more important than one that concerns our eternal soul. We are only one breath away from eternity, and there are only two possible destinations. Perhaps you do not wish to think about it—most people do not—but reality is not based on consensus, it is based on facts. The facts of life are clearly explained in the Bible. I hope I have succeeded in convincing you the importance of studying the Bible. We cannot delegate the responsibility for our souls to someone else; it is our personal responsibility and no one else's. The time for decision is now; if you are not a born-again Christian, this is your hour of decision. Do not put your soul in the hands of someone else because there is no second chance at life. The simple message in the Bible is: (1) turn to God, accept Jesus Christ as Lord and Master of your life, do his will, and spend eternity with him in heaven; (2) Reject God, and spend eternity in hell with Satan, forever separated from God. No matter how many years spent in the seminary or devoted to Bible study, no alternative message will be revealed; it is the truth of the Bible reduced to its most basic purpose.

The Only Hope

On Flag Day, June 14, 1954, President Eisenhower signed into law a bill that added the words "under God" to the Pledge of Allegiance. Upon that occasion, President Eisenhower said, "Of all the weapons we possess in our nation, our spiritual weapons will forever be our country's most powerful resource in both times of peace and war." If you are a freedom-loving, staunch American, with a love of God, family, and country, there is a call to arms, not military arms, but the more powerful arms of prayer, to appeal to the promises of Almighty God.

> The LORD is righteous in all his ways, and holy in all his works. The LORD is nigh unto all them that call upon him, to all that call upon him in truth. He will fulfil the desire of them that fear him: he also will hear their cry, and will save

them. The LORD preserveth all them that love him: but all the wicked will he destroy. My mouth shall speak the praise of the LORD: and let all flesh bless his holy name forever and ever.
—Psalms 145:17–21

A FINAL WORD

There is no way to know the time lapse between the time of this writing and the time you will read it; events are changing so rapidly, it is difficult to keep ahead. As you have seen, this is not a comprehensive study. Every effort has been made to keep things simple because we can make the study of God's word far more complex than is necessary.

> And you hath he quickened, who were dead in trespasses and sins; Wherein in time past ye walked according to the course of this world, according to the prince of the power of the air, the spirit that now worketh in the children of disobedience: Among whom also we all had our conversation in times past in the lusts of our flesh, fulfilling the desires of the flesh and of the mind; and were by nature the children of wrath, even as others. But God, who is rich in mercy, for his great love wherewith he loved us, Even when we were dead in sins, hath quickened us together with Christ, (by grace ye are saved;) And hath raised us up together, and made us sit together in heavenly places in Christ Jesus: That in the ages to come he might shew the exceeding riches of his grace in his kindness toward us through Christ Jesus. For by grace are ye saved through faith; and that not of yourselves: it is the gift of God: Not of works, lest any man should boast. For we are his workmanship, created in Christ Jesus unto good works, which God hath before ordained that we should walk in them.
> —Ephesians 2:1–10

The above verses are repeated to offer encouragement and hope. If you do not feel the above verses are speaking about you, then you can be included if you turn away from man's sinful world and dedicate your life to serving Jesus Christ. There are no downsides to making that decision and the love and joy that God promises is a promise he will keep. We can know the past, but we cannot go back to the past. However, we can look to the future and prepare for it before it, too, becomes the past. Now is the moment of decision; tomorrow may never come.

When faced with the prospect of a coming disaster, it is much easier to wait and see what happens than it is to prepare for it in advance. It is that attitude that accounts for our troubles. Pay attention to the reality of what is transpiring, and educate yourself so you can be prepared for whatever comes.

If you choose to ignore every personal opinion I have expressed, in no way will it disappoint me. However, it is my hope and prayer that you will not ignore the Bible scriptures and other quotes that are included.

> And, behold, I come quickly; and my reward is with me, to give every man according as his work shall be. I am Alpha and Omega, the beginning and the end, the first and the last. Blessed are they that do his commandments, that they may have right to the tree of life, and may enter in through the gates into the city. For without are dogs, and sorcerers, and whoremongers, and murderers, and idolaters, and whosoever loveth and maketh a lie. I Jesus have sent mine angel to testify unto you these things in the churches. I am the root and the offspring of David, and the bright and morning star. And the Spirit and the bride say, Come. And let him that heareth say, Come. And let him that is athirst come. And whosoever will, let him take the water of life freely. For I testify unto every man that heareth the words of the prophecy of this book, If any man shall add unto these things, God shall add unto him the plagues that are written in this book: And if any man shall take away from the words of the book of this prophecy, God shall take away his part out of the book of

life, and out of the holy city, and from the things which are written in this book. He which testifieth these things saith, Surely I come quickly. Amen. Even so, come, Lord Jesus. The grace of our Lord Jesus Christ be with you all. Amen.
—Revelation 22:12–21

In whatever stage you are with your relationship with God, perhaps this book will be of some benefit. From the beginning, I had some doubt about producing a credible work, but desire and motivation caused me to press forward with the task. I accept there are things in this book that are worthy of criticism, but it is important for you to know that every word written by me came from my heart. I did not write this book for everyone, because not everyone will wish to read it. There is only one book in existence that was written for everyone—the Holy Bible.

There is one advantage I have that perhaps in some measure, will compensate for my disadvantages. For the past fifteen years, my wife and I have been privileged to travel this great country in our motor home. This opportunity has provided me with a greater insight into what is happening in America; we have visited almost every state, and some many times. My travels also have provided the opportunity to visit many churches of various denominations and practices. Coupled with my longevity, this experience has made me realize that America is in deep trouble. Liberalism has spread to every hollow and peak. Political correctness is the noose around our necks, and eventually, the trap will be sprung. It gives me no pleasure to refer to this generation as the most inept and uninformed in our history, but it is going to destroy America. We have visited places where God seems to rule and places where, it seems, he does not exist at all; unfortunately, the latter is becoming more prevalent. I am not a purveyor of doom and gloom, but neither am I a purveyor of false optimism. My unique opportunity to observe this country from sea to sea and my knowledge of the Bible, limited as it is, combined or separate, convinces me America is doomed for failure. Unless America's demise is delayed by the hand of God, in less than five years from now, you will look back to today's circumstances as the good old days.

I have emphasized many times the importance of studying the Bible; it is not necessary to know everything there is to know in the Bible—and no one does. The Holy Spirit teaches us what God requires us to know to be part of his family; the Holy Spirit will not misguide anyone. There are many mysteries and areas of confusion in the Bible, especially for those who are new to the study, but do not be discouraged because there are no shortcuts to God. We began as babies taking baby steps, and we only mature through perseverance and devotion. The messages in God's word are very exact and revealing, but we may not fully understand those messages the first time we are exposed to them.

If you have never experienced the spirit of God in your life, it will be natural for you to be skeptical about what I have written. If you are skeptical, I pray you will give him the opportunity to reveal himself to you, and that is not difficult to do. If you have a sincere desire in your heart to surrender your life to him, tell him so, and I promise he will not ignore you. Like every other person on this planet, you are a sinner living in a sinful world. God loves you the same as he loves anyone else, so take him at his word and seek a relationship with Christ; you will not be disappointed. There are born-again Christians in your neighborhood who are eager to welcome you into God's family and to nurture and guide you in your new life. Even the angels in heaven will rejoice over your decision. My motivation for writing this book is to make you aware of things you may not think about, because most people do not, and motivate you to educate yourself on the subjects covered. Because it is my first attempt to write a book, it has taken 14 months to satisfy myself that what I have written may, in some way, help someone. If only one person benefits from my effort, that will be my reward. Hard times are coming to America, and without God in your life, it will be infinitely more difficult to cope.

> For that which I do I allow not: for what I would, that do
> I not; but what I hate, that do I. If then I do that which I
> would not, I consent unto the law that *it is* good. Now then
> it is no more I that do it, but sin that dwelleth in me. For
> I know that in me (that is, in my flesh,) dwelleth no good
> thing: for to will is present with me; but *how* to perform that

which is good I find not. For the good that I would I do not:
but the evil which I would not, that I do. Now if I do that
I would not, it is no more I that do it, but sin that dwelleth
in me. I find then a law, that, when I would do good, evil
is present with me. For I delight in the law of God after the
inward man: But I see another law in my members, warring
against the law of my mind, and bringing me into captivity
to the law of sin which is in my members. O wretched man
that I am! who shall deliver me from the body of this death?
I thank God through Jesus Christ our Lord. So then with
the mind I myself serve the law of God; but with the flesh
the law of sin.
—Romans 7:15-25

Do you recognize yourself in the above verses? I certainly do and I suspect
you do also. Regardless of how we wish to view ourselves, we should never
lose sight of how God sees us: we are poor, wretched, miserable sinners—each
of us. We have not one ounce of righteousness in ourselves, but we have
the opportunity to be covered by the righteousness of Jesus Christ; it is our
choice.

A Positive Observation

Since I began the task, and often agonizingly, of writing this book, I have
seen a glimmer of hope that many American people are awakening from their
slumber and taking note of the precarious state of our country. If I am correct,
and I pray that I am, may God guide us in a revival of the values, and faith
in him, that he ordained for our great country.

If I have misjudged what is happening, do not despair. Remember, our great
merciful God is controlling events in this world and if we remain close to
him, he will lead us to where he wants us to go, and that assurance will keep
us in his sunlight—and we will have nothing to fear.

Regrettably, I found it necessary to cast disparagement against some churches
in America however, there are many God loving and Christ worshiping
churches, in America, as there has always been. We have a solid core of truly

born again Christians that are on the battle line every day holding Christ up to a sinful nation. If you have not already, it is my hope and pray that you will join God's army and change the lives of you and your family forever.

I conclude this chapter, not with my words, but from the word of God from verses in Romans and Revelation:

> For I am not ashamed of the gospel of Christ: for it is the power of God unto salvation to everyone that believeth; to the Jew first, and also to the Greek. For therein is the righteousness of God revealed from faith to faith: as it is written, The just shall live by faith. For the wrath of God is revealed from heaven against all ungodliness and unrighteousness of men, who hold the truth in unrighteousness.
> —Romans 1:16–18

> And he said unto me, These sayings are faithful and true: and the Lord God of the holy prophets sent his angel to shew unto his servants the things which must shortly be done. Behold, I come quickly: blessed is he that keepeth the sayings of the prophecy of this book. And I John saw these things, and heard them. And when I had heard and seen, I fell down to worship before the feet of the angel which shewed me these things. Then saith he unto me, See thou do it not: for I am thy fellowservant, and of thy brethren the prophets, and of them which keep the sayings of this book: worship God. And he saith unto me, Seal not the sayings of the prophecy of this book: for the time is at hand. He that is unjust, let him be unjust still: and he which is filthy, let him be filthy still: and he that is righteous, let him be righteous still: and he that is holy, let him be holy still. And, behold, I come quickly; and my reward is with me, to give every man according as his work shall be. I am Alpha and Omega, the beginning and the end, the first and the last. Blessed are they that do his commandments, that they may have right to the tree of life, and may enter in through the gates into the city.

For without are dogs, and sorcerers, and whoremongers, and murderers, and idolaters, and whosoever loveth and maketh a lie. I Jesus have sent mine angel to testify unto you these things in the churches. I am the root and the offspring of David, and the bright and morning star.

—Revelation 22:6–16

A NOTE TO THE READER

Some readers may be curious about why I do not capitalize "he" and "him," etc., when referring to God. Although it is my personal preference to do so, I opted to be consistent with the scriptures in the King James Version of the Bible, where capitalization is not used.

In the poem, "Pippa's Song", by Robert Browning, the last line reads: "God's in His Heaven, All's Right With the World." God is in his Heaven, but all is certainly not right with the world—someday it will be.

SOURCES

King James Version of The Holy Bible.

Flavius, Josephus,—The complete Works of Flavius Josephus: Publisher, Hendrickson Publishing, Published, 9/1 1980.

Jones, Vernon,—Aesop's Fables: A new translation with introduction by G.K. Chesterton,1912.

Merriam-Webster's Collegiate Dictionary, and Thesaurus—11th eddition.

Inauguration Speeches of American Presidents. http://en.wikipedia.org/wiki/ Inaugural_Addresses_of_the_Presidents_of_the_United_States.

Gibbon, Edward, —History of the Decline and fall of the Roman Empire, with notes by Rev. H.H.Miman.—Kindle for PC, Version: 1.2.1.

King, Martin Luther Jr.— Strength of Love speech. 1963.

Anderson, Hans Christen, —"The Emperor's New Clothes" adapted by Stephen Corrin in Stories for Seven-Year-Olds. London 1964. Reproduced on the website:http://www.mindfully.org/Reform/Emperors-New-Clothes.htm.

United States Constitution.

History Channel:—"First Invasion, the War of 1812", Aired 4/9,2010.

Britannica Concise Encyclopedia..—"Henry Morgenthau, Jr."

Garfield, James,— President of the United States,http://www.brainyquote.com/
quotes/authors/j/james_a_garfield_2.html.

World Christian Encyclopedia.

Herodotus,— A Web addition, from Kindle for PC, Version: 1.2.1., derived from
two different additions. "Volume I" is from the addition dated 1890, published
by MacMillan and Co., Volume II from the eddition dated 1914, published by
MacMillan and Co.

McEvedy, Colin and Jones, Richard,— Atlas of World Population History
1978.

Department of Labor, Bureau of Labor Statistics:—"Unemployment rate."

American Religious Identification Survey. (ARIS).

Folsom, Burton Jr.,— New Deal or Raw Deal: How FDR's Economic Legacy
Has Damaged America" (2008).

Browning, Robert,—"Pippa's Song," a poem.